Garfield
SURVIVAL of the FATTEST

BY JIM DAVIS

Genadi

Ballantine Books • New York

A Ballantine Book
Published by The Random House Publishing Group
Copyright © 2004 by PAWS, Inc. All Rights Reserved.

All rights reserved under International and Pan-American Copyright Conventions. Published in the United States by The Random House Publishing Group, a division of Random House, Inc., New York, and simultaneously in Canada by Random House of Canada Limited, Toronto.

Ballantine is a registered trademark and the Ballantine colophon is a trademark of Random House, Inc.

"GARFIELD" and the GARFIELD characters are registered and unregistered trademarks of PAWS, Inc.

www.ballantinebooks.com

Library of Congress Control Number: 2003096927

ISBN 0-345-46458-3

Manufactured in the United States of America

First Edition: February 2004

10 9 8 7 6 5 4 3 2

Outrageous Outtakes

Never-before-seen, over-the-top strips saved from extinction by our kooky comics conservationists!

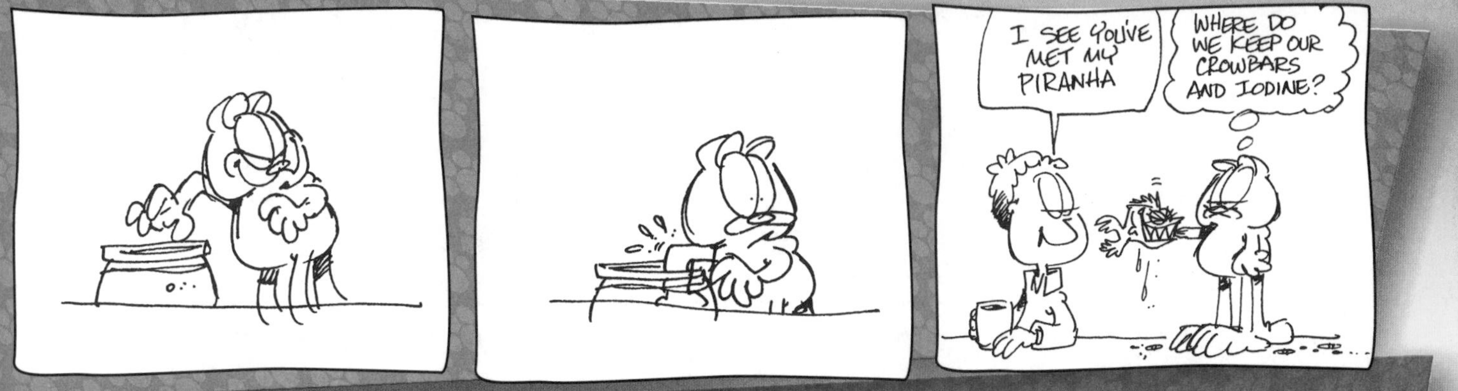
I SEE YOU'VE MET MY PIRANHA
WHERE DO WE KEEP OUR CROWBARS AND IODINE?

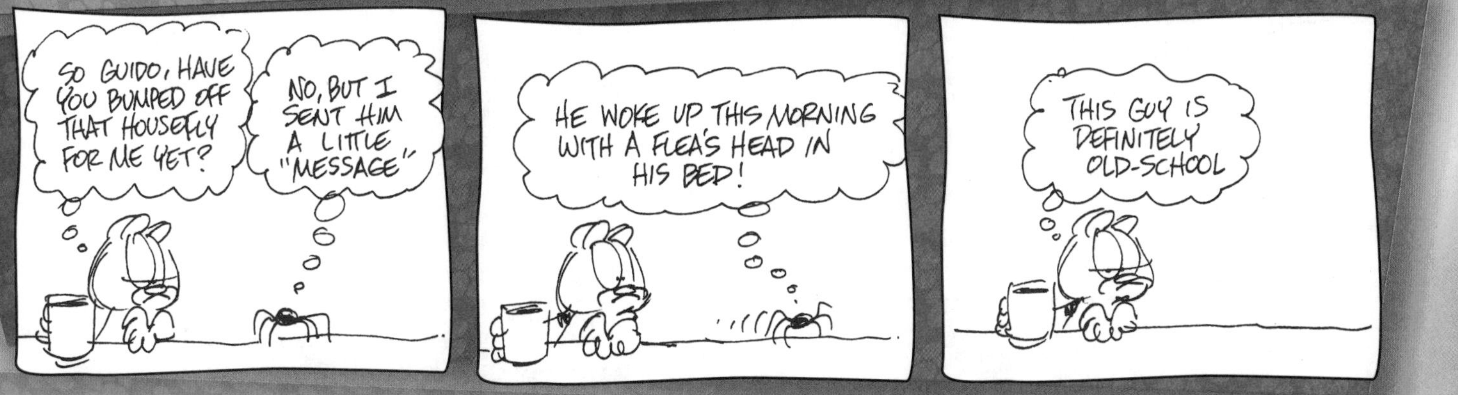
SO GUIDO, HAVE YOU BUMPED OFF THAT HOUSEFLY FOR ME YET?
NO, BUT I SENT HIM A LITTLE "MESSAGE"
HE WOKE UP THIS MORNING WITH A FLEA'S HEAD IN HIS BED!
THIS GUY IS DEFINITELY OLD-SCHOOL

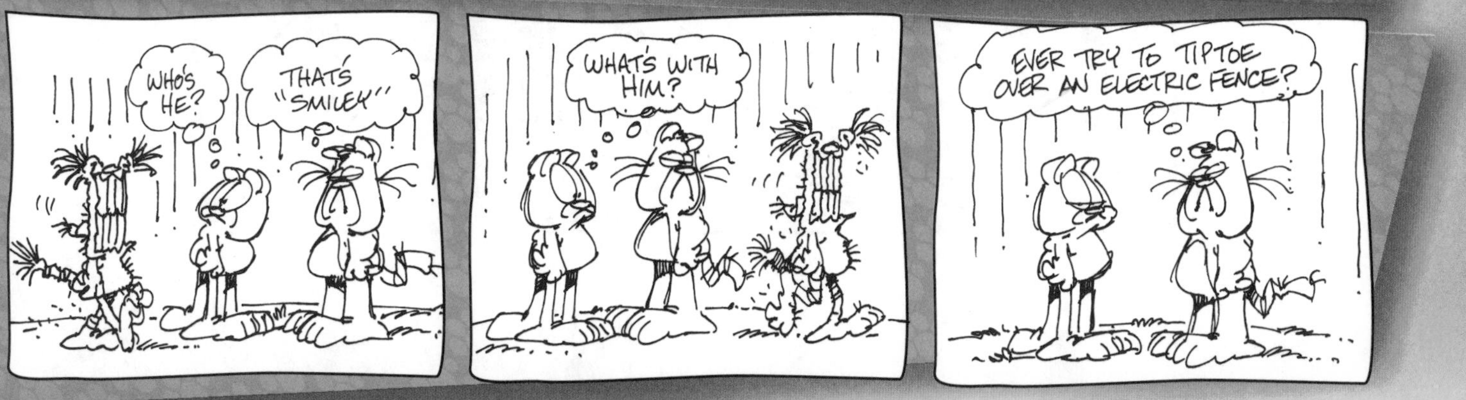
WHO'S HE?
THAT'S "SMILEY"
WHAT'S WITH HIM?
EVER TRY TO TIPTOE OVER AN ELECTRIC FENCE?

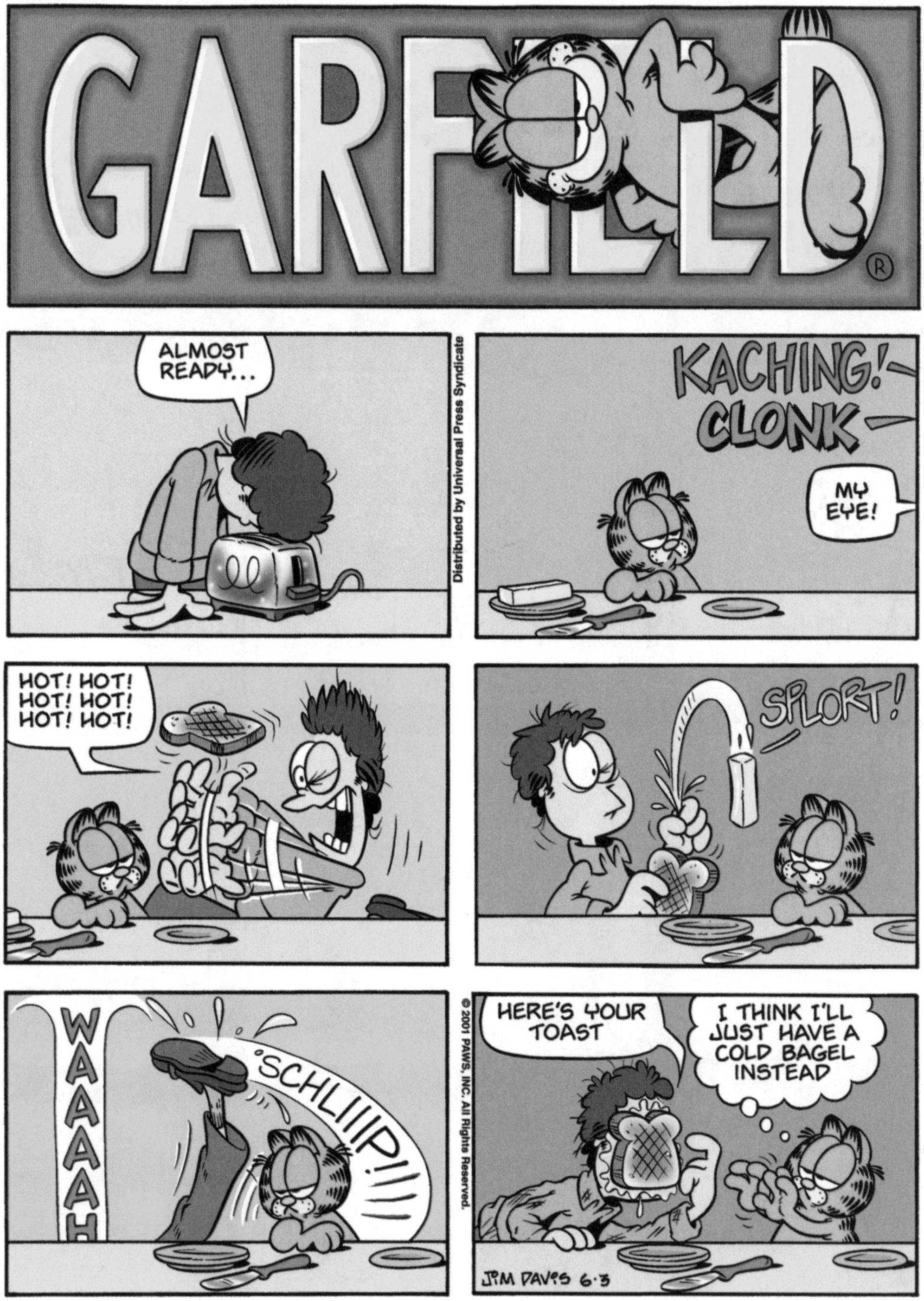
GARFIELD
ALMOST READY...
Distributed by Universal Press Syndicate
KACHING!
CLONK
MY EYE!
HOT! HOT! HOT! HOT! HOT! HOT!
SPLORT!
WAAAAH
SCHLIIIP!
© 2001 PAWS, INC. All Rights Reserved.
HERE'S YOUR TOAST
I THINK I'LL JUST HAVE A COLD BAGEL INSTEAD
JIM DAVIS 6·3

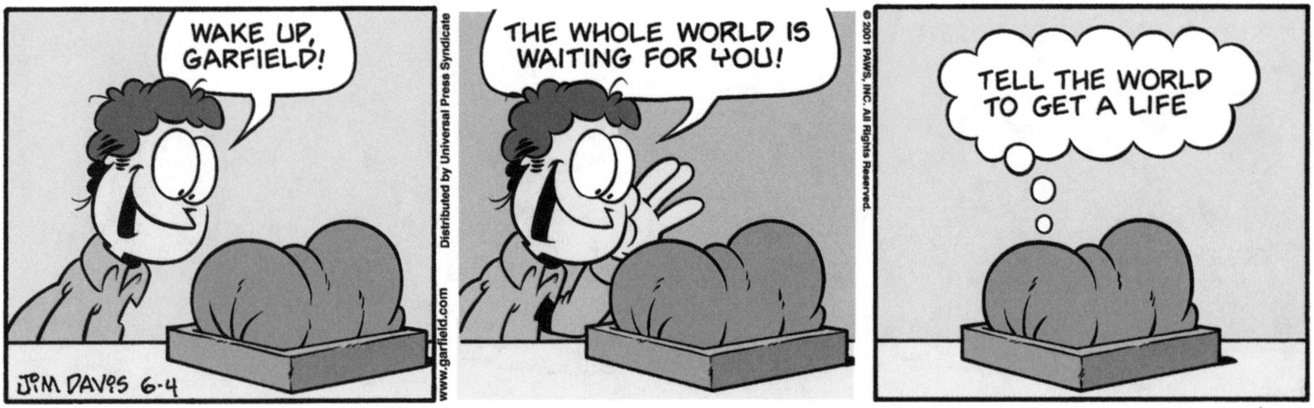
WAKE UP, GARFIELD!
JIM DAVIS 6-4
www.garfield.com Distributed by Universal Press Syndicate
THE WHOLE WORLD IS WAITING FOR YOU!
© 2001 PAWS, INC. All Rights Reserved.
TELL THE WORLD TO GET A LIFE

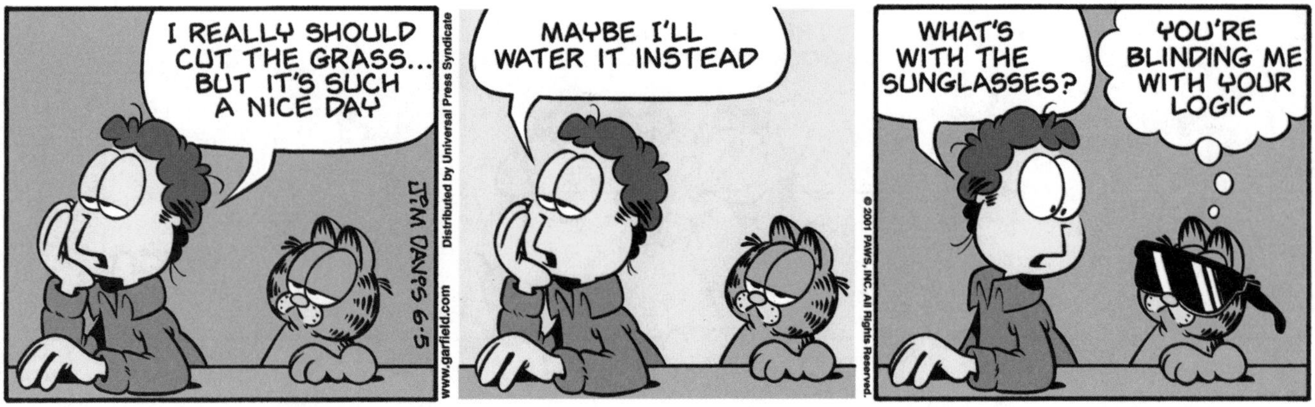
I REALLY SHOULD CUT THE GRASS... BUT IT'S SUCH A NICE DAY
JIM DAVIS 6-5
www.garfield.com Distributed by Universal Press Syndicate
MAYBE I'LL WATER IT INSTEAD
© 2001 PAWS, INC. All Rights Reserved.
WHAT'S WITH THE SUNGLASSES?
YOU'RE BLINDING ME WITH YOUR LOGIC

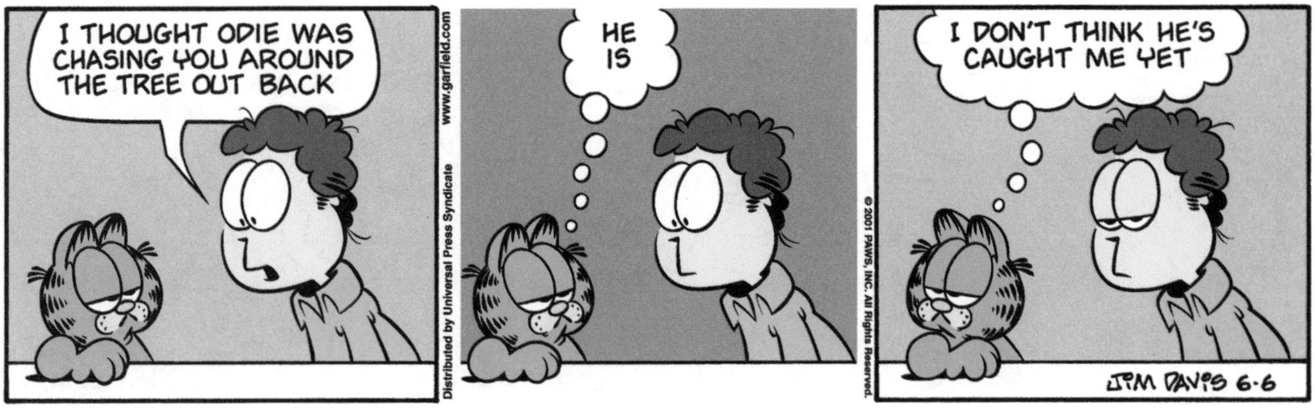
I THOUGHT ODIE WAS CHASING YOU AROUND THE TREE OUT BACK
Distributed by Universal Press Syndicate www.garfield.com
HE IS
© 2001 PAWS, INC. All Rights Reserved.
I DON'T THINK HE'S CAUGHT ME YET
JIM DAVIS 6-6

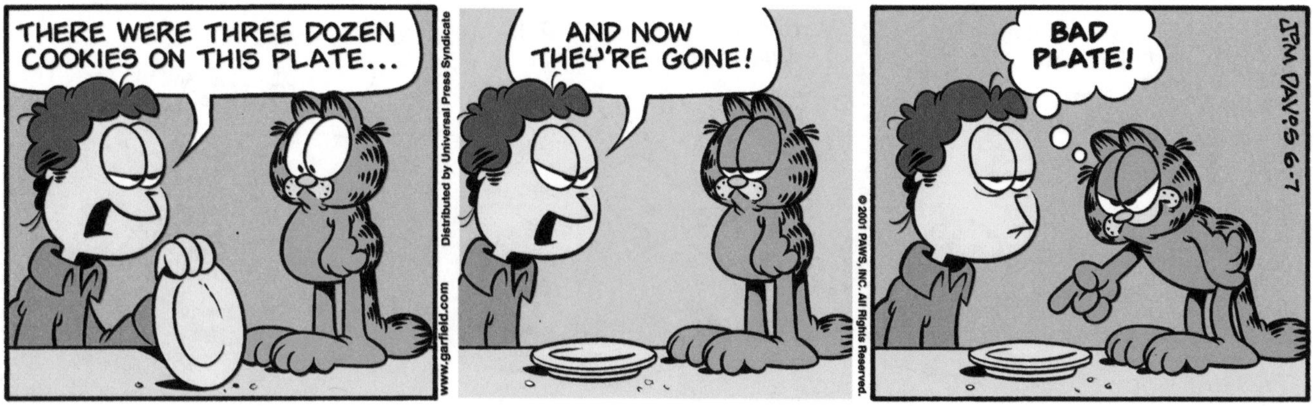
THERE WERE THREE DOZEN COOKIES ON THIS PLATE...
www.garfield.com Distributed by Universal Press Syndicate
AND NOW THEY'RE GONE!
© 2001 PAWS, INC. All Rights Reserved.
BAD PLATE!
JIM DAVIS 6-7

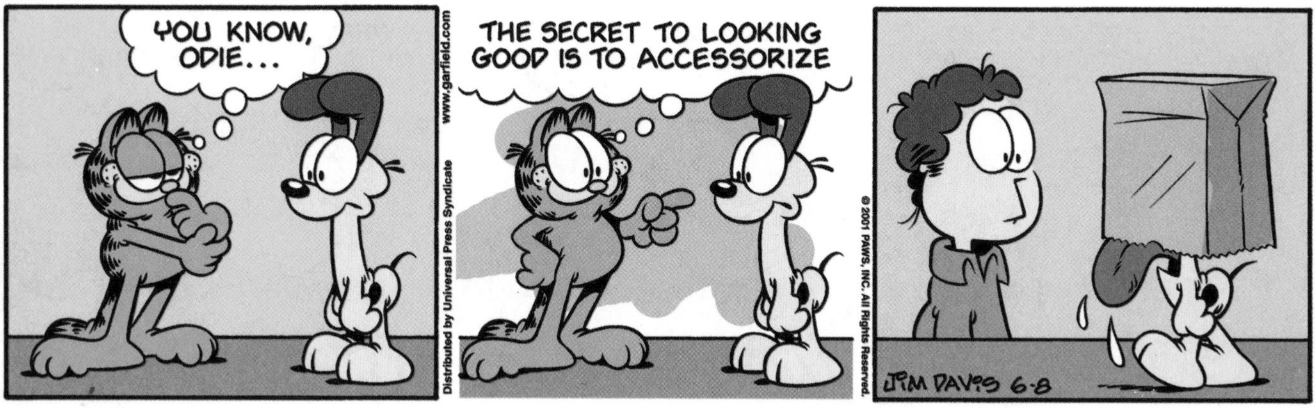
YOU KNOW, ODIE...
www.garfield.com Distributed by Universal Press Syndicate
THE SECRET TO LOOKING GOOD IS TO ACCESSORIZE
© 2001 PAWS, INC. All Rights Reserved.
JIM DAVIS 6-8

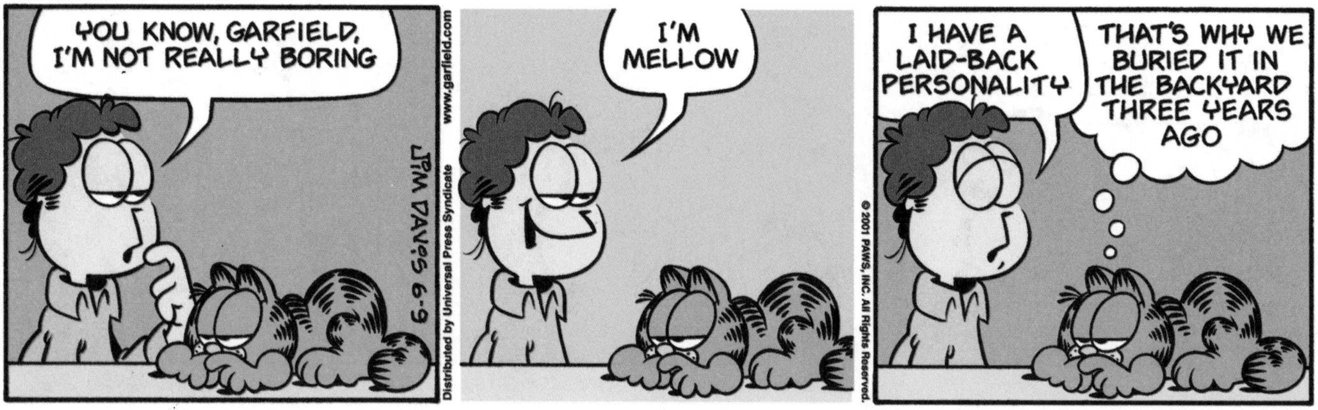
YOU KNOW, GARFIELD, I'M NOT REALLY BORING
JIM DAVIS 6-9
www.garfield.com Distributed by Universal Press Syndicate
I'M MELLOW
© 2001 PAWS, INC. All Rights Reserved.
I HAVE A LAID-BACK PERSONALITY
THAT'S WHY WE BURIED IT IN THE BACKYARD THREE YEARS AGO

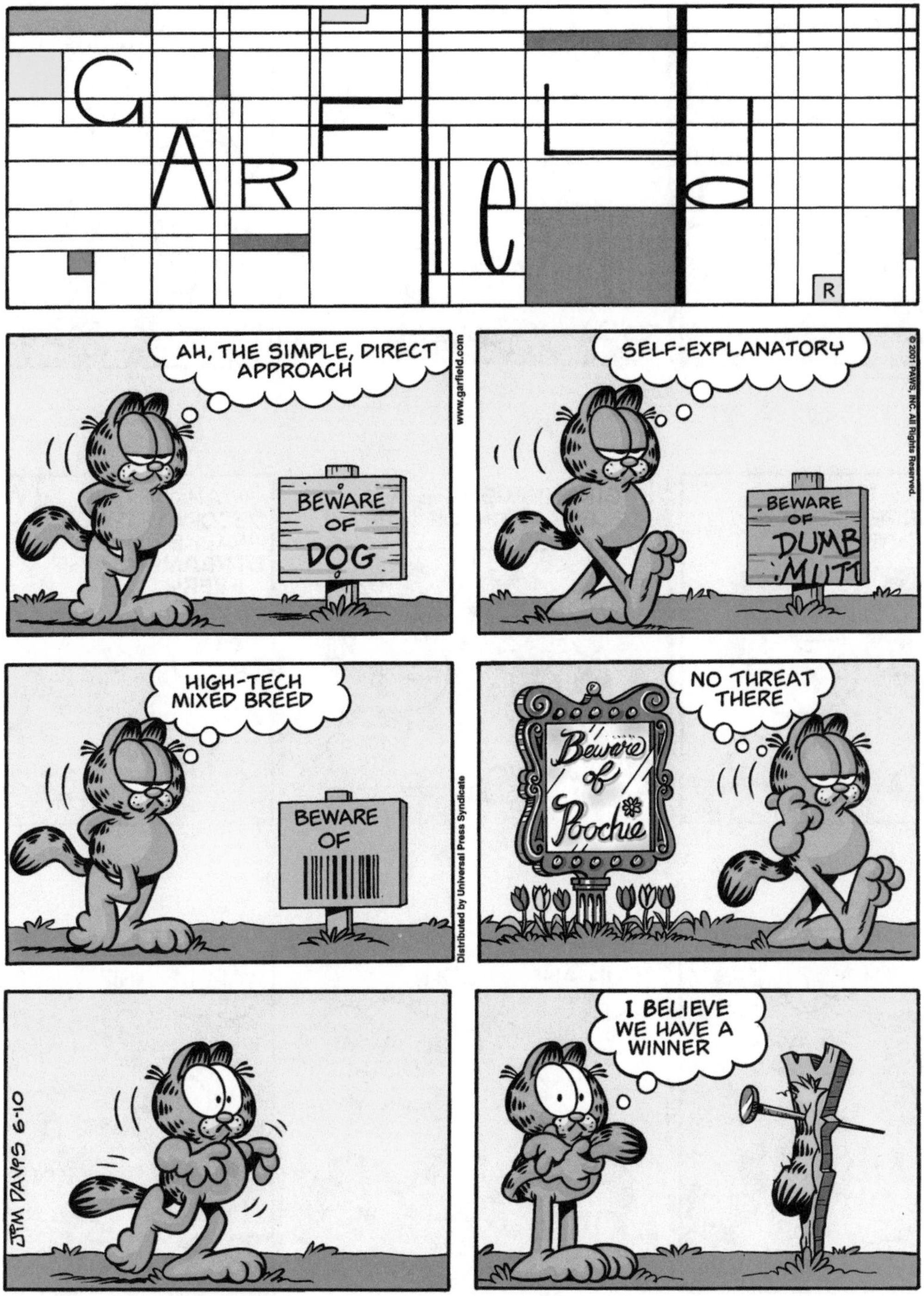
GARFIELD
AH, THE SIMPLE, DIRECT APPROACH
BEWARE OF DOG
www.garfield.com
SELF-EXPLANATORY
BEWARE OF DUMB MUTT
© 2001 PAWS, INC. All Rights Reserved.
HIGH-TECH MIXED BREED
BEWARE OF
Distributed by Universal Press Syndicate
NO THREAT THERE
Beware of Poochie
JIM DAVIS 6-10
I BELIEVE WE HAVE A WINNER

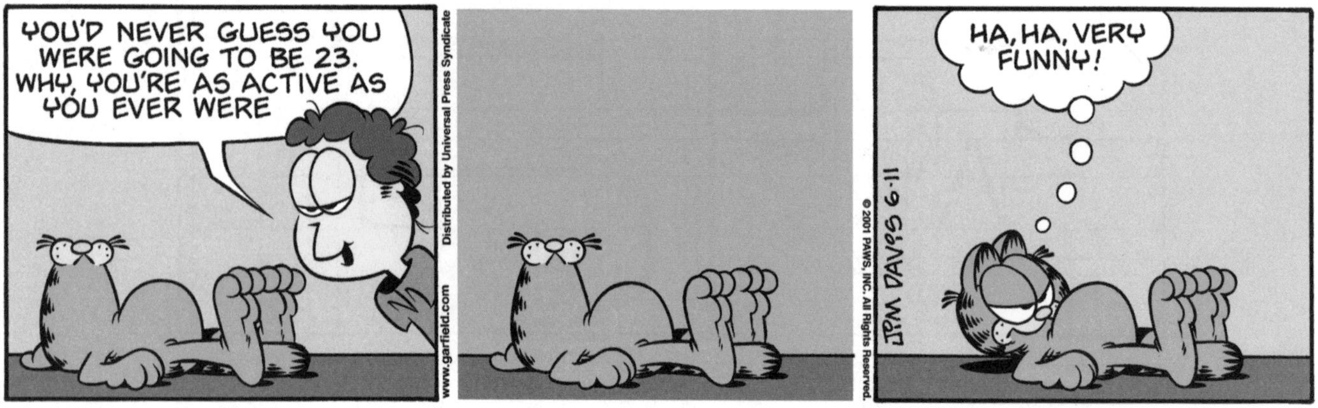
YOU'D NEVER GUESS YOU WERE GOING TO BE 23. WHY, YOU'RE AS ACTIVE AS YOU EVER WERE
HA, HA, VERY FUNNY!
JPM DAVIS 6-11
www.garfield.com Distributed by Universal Press Syndicate
© 2001 PAWS, INC. All Rights Reserved.

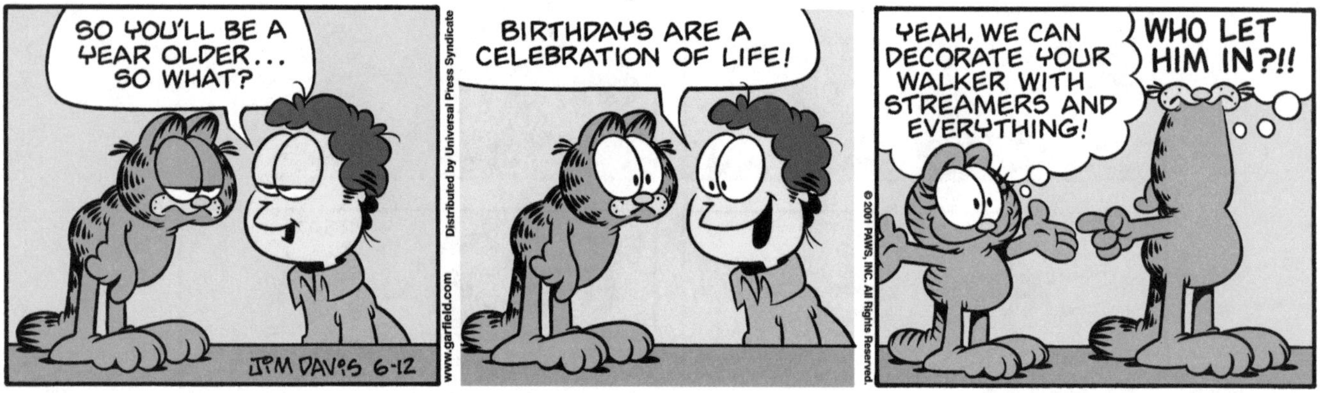
SO YOU'LL BE A YEAR OLDER... SO WHAT?
JPM DAVIS 6-12
BIRTHDAYS ARE A CELEBRATION OF LIFE!
YEAH, WE CAN DECORATE YOUR WALKER WITH STREAMERS AND EVERYTHING!
WHO LET HIM IN?!!
www.garfield.com Distributed by Universal Press Syndicate
© 2001 PAWS, INC. All Rights Reserved.

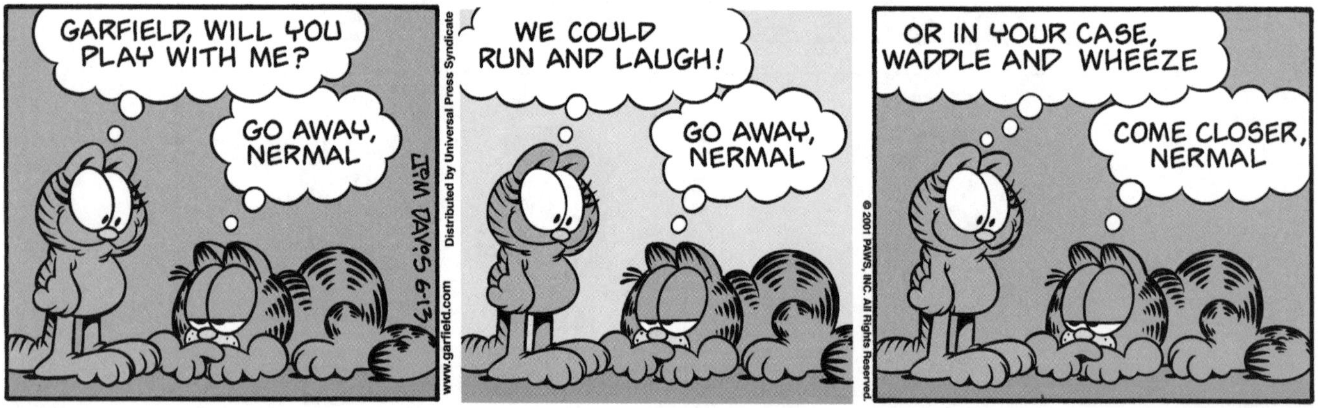
GARFIELD, WILL YOU PLAY WITH ME?
GO AWAY, NERMAL
JPM DAVIS 6-13
WE COULD RUN AND LAUGH!
GO AWAY, NERMAL
OR IN YOUR CASE, WADDLE AND WHEEZE
COME CLOSER, NERMAL
www.garfield.com Distributed by Universal Press Syndicate
© 2001 PAWS, INC. All Rights Reserved.

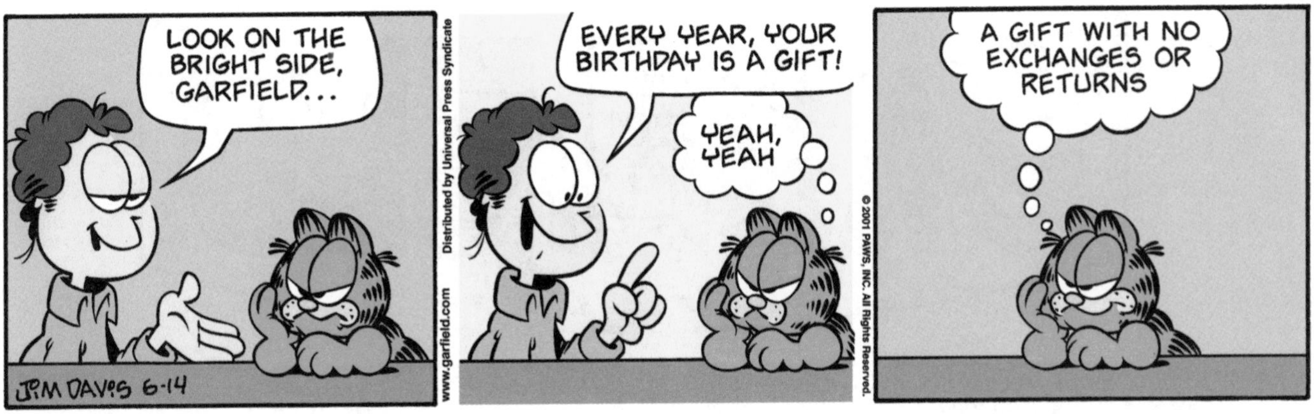
LOOK ON THE BRIGHT SIDE, GARFIELD...
JIM DAVIS 6-14
www.garfield.com Distributed by Universal Press Syndicate
EVERY YEAR, YOUR BIRTHDAY IS A GIFT!
YEAH, YEAH
© 2001 PAWS, INC. All Rights Reserved.
A GIFT WITH NO EXCHANGES OR RETURNS

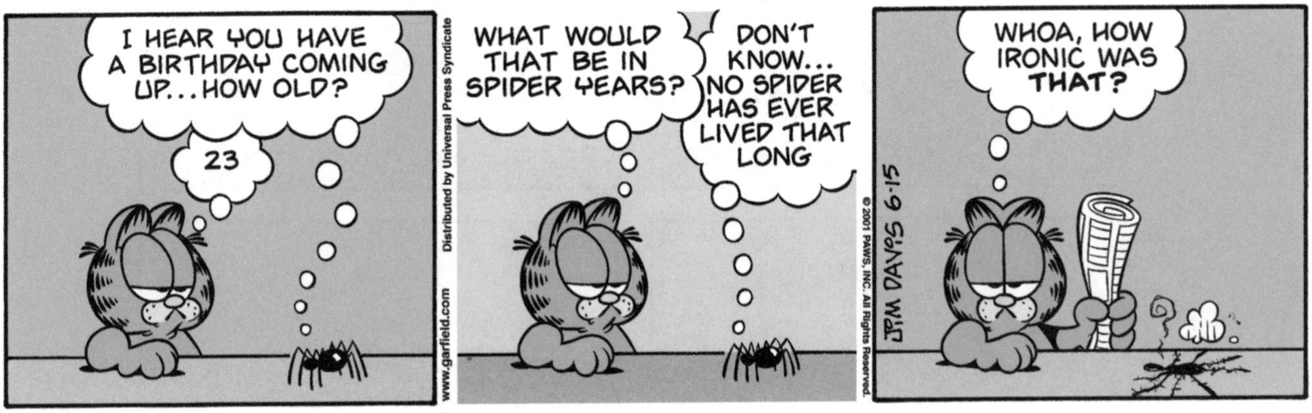
I HEAR YOU HAVE A BIRTHDAY COMING UP...HOW OLD?
23
www.garfield.com Distributed by Universal Press Syndicate
WHAT WOULD THAT BE IN SPIDER YEARS?
DON'T KNOW... NO SPIDER HAS EVER LIVED THAT LONG
© 2001 PAWS, INC. All Rights Reserved.
JIM DAVIS 6-15
WHOA, HOW IRONIC WAS **THAT?**

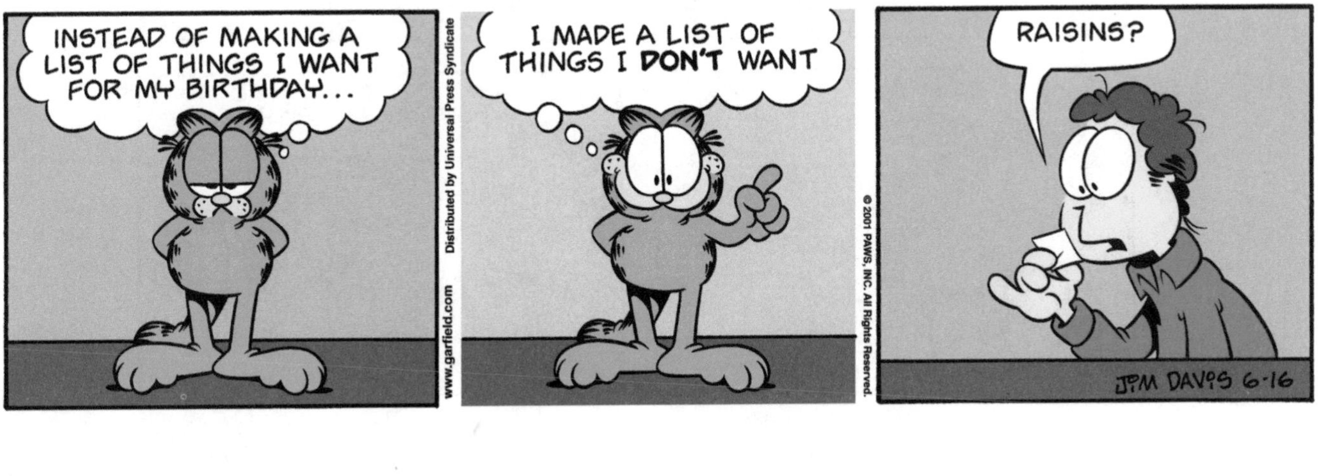
INSTEAD OF MAKING A LIST OF THINGS I WANT FOR MY BIRTHDAY...
www.garfield.com Distributed by Universal Press Syndicate
I MADE A LIST OF THINGS I **DON'T** WANT
© 2001 PAWS, INC. All Rights Reserved.
RAISINS?
JIM DAVIS 6-16

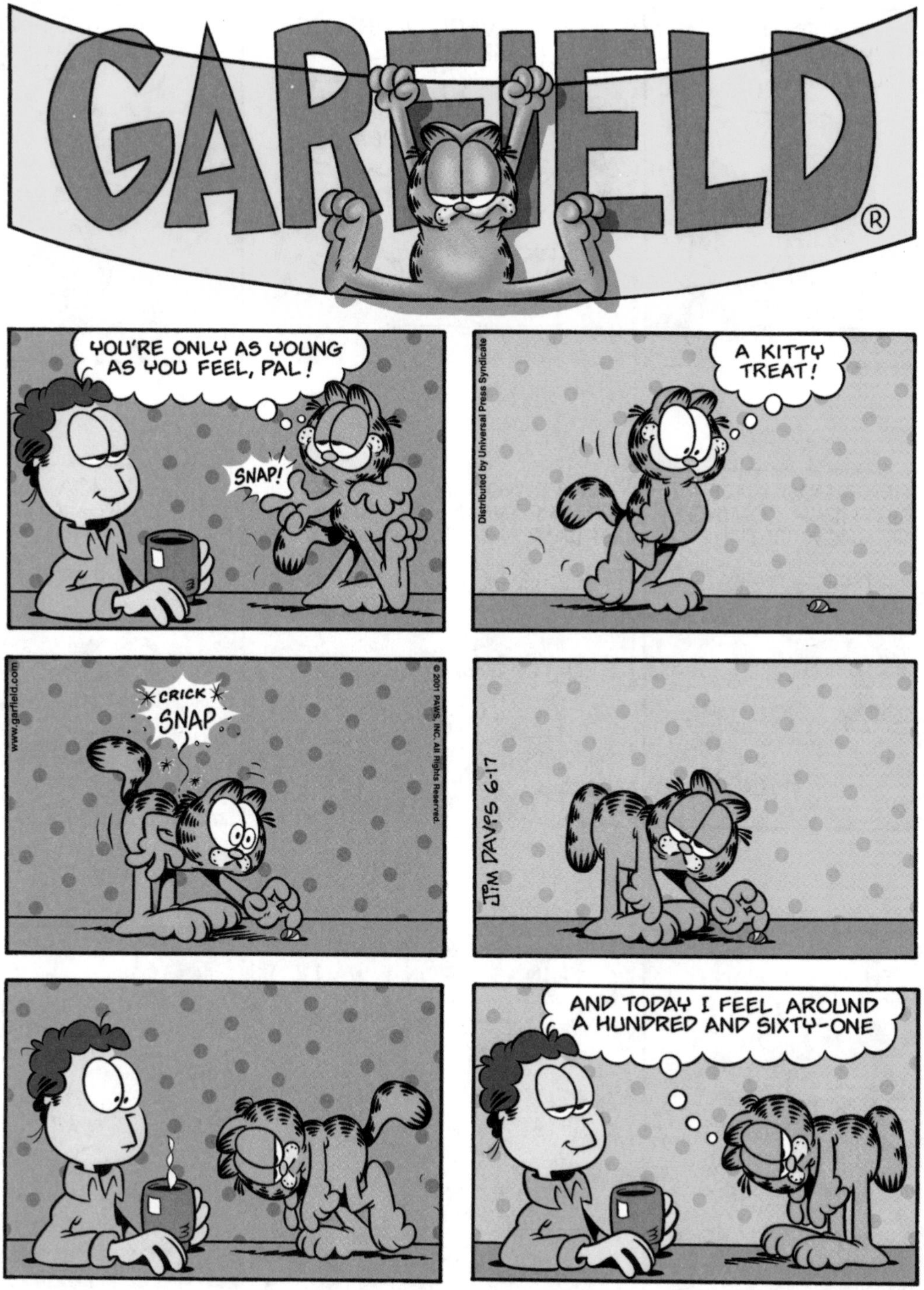
GARFIELD
YOU'RE ONLY AS YOUNG AS YOU FEEL, PAL!
SNAP!
Distributed by Universal Press Syndicate
A KITTY TREAT!
www.garfield.com
CRICK SNAP
© 2001 PAWS, INC. All Rights Reserved.
JIM DAVIS 6-17
AND TODAY I FEEL AROUND A HUNDRED AND SIXTY-ONE

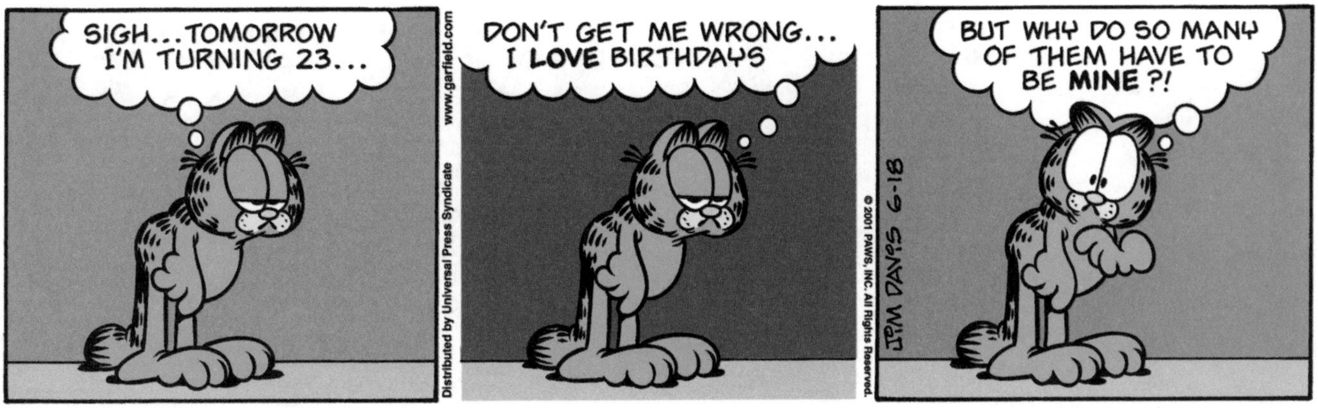
SIGH...TOMORROW I'M TURNING 23...
DON'T GET ME WRONG... I LOVE BIRTHDAYS
BUT WHY DO SO MANY OF THEM HAVE TO BE MINE?!
Distributed by Universal Press Syndicate www.garfield.com
© 2001 PAWS, INC. All Rights Reserved.
JIM DAVIS 6-18

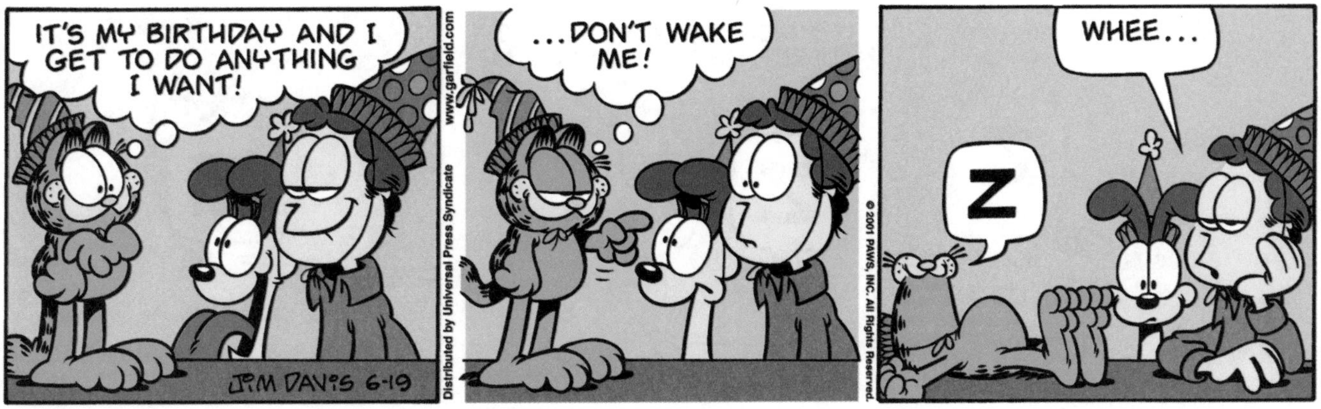
IT'S MY BIRTHDAY AND I GET TO DO ANYTHING I WANT!
...DON'T WAKE ME!
Z
WHEE...
JIM DAVIS 6-19
Distributed by Universal Press Syndicate www.garfield.com
© 2001 PAWS, INC. All Rights Reserved.

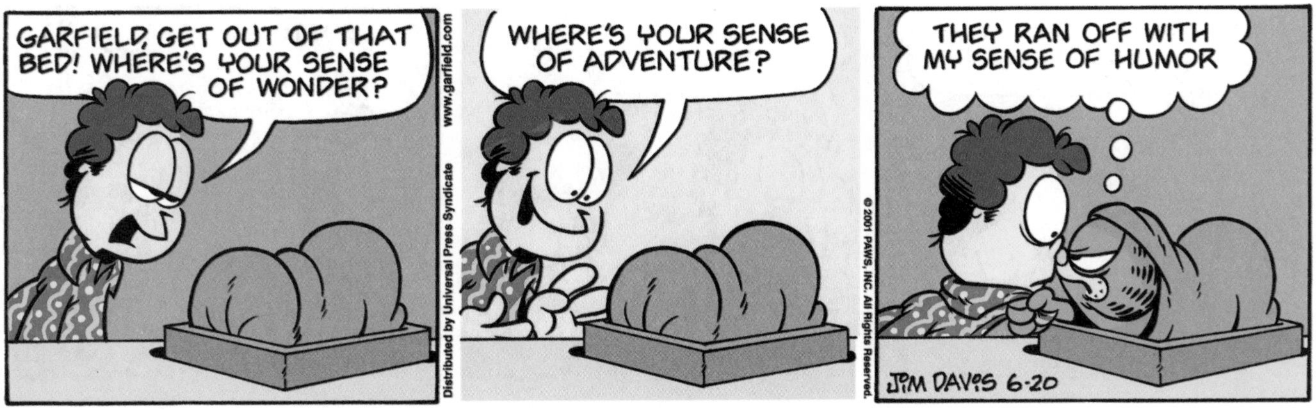
GARFIELD, GET OUT OF THAT BED! WHERE'S YOUR SENSE OF WONDER?
WHERE'S YOUR SENSE OF ADVENTURE?
THEY RAN OFF WITH MY SENSE OF HUMOR
Distributed by Universal Press Syndicate www.garfield.com
© 2001 PAWS, INC. All Rights Reserved.
JIM DAVIS 6-20

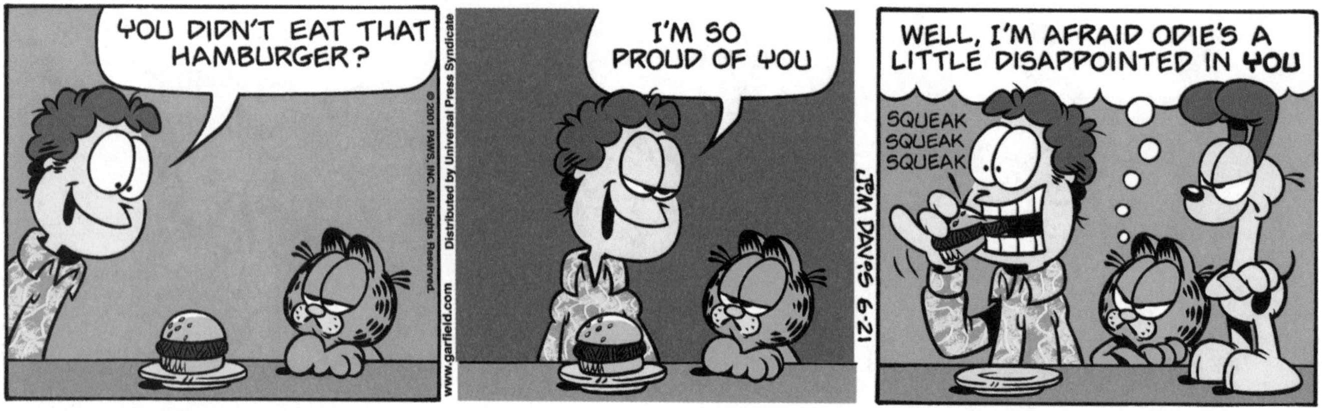
YOU DIDN'T EAT THAT HAMBURGER?
© 2001 PAWS, INC. All Rights Reserved.
Distributed by Universal Press Syndicate
www.garfield.com
I'M SO PROUD OF YOU
JPM DAVPS 6-21
WELL, I'M AFRAID ODIE'S A LITTLE DISAPPOINTED IN YOU
SQUEAK SQUEAK SQUEAK

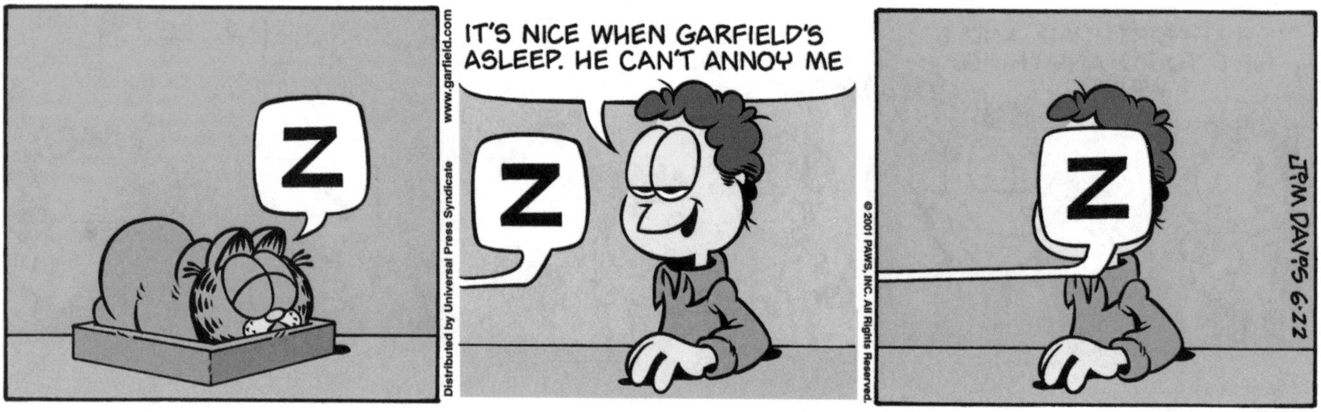
Z
Distributed by Universal Press Syndicate
www.garfield.com
IT'S NICE WHEN GARFIELD'S ASLEEP. HE CAN'T ANNOY ME
Z
© 2001 PAWS, INC. All Rights Reserved.
Z
JPM DAVPS 6-22

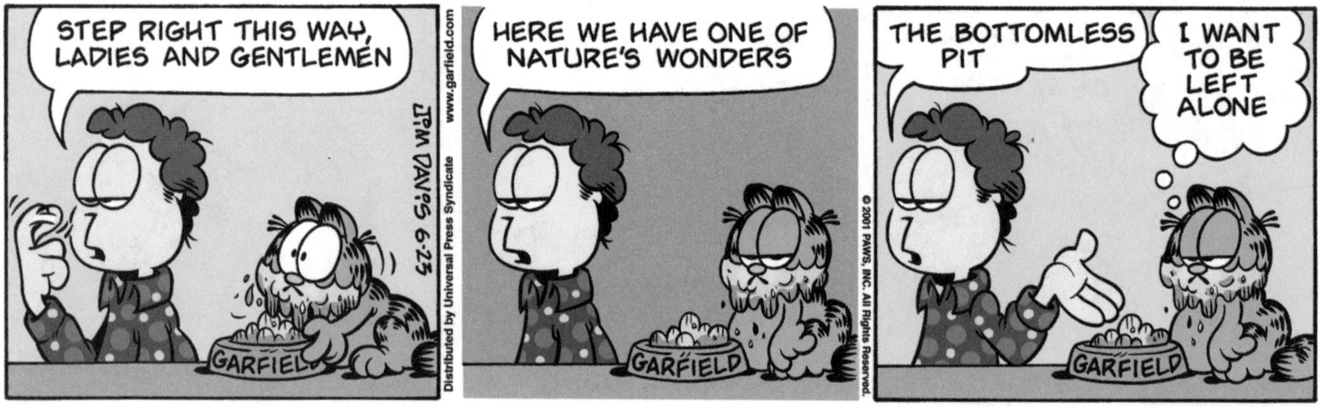
STEP RIGHT THIS WAY, LADIES AND GENTLEMEN
JPM DAVPS 6-23
GARFIEL
Distributed by Universal Press Syndicate
www.garfield.com
HERE WE HAVE ONE OF NATURE'S WONDERS
GARFIELD
© 2001 PAWS, INC. All Rights Reserved.
THE BOTTOMLESS PIT
I WANT TO BE LEFT ALONE
GARFIELD

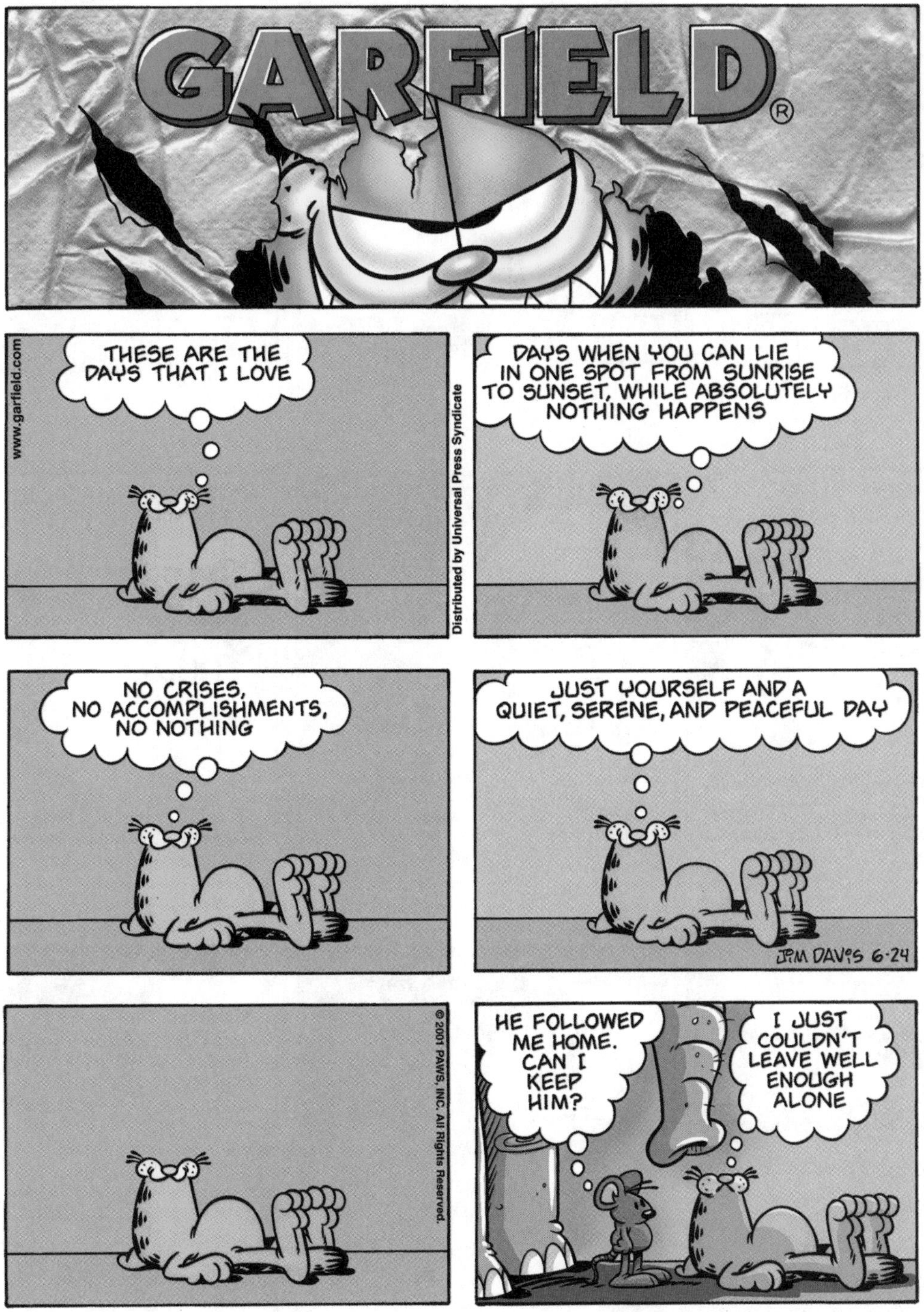
GARFIELD®
www.garfield.com
THESE ARE THE DAYS THAT I LOVE
Distributed by Universal Press Syndicate
DAYS WHEN YOU CAN LIE IN ONE SPOT FROM SUNRISE TO SUNSET, WHILE ABSOLUTELY NOTHING HAPPENS
NO CRISES, NO ACCOMPLISHMENTS, NO NOTHING
JUST YOURSELF AND A QUIET, SERENE, AND PEACEFUL DAY
JIM DAVIS 6·24
© 2001 PAWS, INC. All Rights Reserved.
HE FOLLOWED ME HOME. CAN I KEEP HIM?
I JUST COULDN'T LEAVE WELL ENOUGH ALONE

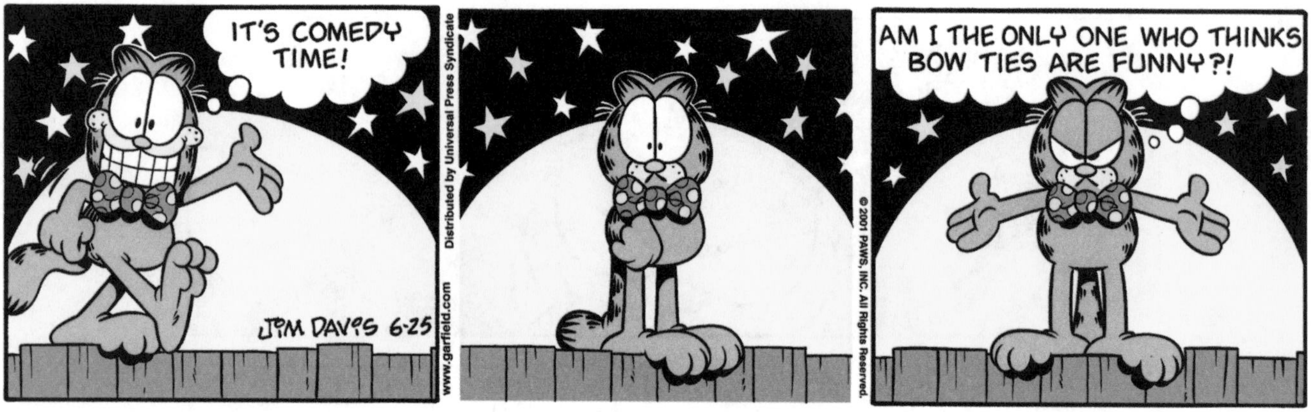
IT'S COMEDY TIME!
JIM DAVIS 6-25
Distributed by Universal Press Syndicate www.garfield.com
AM I THE ONLY ONE WHO THINKS BOW TIES ARE FUNNY?!
© 2001 PAWS, INC. All Rights Reserved.

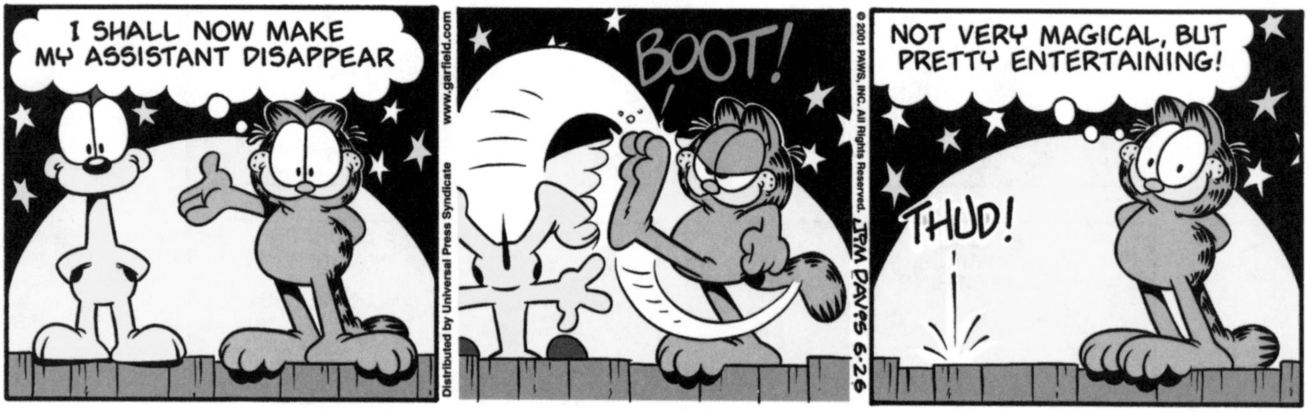
I SHALL NOW MAKE MY ASSISTANT DISAPPEAR
Distributed by Universal Press Syndicate www.garfield.com
BOOT!
© 2001 PAWS, INC. All Rights Reserved.
JIM DAVIS 6-26
NOT VERY MAGICAL, BUT PRETTY ENTERTAINING!
THUD!

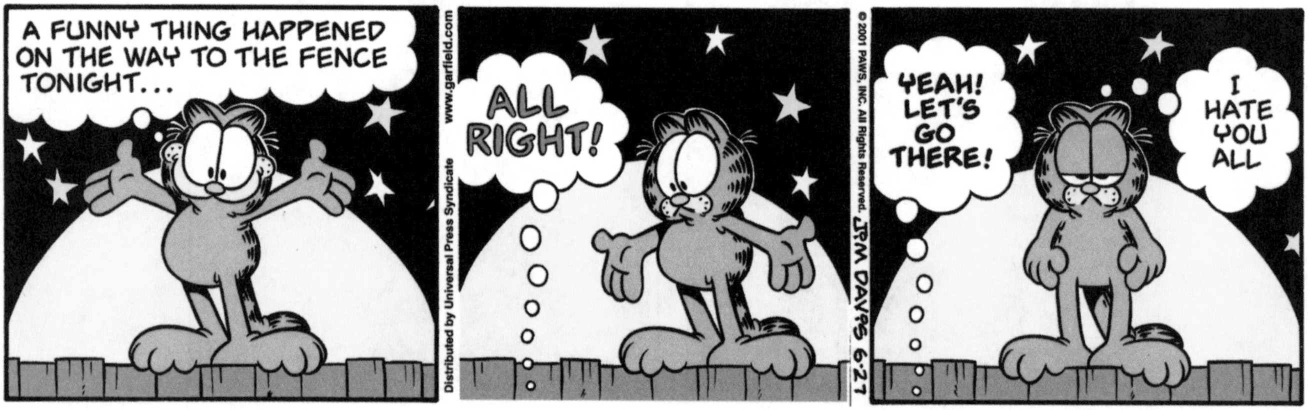
A FUNNY THING HAPPENED ON THE WAY TO THE FENCE TONIGHT...
Distributed by Universal Press Syndicate www.garfield.com
ALL RIGHT!
© 2001 PAWS, INC. All Rights Reserved.
JIM DAVIS 6-27
YEAH! LET'S GO THERE!
I HATE YOU ALL

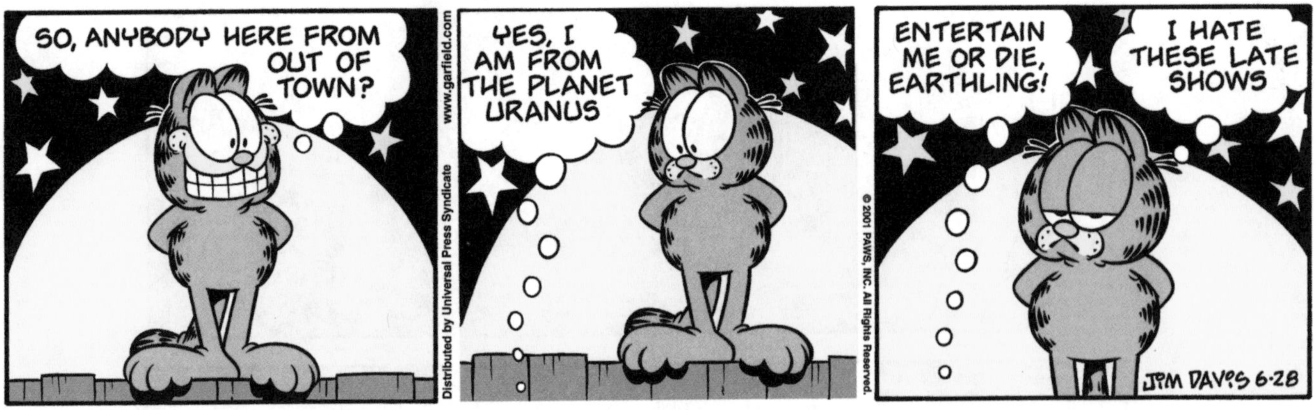
SO, ANYBODY HERE FROM OUT OF TOWN?
www.garfield.com Distributed by Universal Press Syndicate
YES, I AM FROM THE PLANET URANUS
© 2001 PAWS, INC. All Rights Reserved.
ENTERTAIN ME OR DIE, EARTHLING!
I HATE THESE LATE SHOWS
JIM DAVIS 6-28

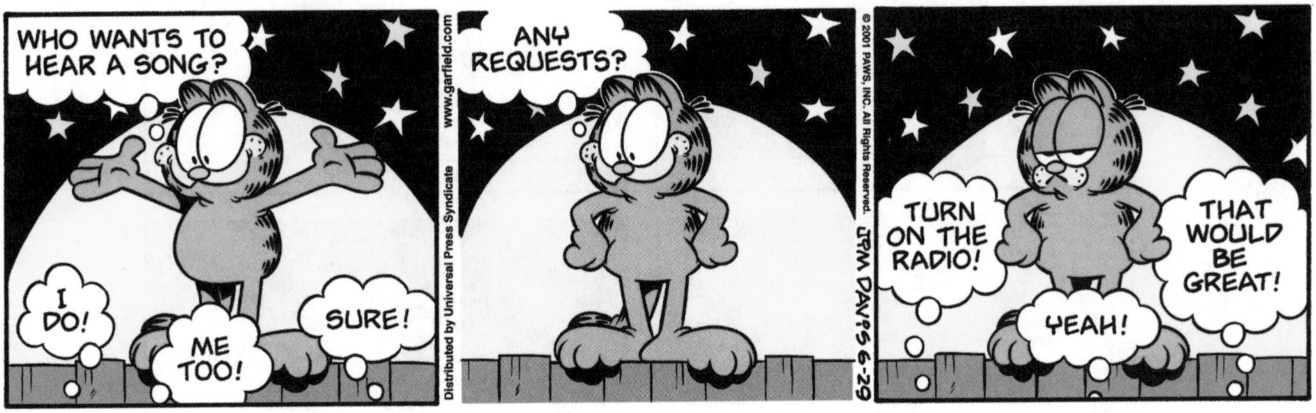
WHO WANTS TO HEAR A SONG?
I DO!
ME TOO!
SURE!
www.garfield.com Distributed by Universal Press Syndicate
ANY REQUESTS?
© 2001 PAWS, INC. All Rights Reserved.
JIM DAVIS 6-29
TURN ON THE RADIO!
YEAH!
THAT WOULD BE GREAT!

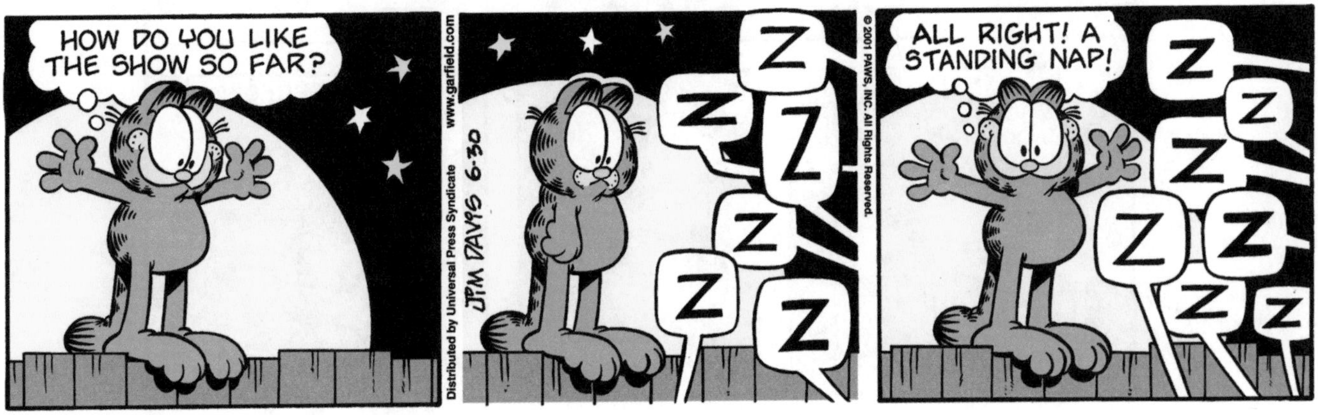
HOW DO YOU LIKE THE SHOW SO FAR?
www.garfield.com Distributed by Universal Press Syndicate
JIM DAVIS 6-30
Z Z Z Z Z Z
© 2001 PAWS, INC. All Rights Reserved.
ALL RIGHT! A STANDING NAP!
Z Z Z Z Z Z Z Z

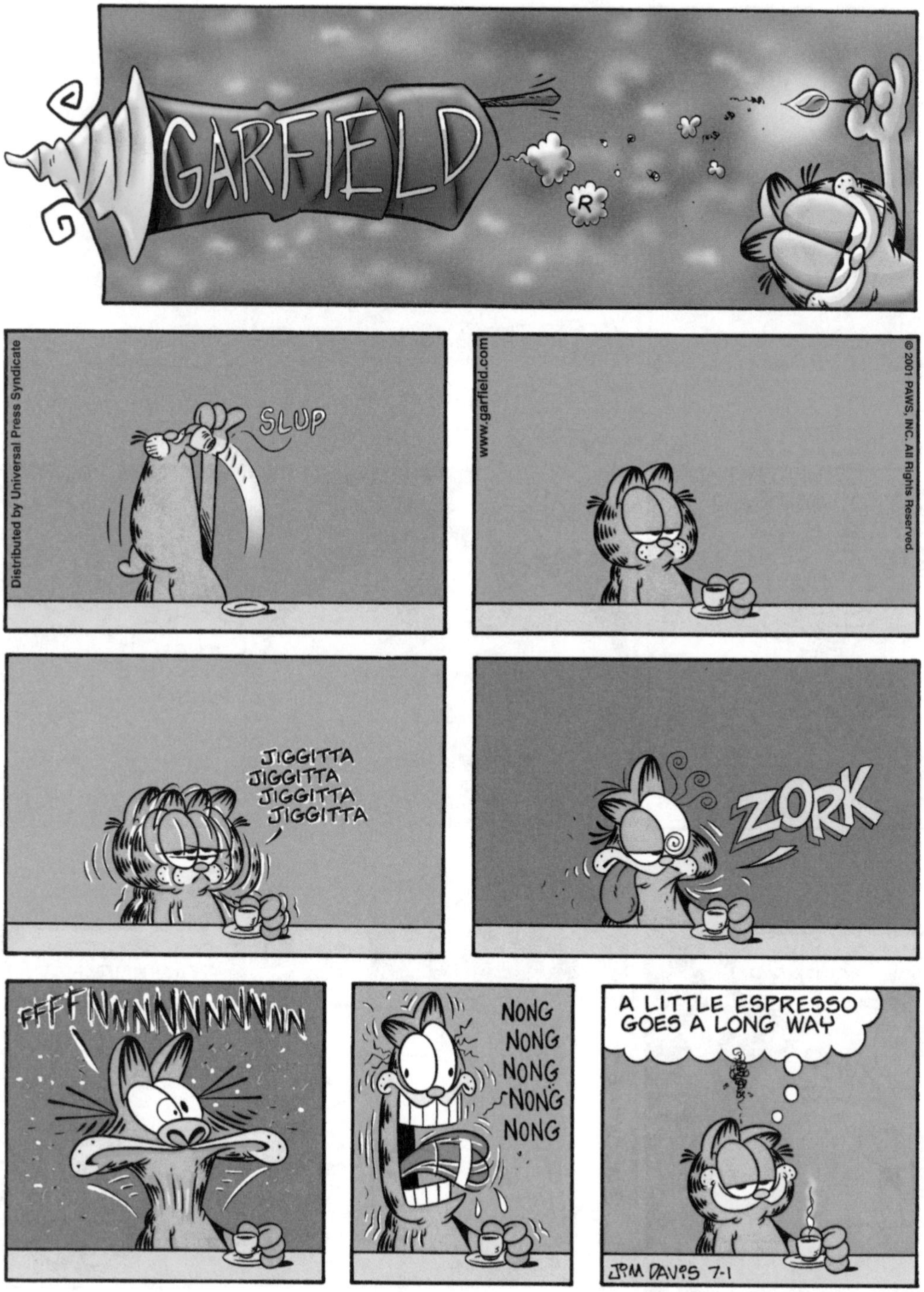
GARFIELD
R
Distributed by Universal Press Syndicate
SLUP
www.garfield.com
© 2001 PAWS, INC. All Rights Reserved.
JIGGITTA
JIGGITTA
JIGGITTA
JIGGITTA
ZORK
FFFFNNNNNNNNNNNN
NONG
NONG
NONG
NONG
NONG
A LITTLE ESPRESSO GOES A LONG WAY
JIM DAVIS 7-1

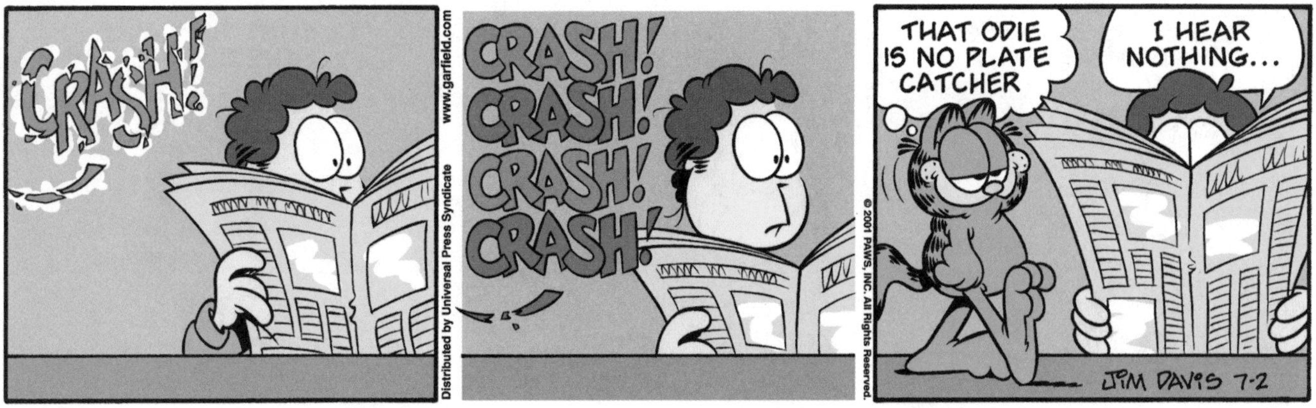
CRASH!
CRASH! CRASH! CRASH! CRASH!
THAT ODIE IS NO PLATE CATCHER
I HEAR NOTHING...
JIM DAVIS 7-2
Distributed by Universal Press Syndicate www.garfield.com
© 2001 PAWS, INC. All Rights Reserved.

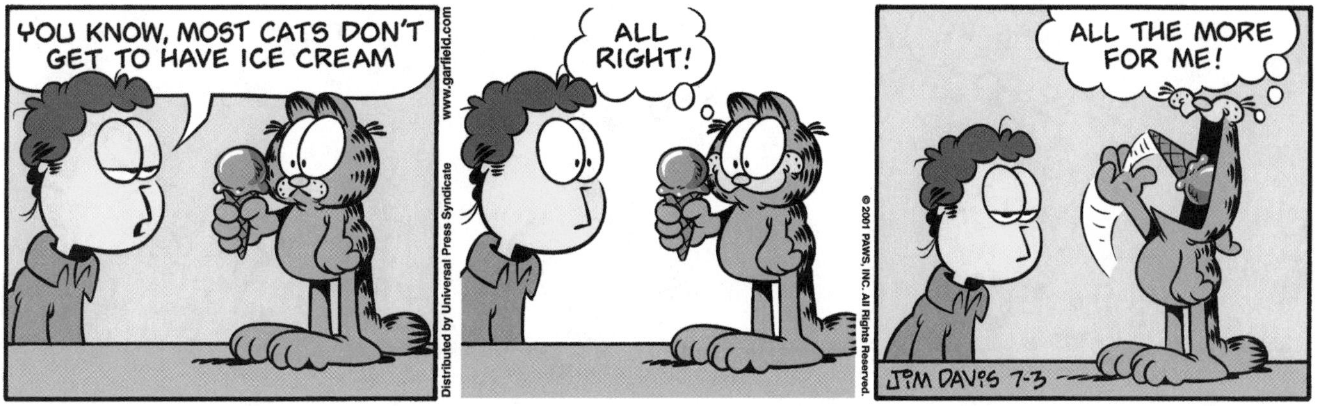
YOU KNOW, MOST CATS DON'T GET TO HAVE ICE CREAM
ALL RIGHT!
ALL THE MORE FOR ME!
JIM DAVIS 7-3
Distributed by Universal Press Syndicate www.garfield.com
© 2001 PAWS, INC. All Rights Reserved.

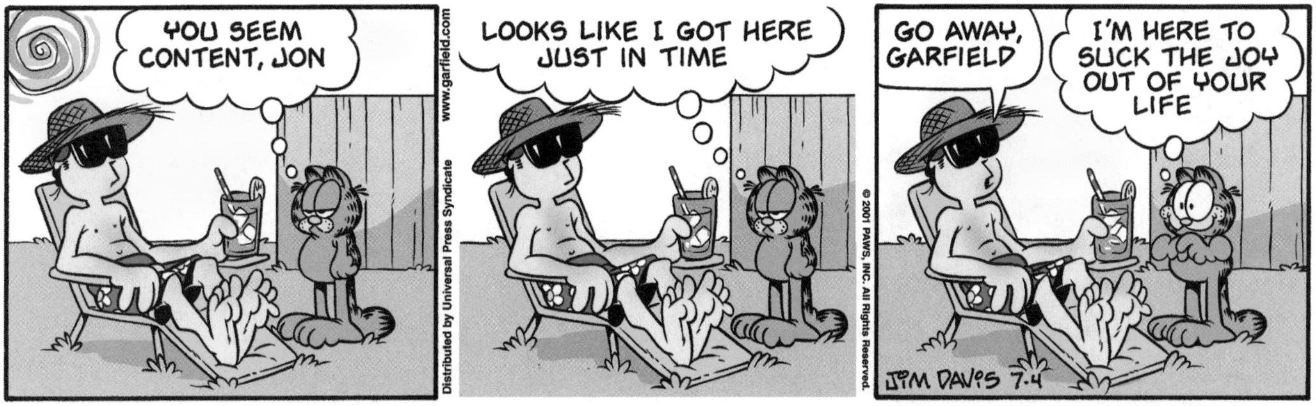
YOU SEEM CONTENT, JON
LOOKS LIKE I GOT HERE JUST IN TIME
GO AWAY, GARFIELD
I'M HERE TO SUCK THE JOY OUT OF YOUR LIFE
JIM DAVIS 7-4
Distributed by Universal Press Syndicate www.garfield.com
© 2001 PAWS, INC. All Rights Reserved.

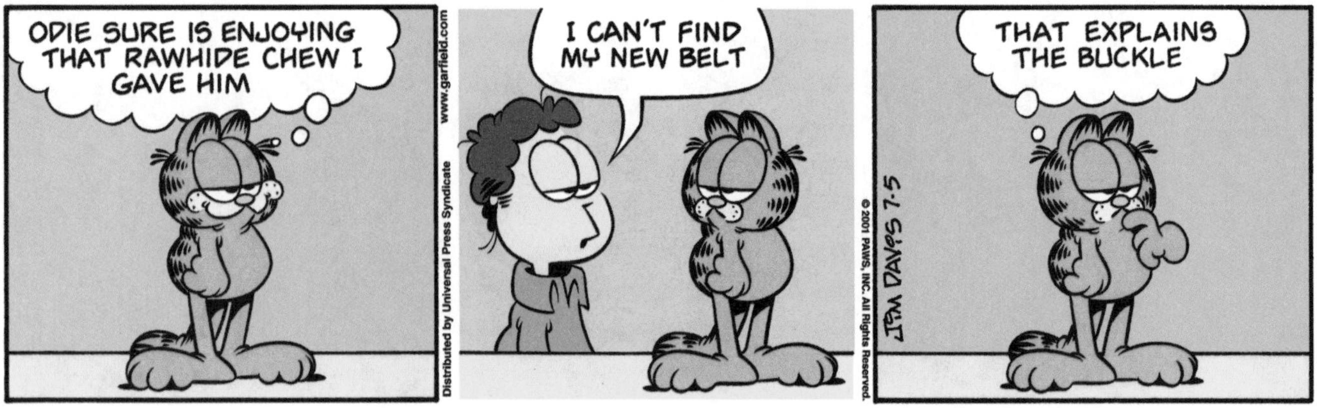
ODIE SURE IS ENJOYING THAT RAWHIDE CHEW I GAVE HIM
Distributed by Universal Press Syndicate www.garfield.com
I CAN'T FIND MY NEW BELT
© 2001 PAWS, INC. All Rights Reserved.
THAT EXPLAINS THE BUCKLE
JIM DAVIS 7-5

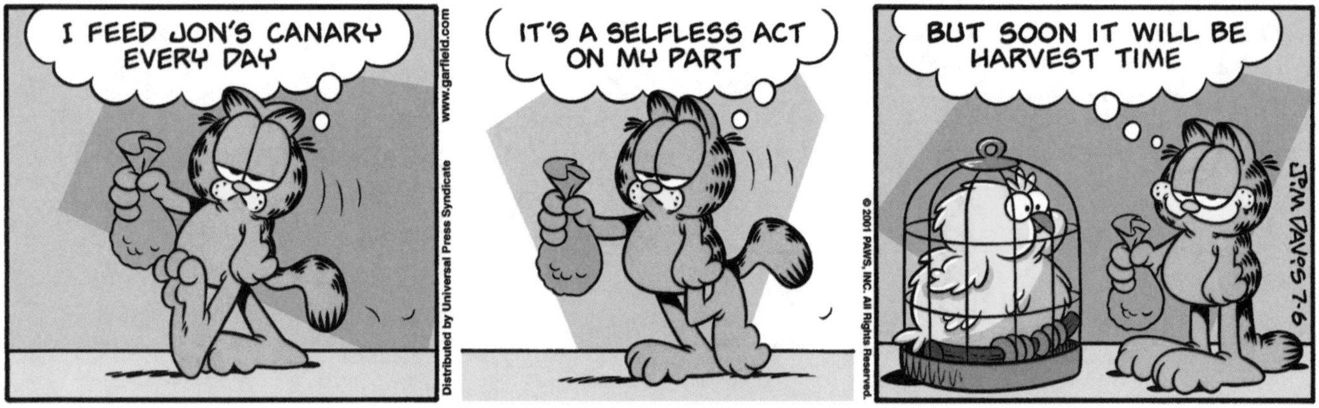
I FEED JON'S CANARY EVERY DAY
Distributed by Universal Press Syndicate www.garfield.com
IT'S A SELFLESS ACT ON MY PART
© 2001 PAWS, INC. All Rights Reserved.
BUT SOON IT WILL BE HARVEST TIME
JIM DAVIS 7-6

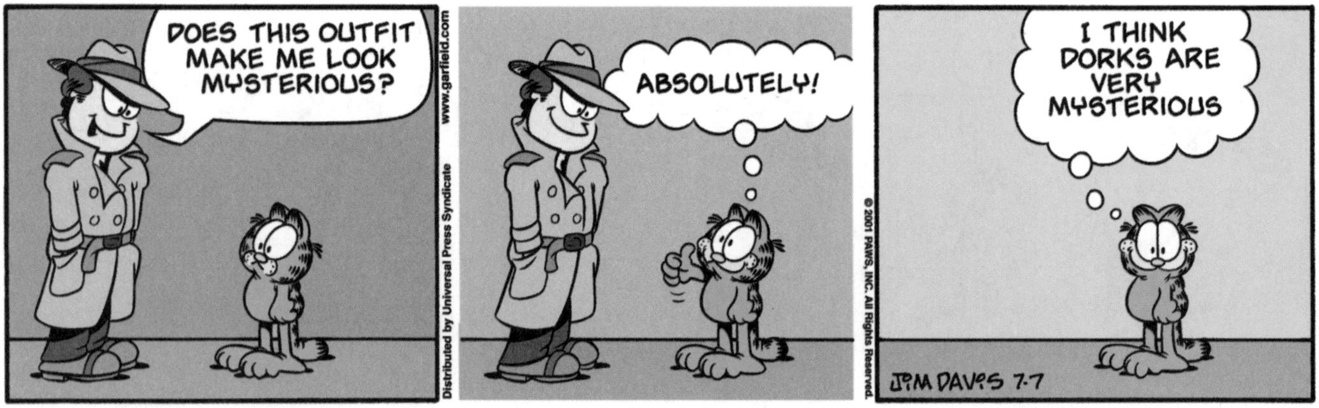
DOES THIS OUTFIT MAKE ME LOOK MYSTERIOUS?
Distributed by Universal Press Syndicate www.garfield.com
ABSOLUTELY!
© 2001 PAWS, INC. All Rights Reserved.
I THINK DORKS ARE VERY MYSTERIOUS
JIM DAVIS 7-7

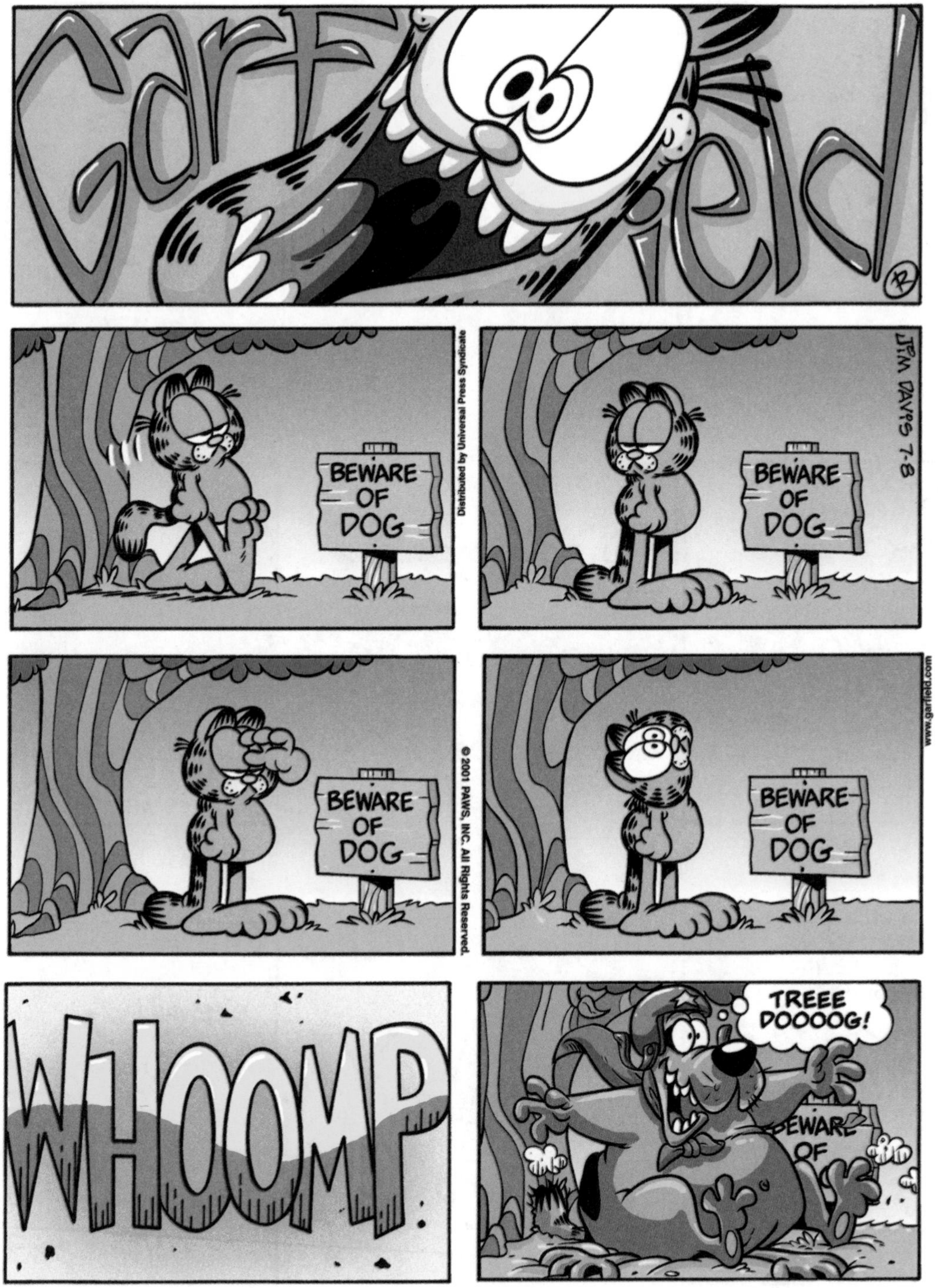
Garfield®
JIM DAVIS 7-8
Distributed by Universal Press Syndicate
BEWARE OF DOG
BEWARE OF DOG
BEWARE OF DOG
© 2001 PAWS, INC. All Rights Reserved.
www.garfield.com
BEWARE OF DOG
WHOOMP
TREEE DOOOOG!
BEWARE OF

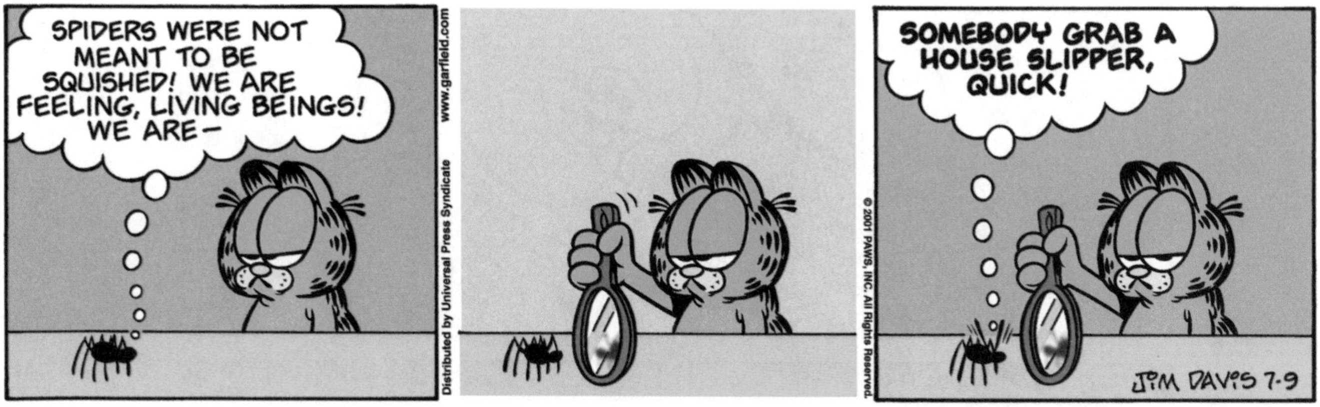
SPIDERS WERE NOT MEANT TO BE SQUISHED! WE ARE FEELING, LIVING BEINGS! WE ARE—
SOMEBODY GRAB A HOUSE SLIPPER, QUICK!
JIM DAVIS 7-9
Distributed by Universal Press Syndicate www.garfield.com
© 2001 PAWS, INC. All Rights Reserved.

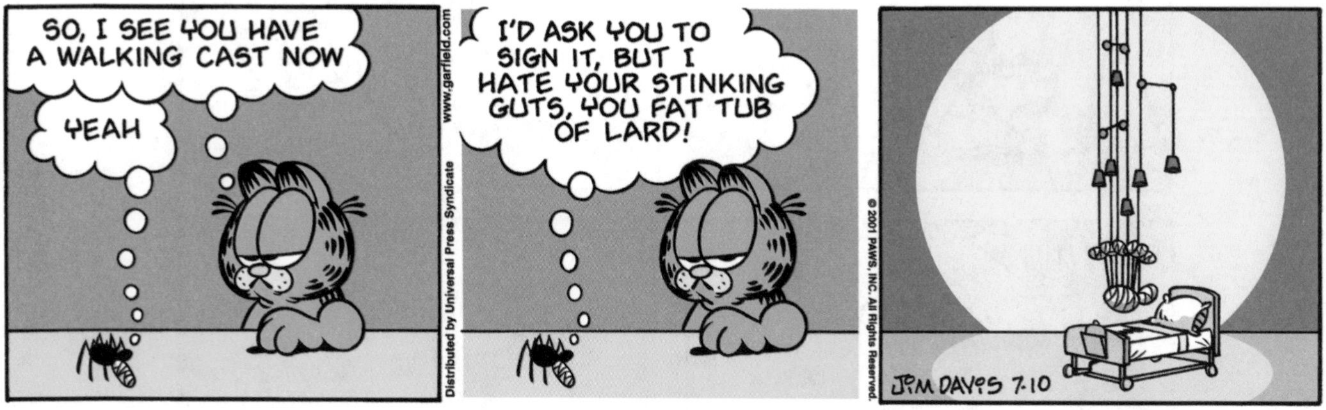
SO, I SEE YOU HAVE A WALKING CAST NOW
YEAH
I'D ASK YOU TO SIGN IT, BUT I HATE YOUR STINKING GUTS, YOU FAT TUB OF LARD!
JIM DAVIS 7-10
Distributed by Universal Press Syndicate www.garfield.com
© 2001 PAWS, INC. All Rights Reserved.

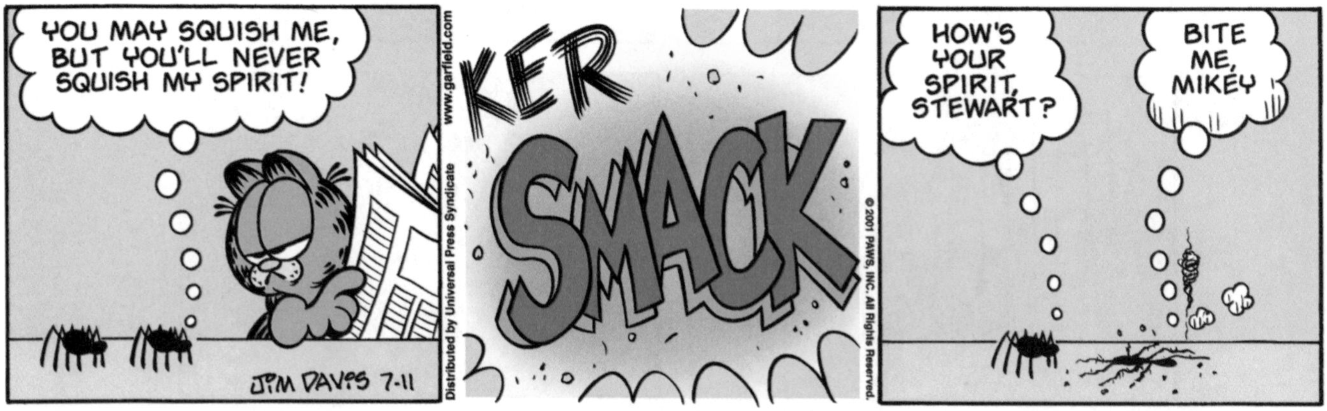
YOU MAY SQUISH ME, BUT YOU'LL NEVER SQUISH MY SPIRIT!
JIM DAVIS 7-11
KER SMACK
HOW'S YOUR SPIRIT, STEWART?
BITE ME, MIKEY
Distributed by Universal Press Syndicate www.garfield.com
© 2001 PAWS, INC. All Rights Reserved.

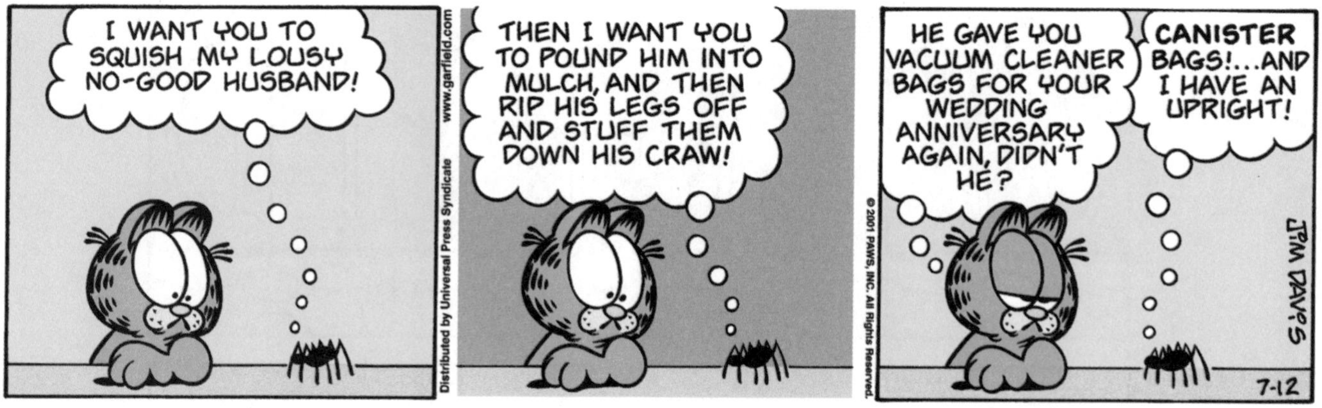
I WANT YOU TO SQUISH MY LOUSY NO-GOOD HUSBAND!
www.garfield.com
Distributed by Universal Press Syndicate
THEN I WANT YOU TO POUND HIM INTO MULCH, AND THEN RIP HIS LEGS OFF AND STUFF THEM DOWN HIS CRAW!
© 2001 PAWS, INC. All Rights Reserved.
HE GAVE YOU VACUUM CLEANER BAGS FOR YOUR WEDDING ANNIVERSARY AGAIN, DIDN'T HE?
CANISTER BAGS!...AND I HAVE AN UPRIGHT!
JIM DAVIS
7-12

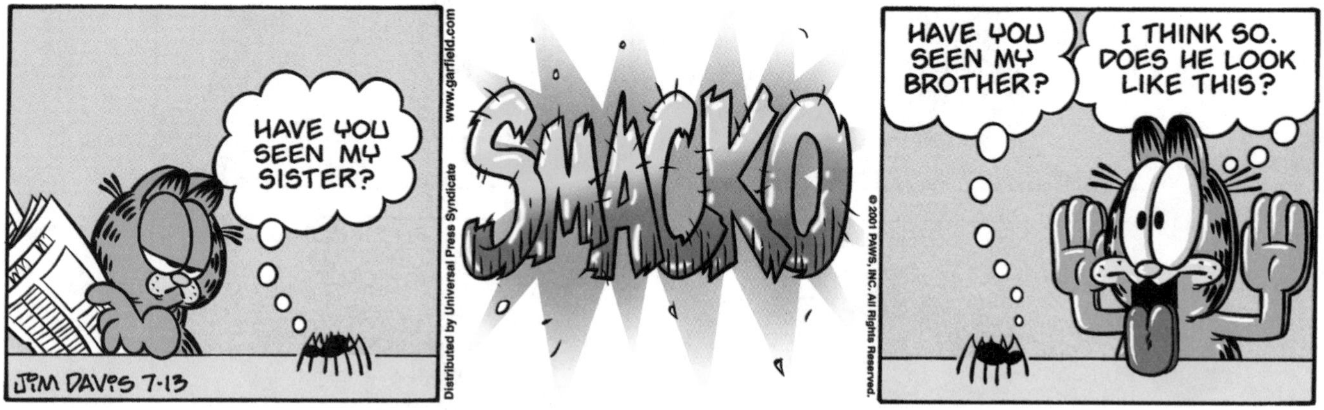
HAVE YOU SEEN MY SISTER?
JIM DAVIS 7-13
www.garfield.com
Distributed by Universal Press Syndicate
SMACKO
© 2001 PAWS, INC. All Rights Reserved.
HAVE YOU SEEN MY BROTHER?
I THINK SO. DOES HE LOOK LIKE THIS?

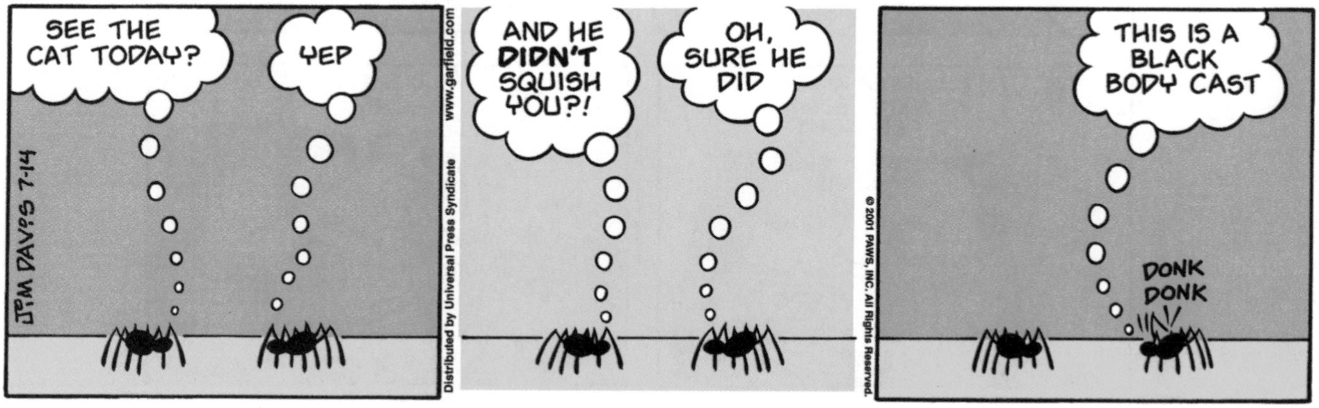
SEE THE CAT TODAY?
YEP
JIM DAVIS 7-14
www.garfield.com
Distributed by Universal Press Syndicate
AND HE **DIDN'T** SQUISH YOU?!
OH, SURE HE DID
© 2001 PAWS, INC. All Rights Reserved.
THIS IS A BLACK BODY CAST
DONK
DONK

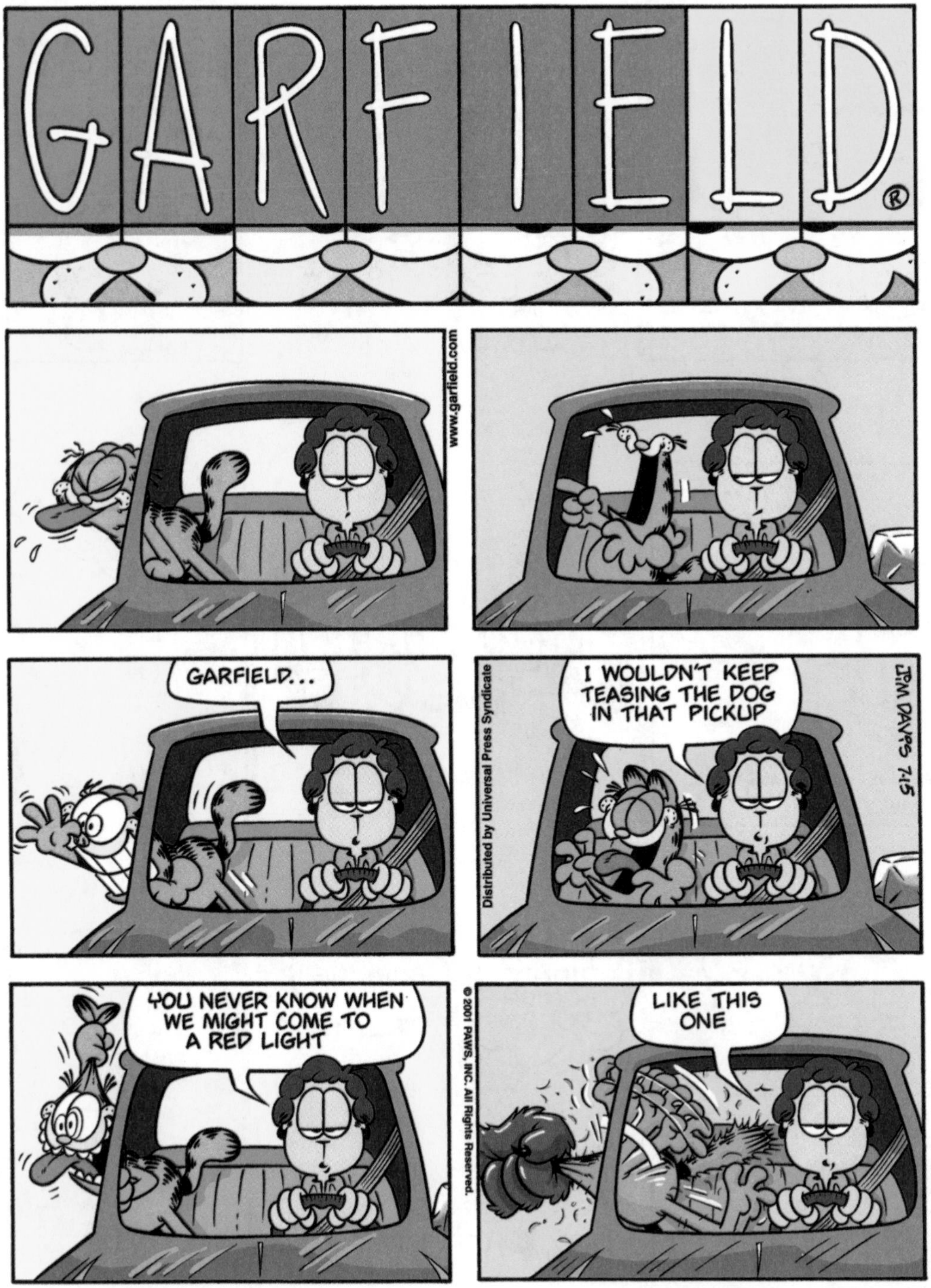
GARFIELD®
www.garfield.com
GARFIELD...
I WOULDN'T KEEP TEASING THE DOG IN THAT PICKUP
JIM DAVIS 7-15
Distributed by Universal Press Syndicate
YOU NEVER KNOW WHEN WE MIGHT COME TO A RED LIGHT
© 2001 PAWS, INC. All Rights Reserved.
LIKE THIS ONE

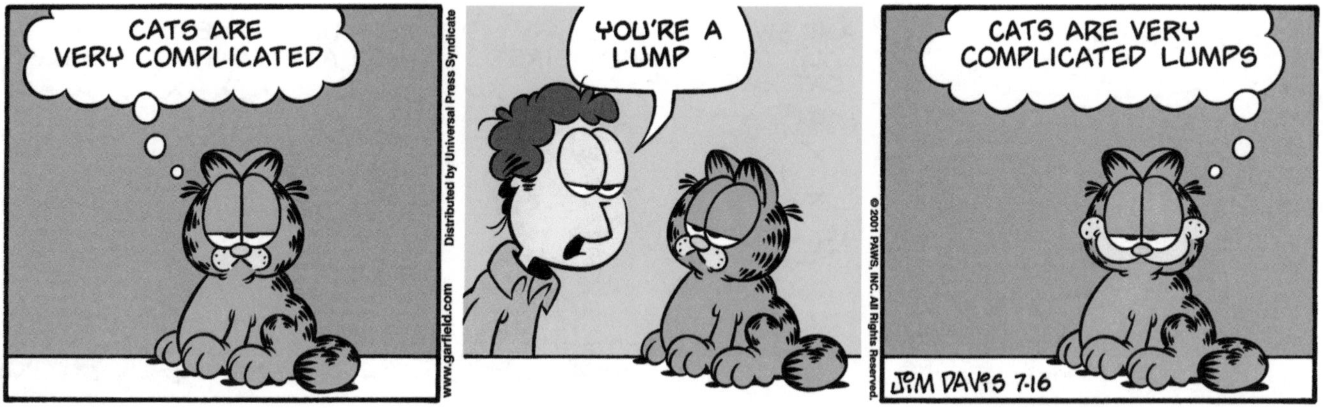
CATS ARE VERY COMPLICATED
YOU'RE A LUMP
CATS ARE VERY COMPLICATED LUMPS
JIM DAVIS 7-16
www.garfield.com Distributed by Universal Press Syndicate
© 2001 PAWS, INC. All Rights Reserved.

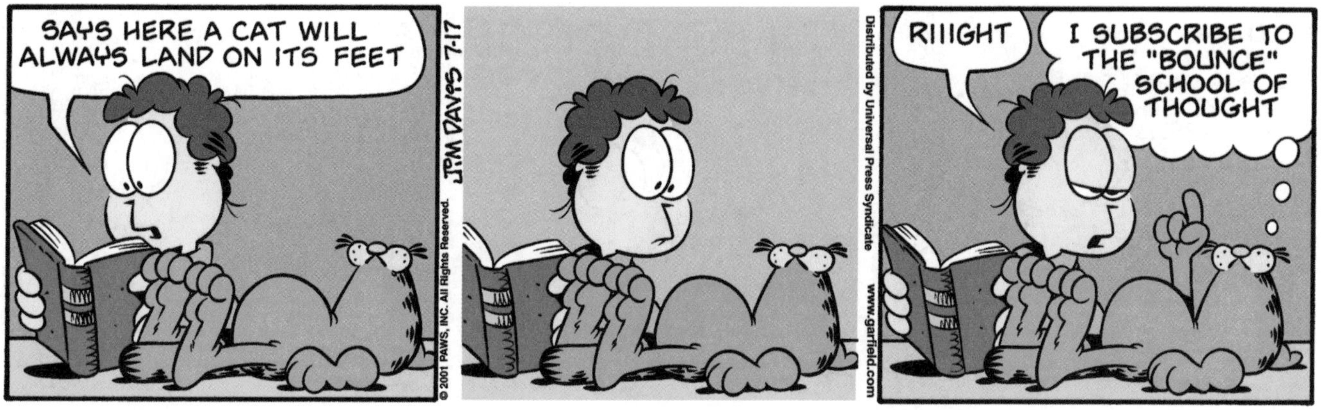
SAYS HERE A CAT WILL ALWAYS LAND ON ITS FEET
RIIIGHT
I SUBSCRIBE TO THE "BOUNCE" SCHOOL OF THOUGHT
JIM DAVIS 7-17
© 2001 PAWS, INC. All Rights Reserved.
Distributed by Universal Press Syndicate www.garfield.com

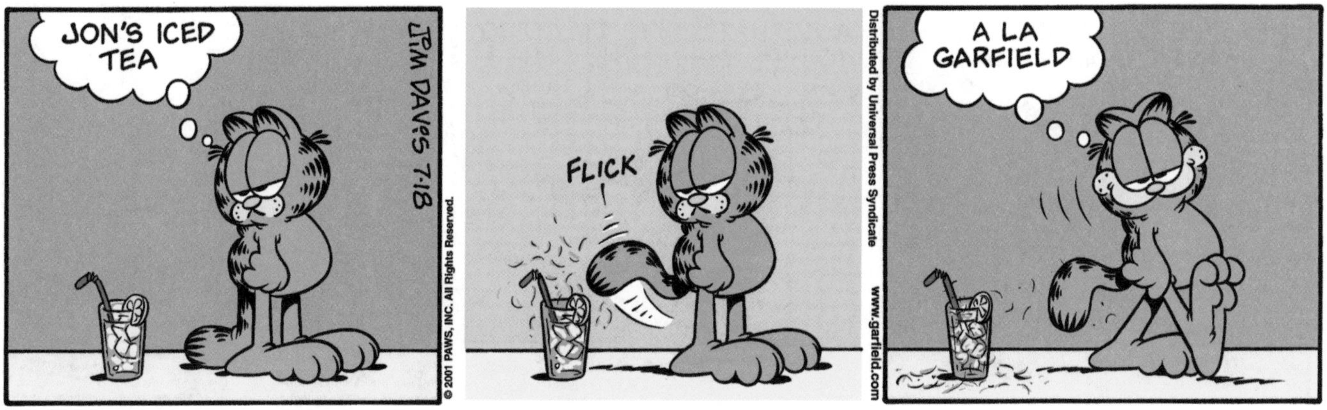
JON'S ICED TEA
FLICK
A LA GARFIELD
JIM DAVIS 7-18
© 2001 PAWS, INC. All Rights Reserved.
Distributed by Universal Press Syndicate www.garfield.com

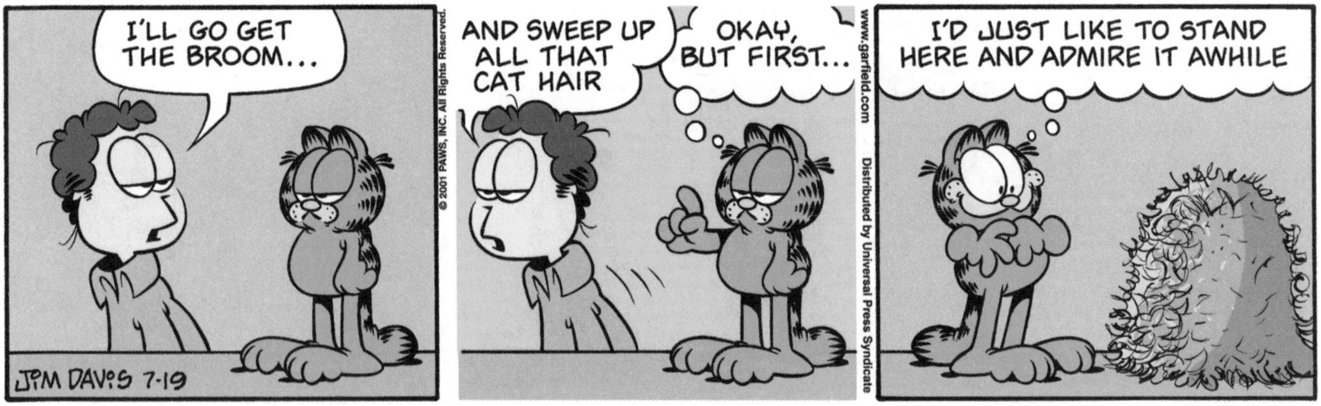
I'LL GO GET THE BROOM...
AND SWEEP UP ALL THAT CAT HAIR
OKAY, BUT FIRST...
I'D JUST LIKE TO STAND HERE AND ADMIRE IT AWHILE
JIM DAVIS 7-19
© 2001 PAWS, INC. All Rights Reserved.
www.garfield.com Distributed by Universal Press Syndicate

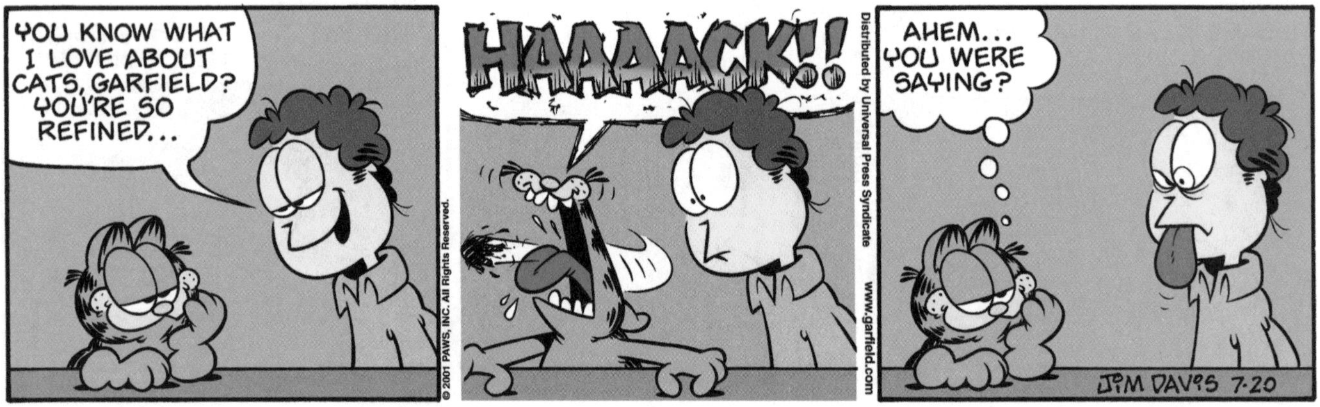
YOU KNOW WHAT I LOVE ABOUT CATS, GARFIELD? YOU'RE SO REFINED...
HAAAACK!!
AHEM... YOU WERE SAYING?
JIM DAVIS 7-20
© 2001 PAWS, INC. All Rights Reserved.
Distributed by Universal Press Syndicate www.garfield.com

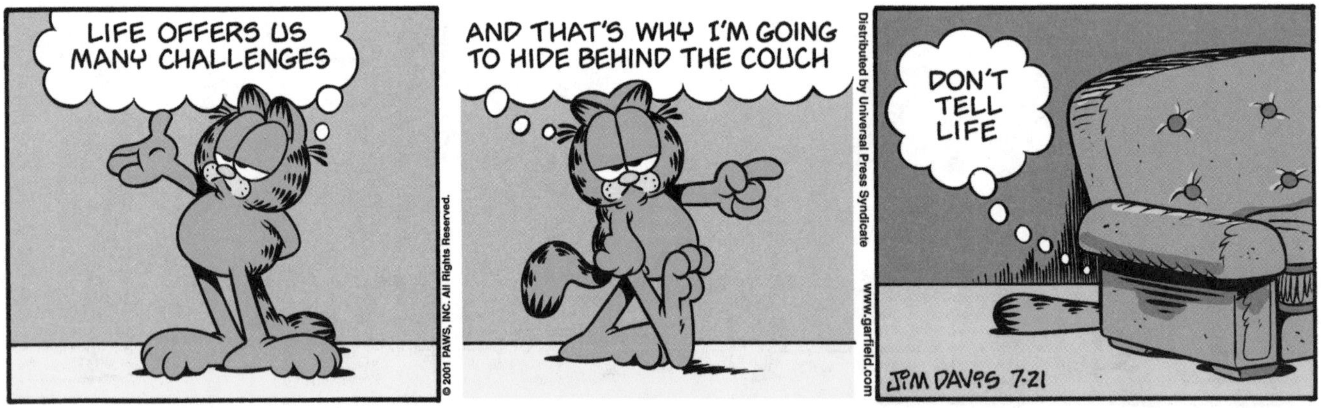
LIFE OFFERS US MANY CHALLENGES
AND THAT'S WHY I'M GOING TO HIDE BEHIND THE COUCH
DON'T TELL LIFE
JIM DAVIS 7-21
© 2001 PAWS, INC. All Rights Reserved.
Distributed by Universal Press Syndicate www.garfield.com

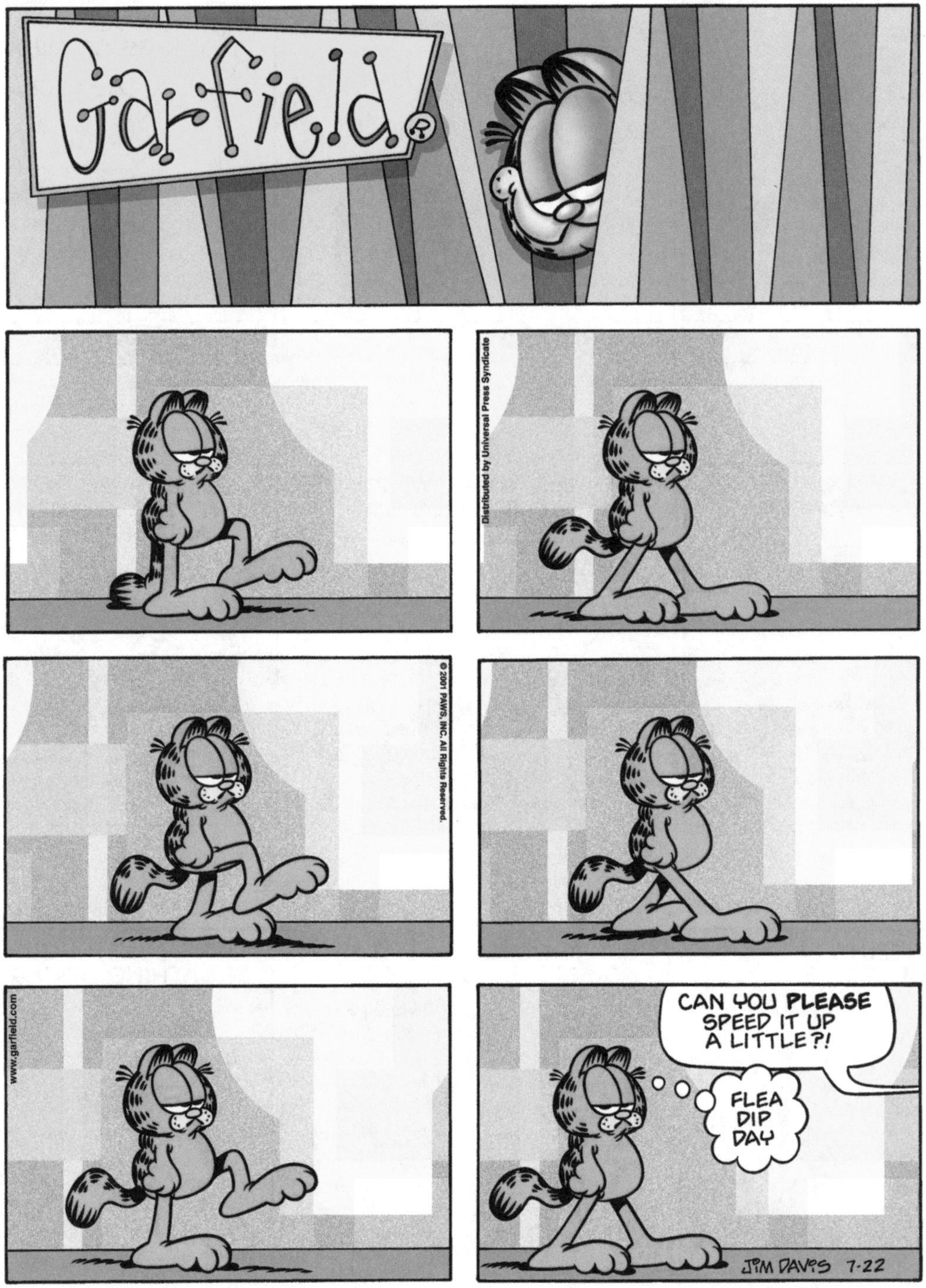
Garfield®
Distributed by Universal Press Syndicate
© 2001 PAWS, INC. All Rights Reserved.
www.garfield.com
CAN YOU PLEASE SPEED IT UP A LITTLE?!
FLEA DIP DAY
JIM DAVIS 7-22

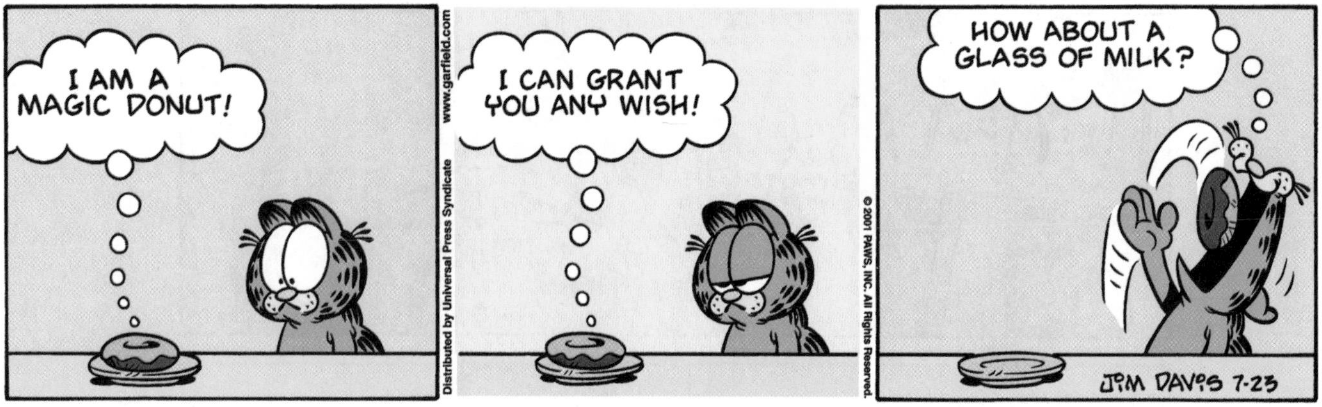
I AM A MAGIC DONUT!
I CAN GRANT YOU ANY WISH!
HOW ABOUT A GLASS OF MILK?
Distributed by Universal Press Syndicate www.garfield.com
© 2001 PAWS, INC. All Rights Reserved.
JIM DAVIS 7-23

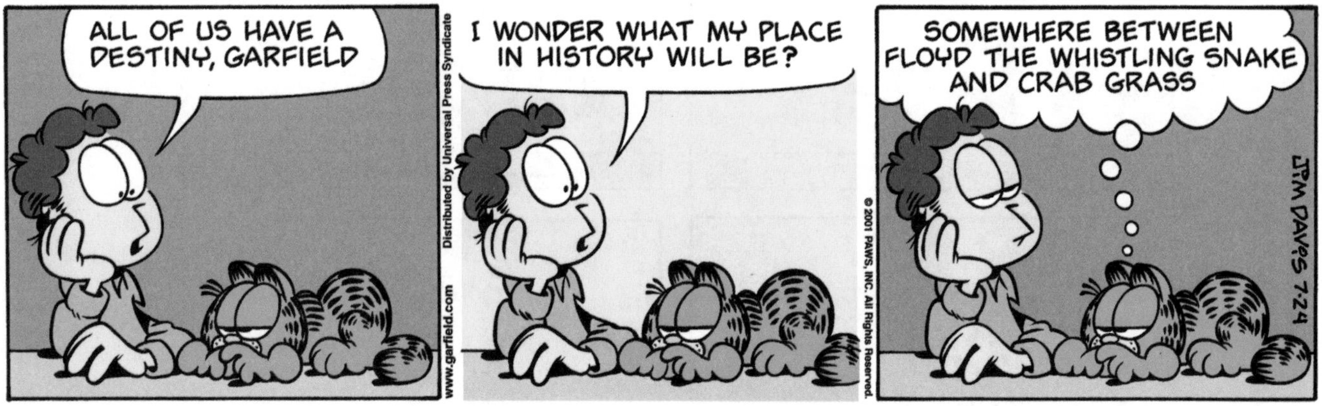
ALL OF US HAVE A DESTINY, GARFIELD
I WONDER WHAT MY PLACE IN HISTORY WILL BE?
SOMEWHERE BETWEEN FLOYD THE WHISTLING SNAKE AND CRAB GRASS
Distributed by Universal Press Syndicate www.garfield.com
© 2001 PAWS, INC. All Rights Reserved.
JIM DAVIS 7-24

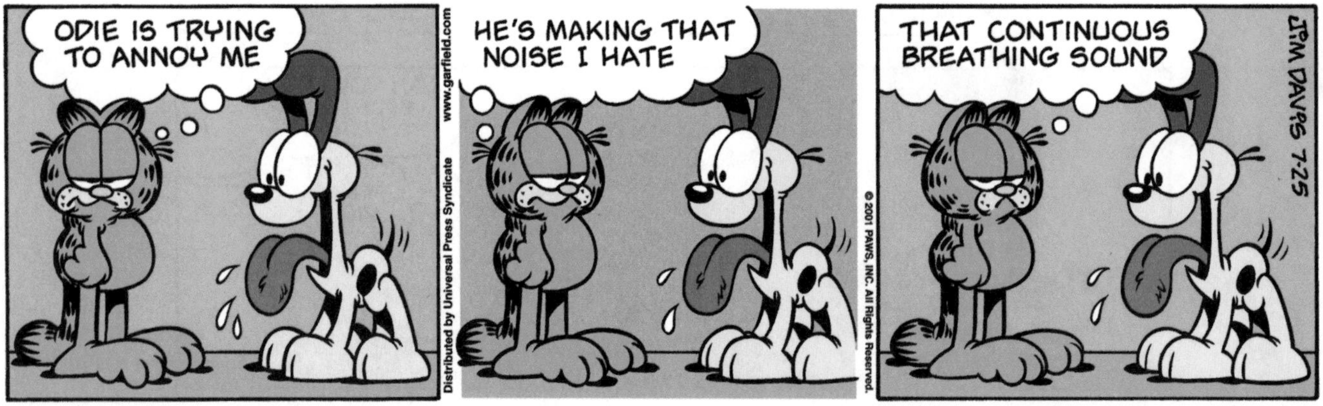
ODIE IS TRYING TO ANNOY ME
HE'S MAKING THAT NOISE I HATE
THAT CONTINUOUS BREATHING SOUND
Distributed by Universal Press Syndicate www.garfield.com
© 2001 PAWS, INC. All Rights Reserved.
JIM DAVIS 7-25

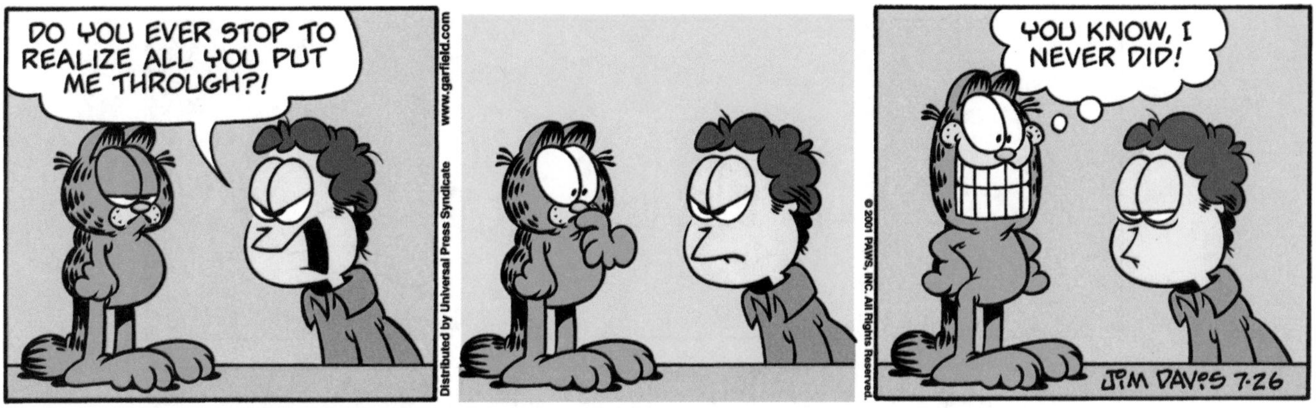
DO YOU EVER STOP TO REALIZE ALL YOU PUT ME THROUGH?!
YOU KNOW, I NEVER DID!
JIM DAVIS 7-26
www.garfield.com
Distributed by Universal Press Syndicate
© 2001 PAWS, INC. All Rights Reserved.

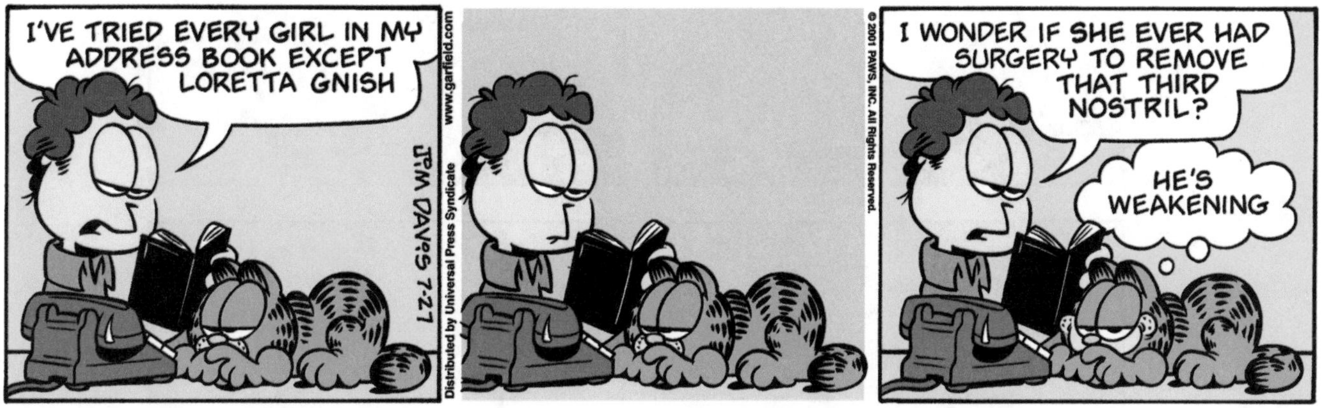
I'VE TRIED EVERY GIRL IN MY ADDRESS BOOK EXCEPT LORETTA GNISH
I WONDER IF SHE EVER HAD SURGERY TO REMOVE THAT THIRD NOSTRIL?
HE'S WEAKENING
JIM DAVIS 7-27
www.garfield.com
Distributed by Universal Press Syndicate
© 2001 PAWS, INC. All Rights Reserved.

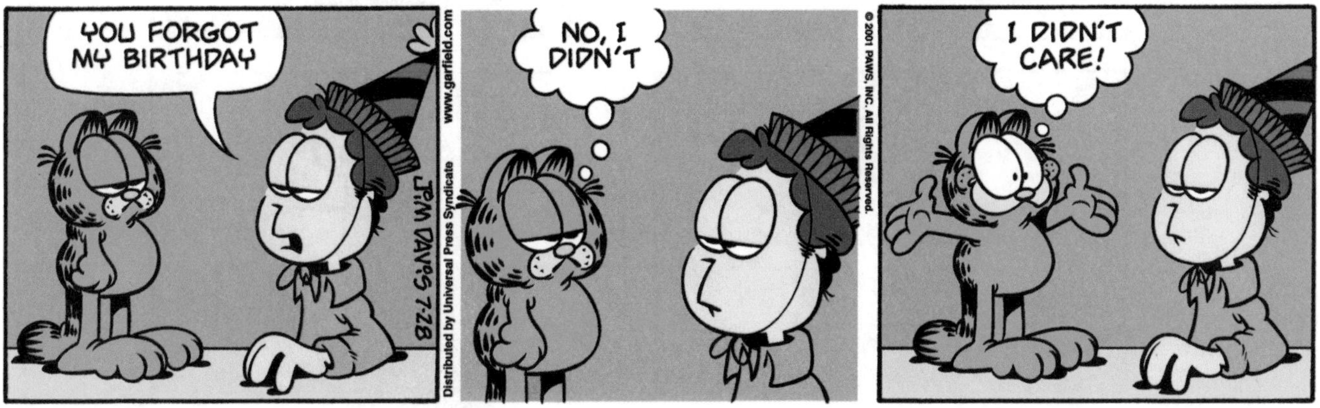
YOU FORGOT MY BIRTHDAY
NO, I DIDN'T
I DIDN'T CARE!
JIM DAVIS 7-28
www.garfield.com
Distributed by Universal Press Syndicate
© 2001 PAWS, INC. All Rights Reserved.

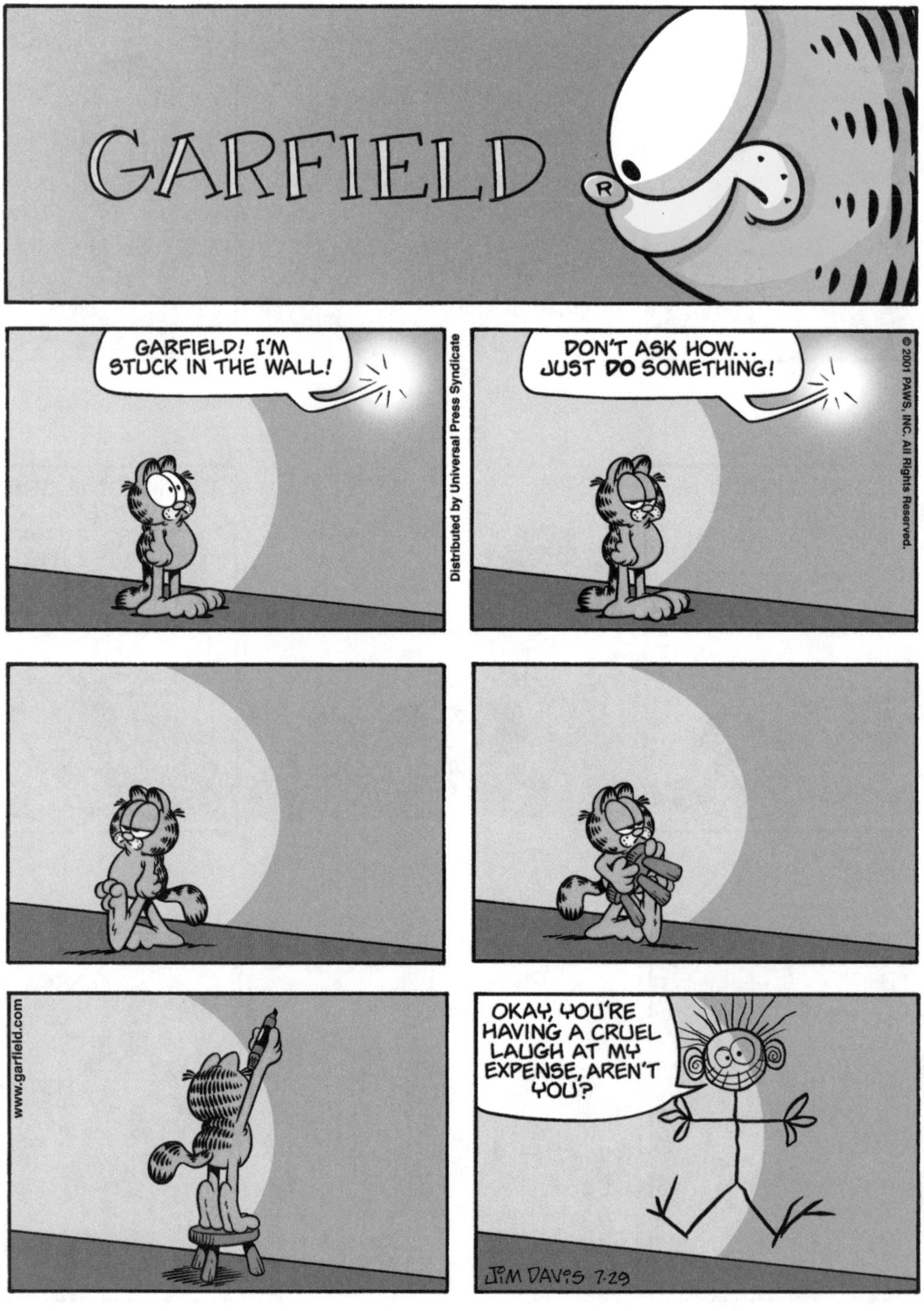
GARFIELD®
GARFIELD! I'M STUCK IN THE WALL!
Distributed by Universal Press Syndicate
DON'T ASK HOW... JUST DO SOMETHING!
© 2001 PAWS, INC. All Rights Reserved.
www.garfield.com
OKAY, YOU'RE HAVING A CRUEL LAUGH AT MY EXPENSE, AREN'T YOU?
JIM DAVIS 7-29

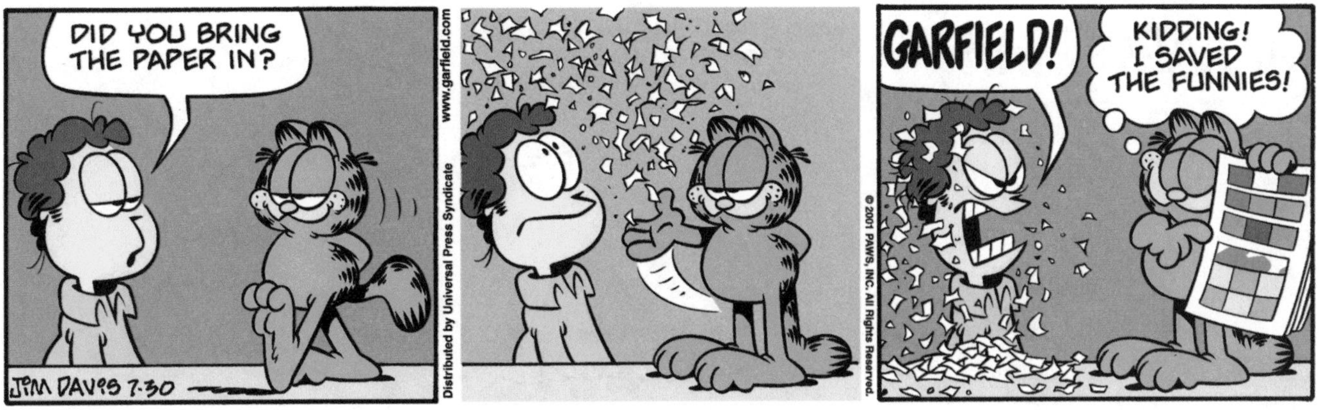
DID YOU BRING THE PAPER IN?
JIM DAVIS 7-30
www.garfield.com
Distributed by Universal Press Syndicate
GARFIELD!
KIDDING! I SAVED THE FUNNIES!
© 2001 PAWS, INC. All Rights Reserved.

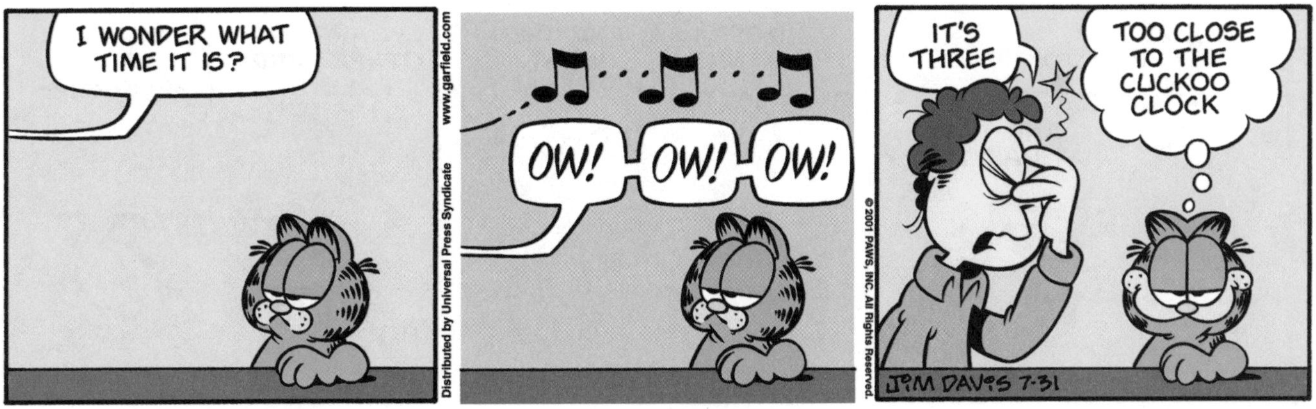
I WONDER WHAT TIME IT IS?
www.garfield.com
Distributed by Universal Press Syndicate
OW! OW! OW!
IT'S THREE
TOO CLOSE TO THE CUCKOO CLOCK
© 2001 PAWS, INC. All Rights Reserved.
JIM DAVIS 7-31

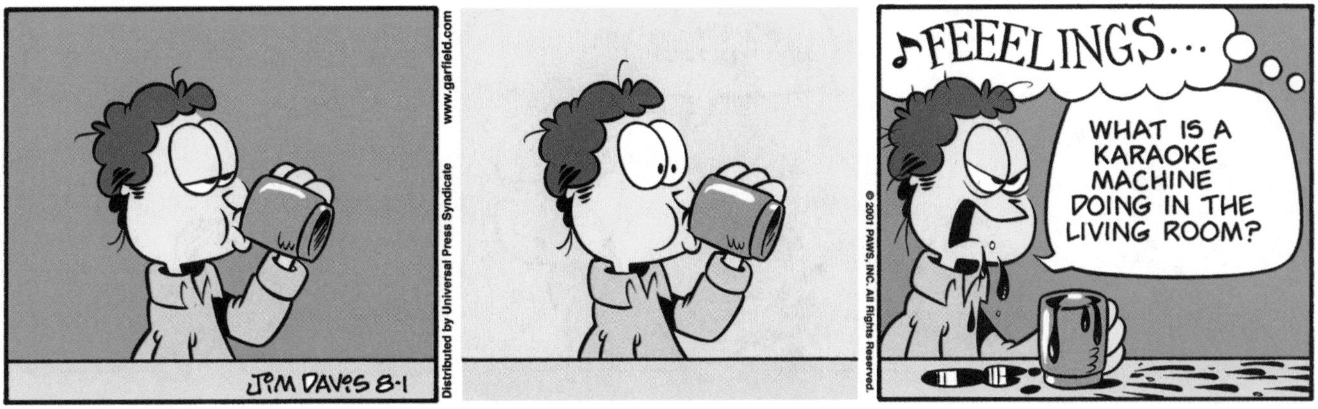
JIM DAVIS 8-1
www.garfield.com
Distributed by Universal Press Syndicate
♪FEEELINGS...
WHAT IS A KARAOKE MACHINE DOING IN THE LIVING ROOM?
© 2001 PAWS, INC. All Rights Reserved.

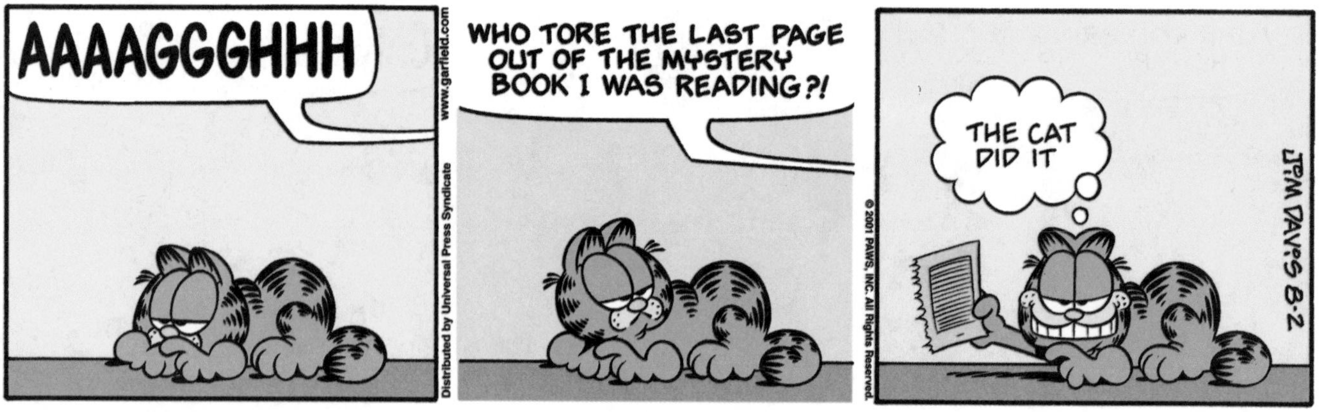
AAAAGGGHHH
WHO TORE THE LAST PAGE OUT OF THE MYSTERY BOOK I WAS READING?!
THE CAT DID IT
JIM DAVIS 8-2
www.garfield.com
Distributed by Universal Press Syndicate
© 2001 PAWS, INC. All Rights Reserved.

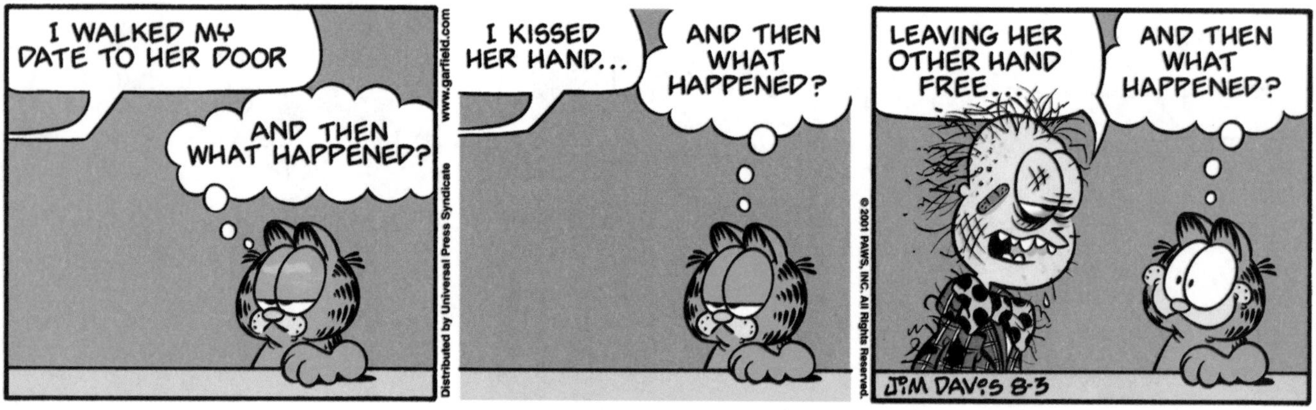
I WALKED MY DATE TO HER DOOR
AND THEN WHAT HAPPENED?
I KISSED HER HAND...
AND THEN WHAT HAPPENED?
LEAVING HER OTHER HAND FREE...
AND THEN WHAT HAPPENED?
JIM DAVIS 8-3
www.garfield.com
Distributed by Universal Press Syndicate
© 2001 PAWS, INC. All Rights Reserved.

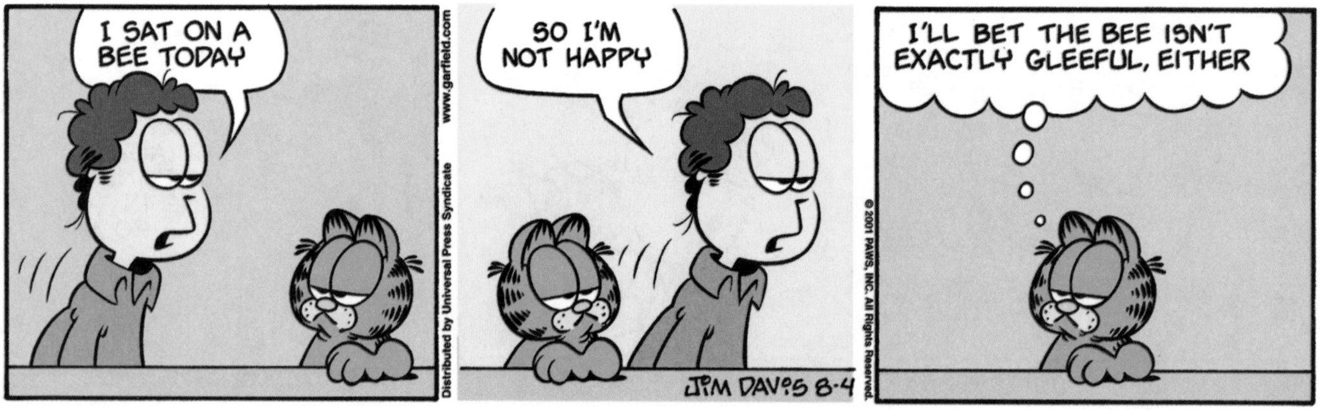
I SAT ON A BEE TODAY
SO I'M NOT HAPPY
I'LL BET THE BEE ISN'T EXACTLY GLEEFUL, EITHER
JIM DAVIS 8-4
www.garfield.com
Distributed by Universal Press Syndicate
© 2001 PAWS, INC. All Rights Reserved.

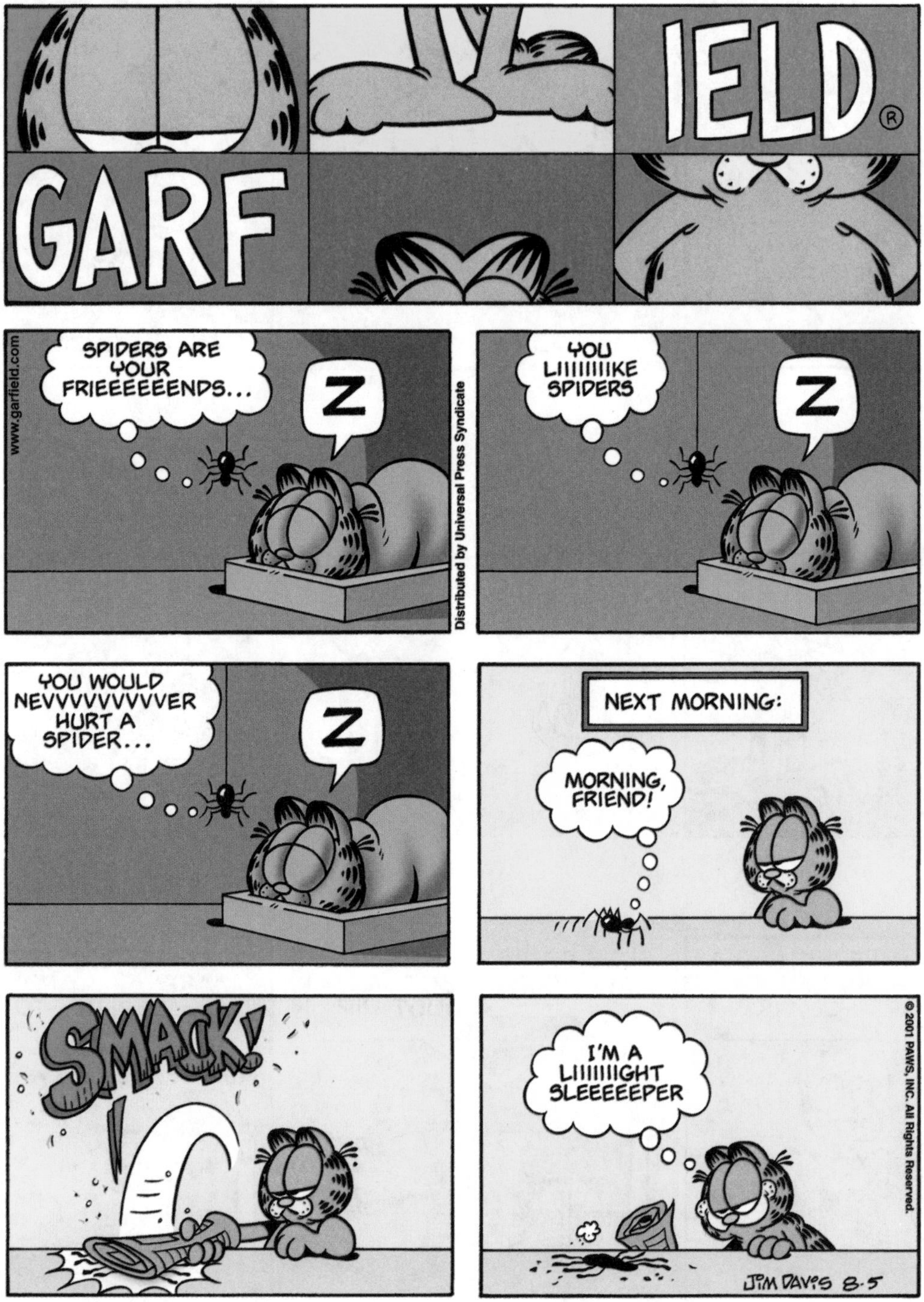
GARF
IELD®
www.garfield.com
SPIDERS ARE YOUR FRIEEEEEENDS...
Z
Distributed by Universal Press Syndicate
YOU LIIIIIIIIKE SPIDERS
Z
YOU WOULD NEVVVVVVVVVVER HURT A SPIDER...
Z
NEXT MORNING:
MORNING, FRIEND!
SMACK!
I'M A LIIIIIIIGHT SLEEEEEPER
© 2001 PAWS, INC. All Rights Reserved.
JIM DAVIS 8-5

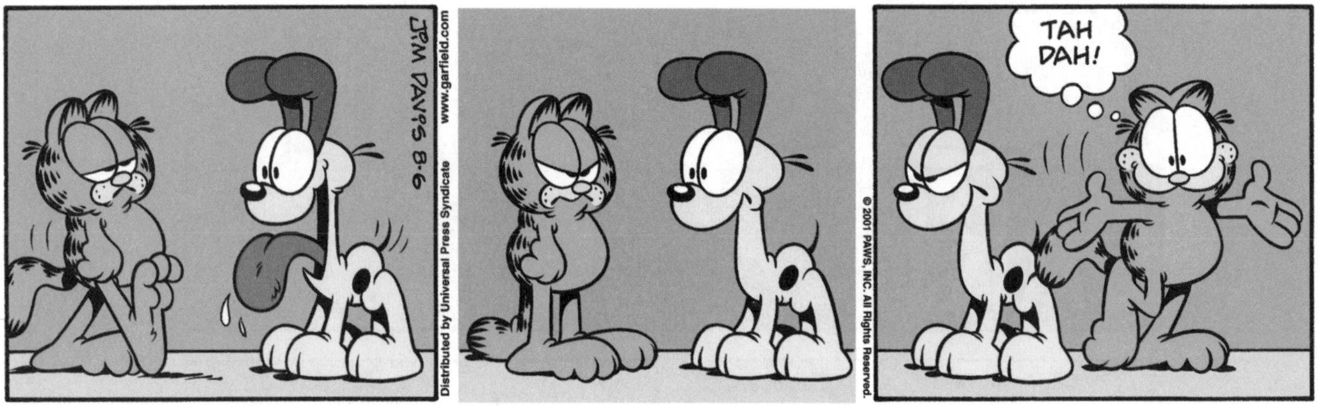
JIM DAVIS 8-6
www.garfield.com
Distributed by Universal Press Syndicate
© 2001 PAWS, INC. All Rights Reserved.
TAH DAH!

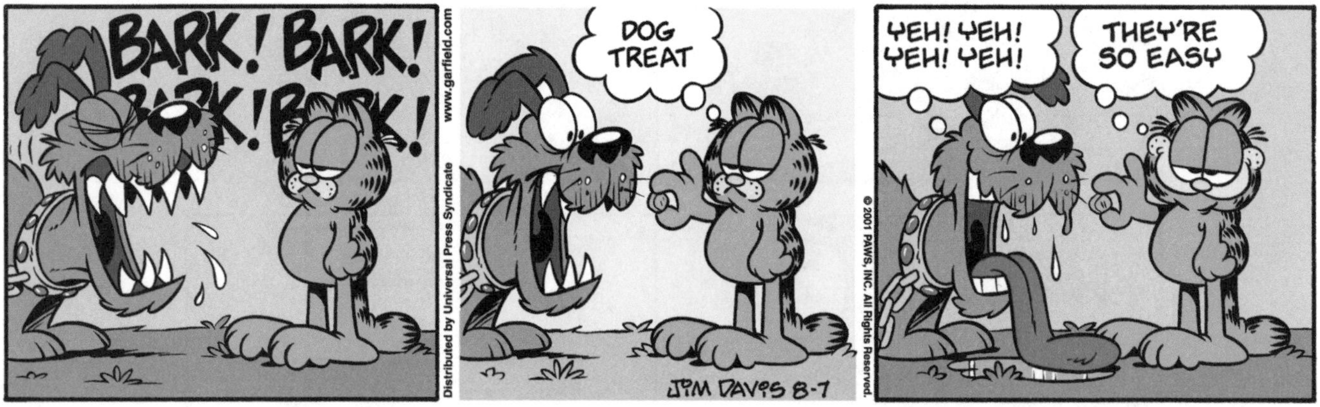
BARK! BARK! BARK! BARK!
www.garfield.com
Distributed by Universal Press Syndicate
DOG TREAT
JIM DAVIS 8-7
© 2001 PAWS, INC. All Rights Reserved.
YEH! YEH! YEH! YEH!
THEY'RE SO EASY

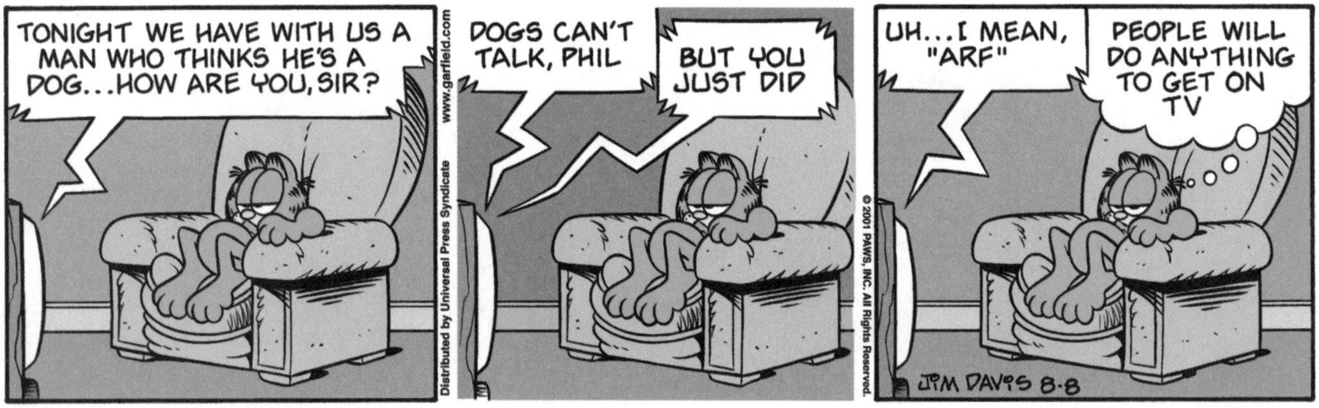
TONIGHT WE HAVE WITH US A MAN WHO THINKS HE'S A DOG...HOW ARE YOU, SIR?
www.garfield.com
Distributed by Universal Press Syndicate
DOGS CAN'T TALK, PHIL
BUT YOU JUST DID
© 2001 PAWS, INC. All Rights Reserved.
UH...I MEAN, "ARF"
PEOPLE WILL DO ANYTHING TO GET ON TV
JIM DAVIS 8-8

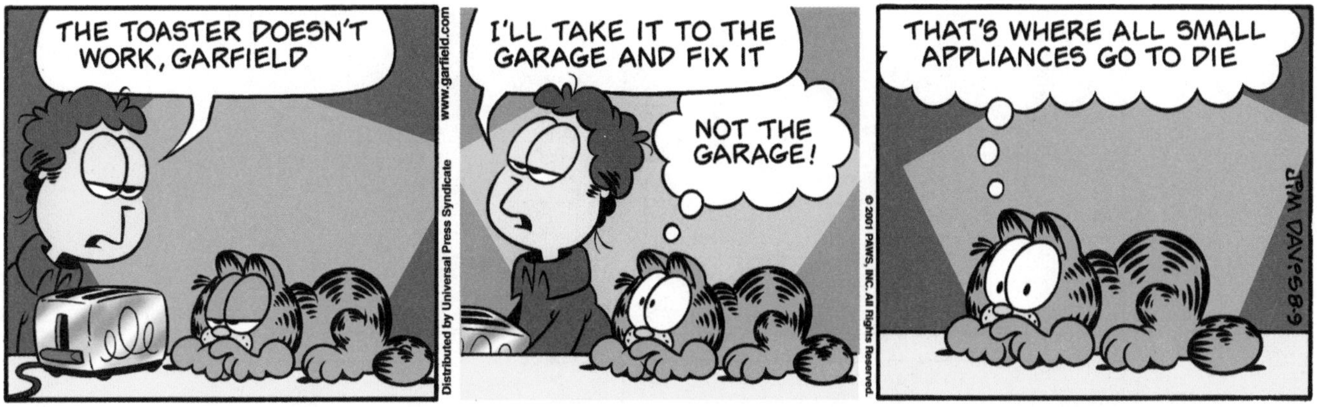
THE TOASTER DOESN'T WORK, GARFIELD
Distributed by Universal Press Syndicate www.garfield.com
I'LL TAKE IT TO THE GARAGE AND FIX IT
NOT THE GARAGE!
© 2001 PAWS, INC. All Rights Reserved.
THAT'S WHERE ALL SMALL APPLIANCES GO TO DIE
JIM DAVIS 8-9

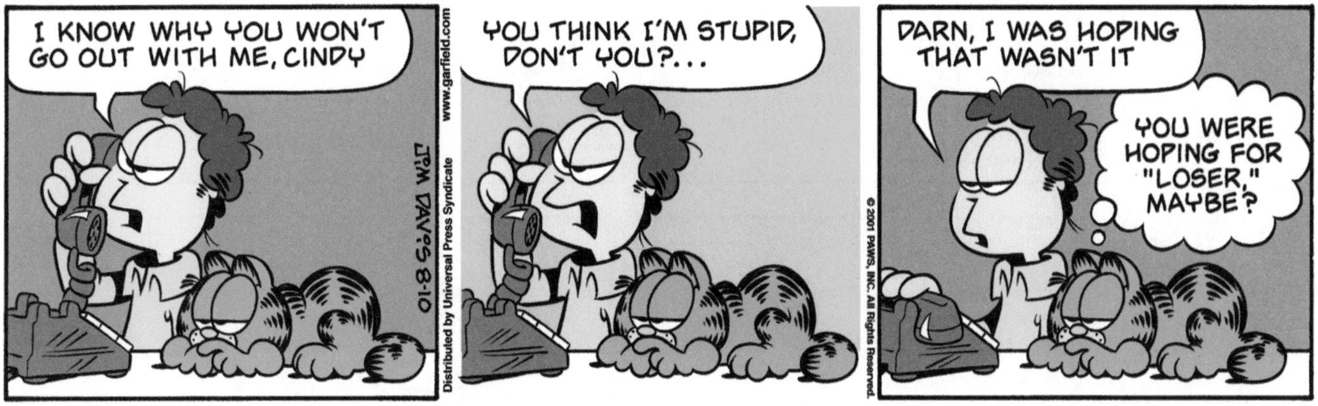
I KNOW WHY YOU WON'T GO OUT WITH ME, CINDY
JIM DAVIS 8-10
Distributed by Universal Press Syndicate www.garfield.com
YOU THINK I'M STUPID, DON'T YOU?...
© 2001 PAWS, INC. All Rights Reserved.
DARN, I WAS HOPING THAT WASN'T IT
YOU WERE HOPING FOR "LOSER," MAYBE?

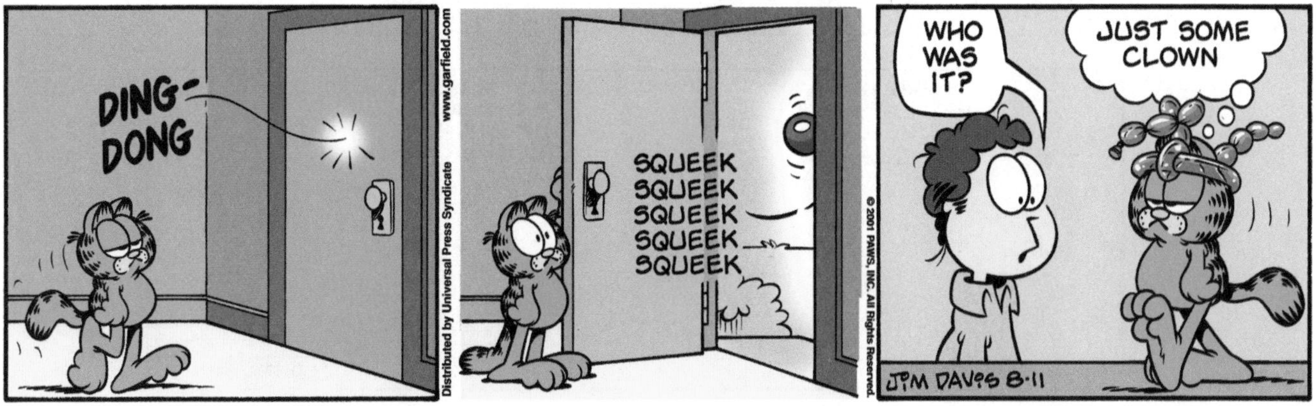
DING-DONG
Distributed by Universal Press Syndicate www.garfield.com
SQUEEK SQUEEK SQUEEK SQUEEK SQUEEK
© 2001 PAWS, INC. All Rights Reserved.
WHO WAS IT?
JUST SOME CLOWN
JIM DAVIS 8-11

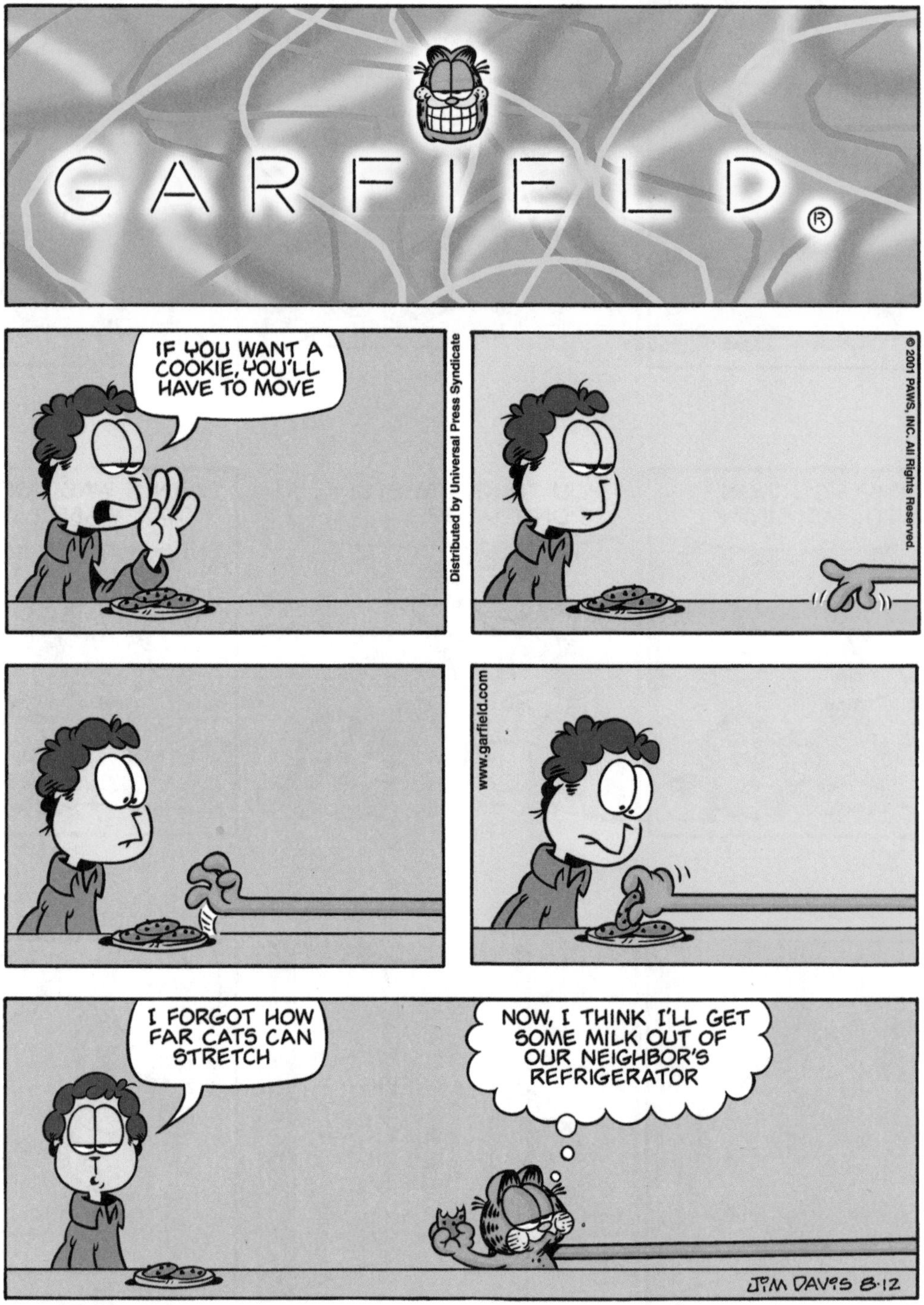
GARFIELD®
IF YOU WANT A COOKIE, YOU'LL HAVE TO MOVE
Distributed by Universal Press Syndicate
© 2001 PAWS, INC. All Rights Reserved.
www.garfield.com
I FORGOT HOW FAR CATS CAN STRETCH
NOW, I THINK I'LL GET SOME MILK OUT OF OUR NEIGHBOR'S REFRIGERATOR
JIM DAVIS 8-12

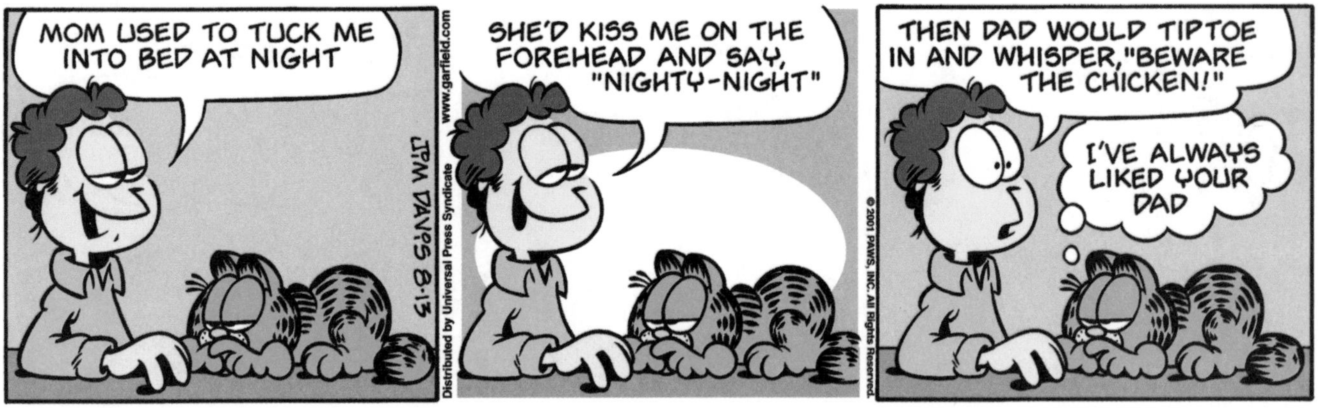
MOM USED TO TUCK ME INTO BED AT NIGHT
JIM DAVIS 8-13
Distributed by Universal Press Syndicate www.garfield.com
SHE'D KISS ME ON THE FOREHEAD AND SAY, "NIGHTY-NIGHT"
© 2001 PAWS, INC. All Rights Reserved.
THEN DAD WOULD TIPTOE IN AND WHISPER, "BEWARE THE CHICKEN!"
I'VE ALWAYS LIKED YOUR DAD

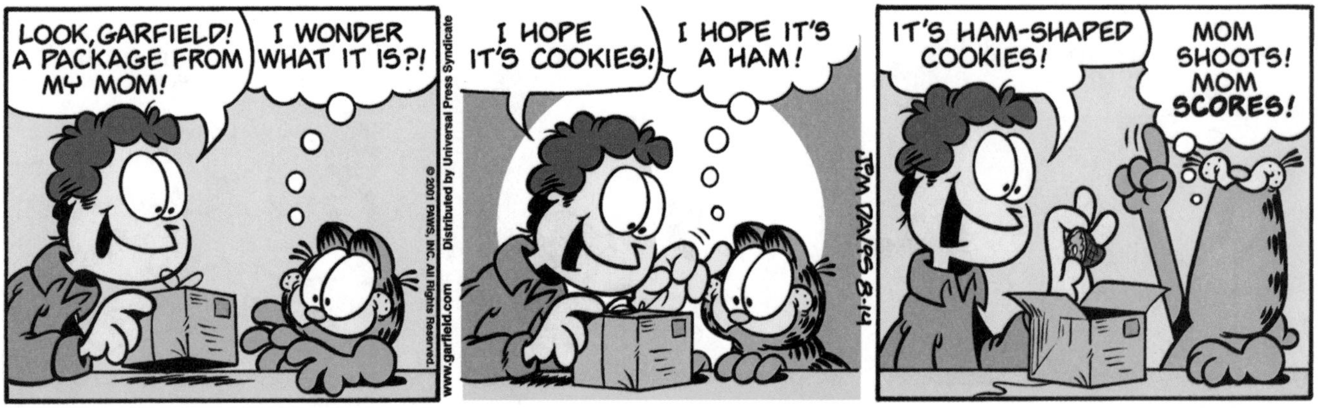
LOOK, GARFIELD! A PACKAGE FROM MY MOM!
I WONDER WHAT IT IS?!
© 2001 PAWS, INC. All Rights Reserved. Distributed by Universal Press Syndicate www.garfield.com
I HOPE IT'S COOKIES!
I HOPE IT'S A HAM!
JIM DAVIS 8-14
IT'S HAM-SHAPED COOKIES!
MOM SHOOTS! MOM SCORES!

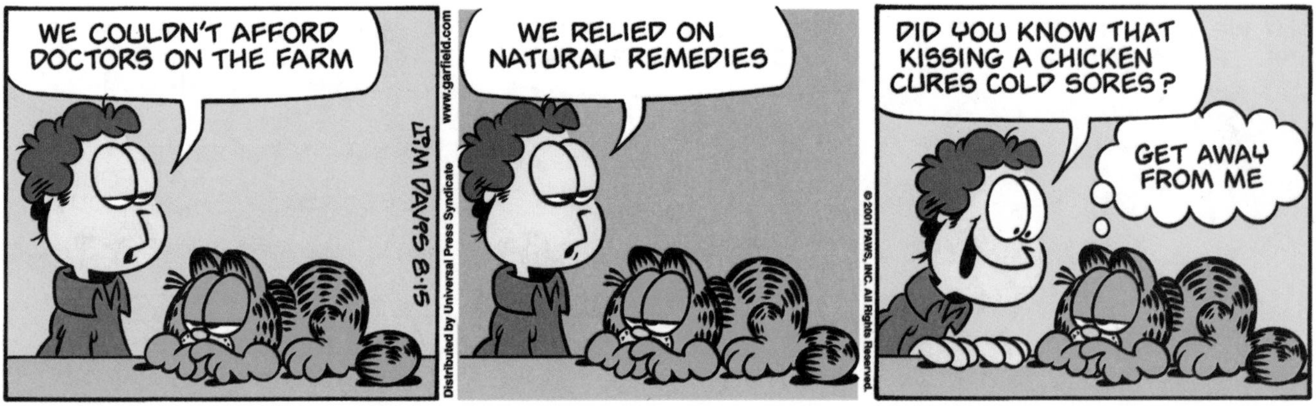
WE COULDN'T AFFORD DOCTORS ON THE FARM
JIM DAVIS 8-15
Distributed by Universal Press Syndicate www.garfield.com
WE RELIED ON NATURAL REMEDIES
© 2001 PAWS, INC. All Rights Reserved.
DID YOU KNOW THAT KISSING A CHICKEN CURES COLD SORES?
GET AWAY FROM ME

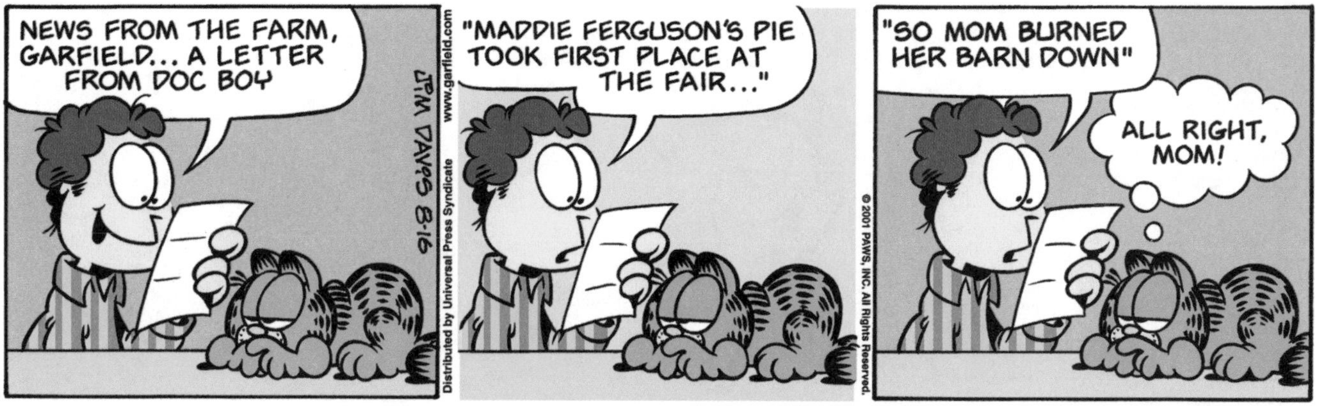
NEWS FROM THE FARM, GARFIELD... A LETTER FROM DOC BOY
JIM DAVIS 8-16
www.garfield.com
Distributed by Universal Press Syndicate
"MADDIE FERGUSON'S PIE TOOK FIRST PLACE AT THE FAIR..."
© 2001 PAWS, INC. All Rights Reserved.
"SO MOM BURNED HER BARN DOWN"
ALL RIGHT, MOM!

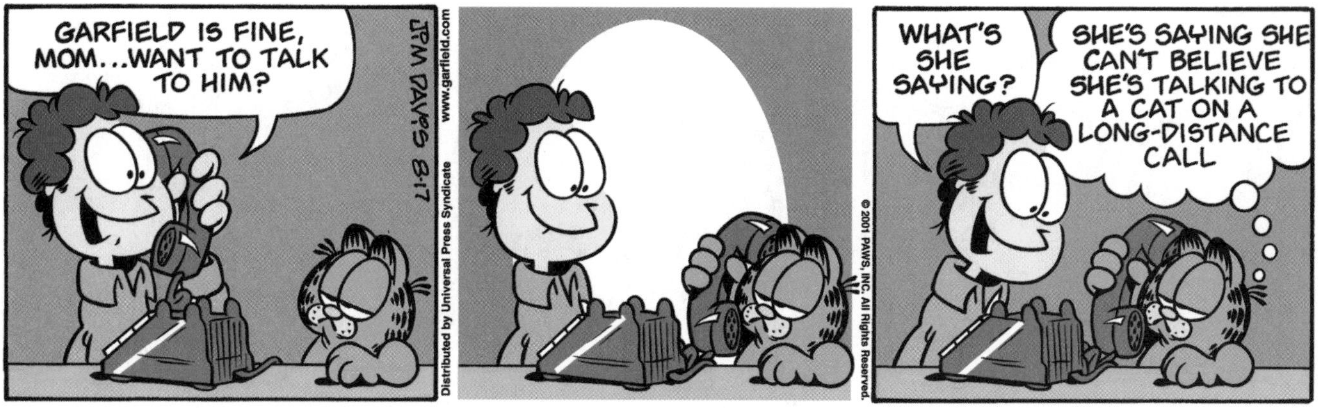
GARFIELD IS FINE, MOM...WANT TO TALK TO HIM?
JIM DAVIS 8-17
www.garfield.com
Distributed by Universal Press Syndicate
© 2001 PAWS, INC. All Rights Reserved.
WHAT'S SHE SAYING?
SHE'S SAYING SHE CAN'T BELIEVE SHE'S TALKING TO A CAT ON A LONG-DISTANCE CALL

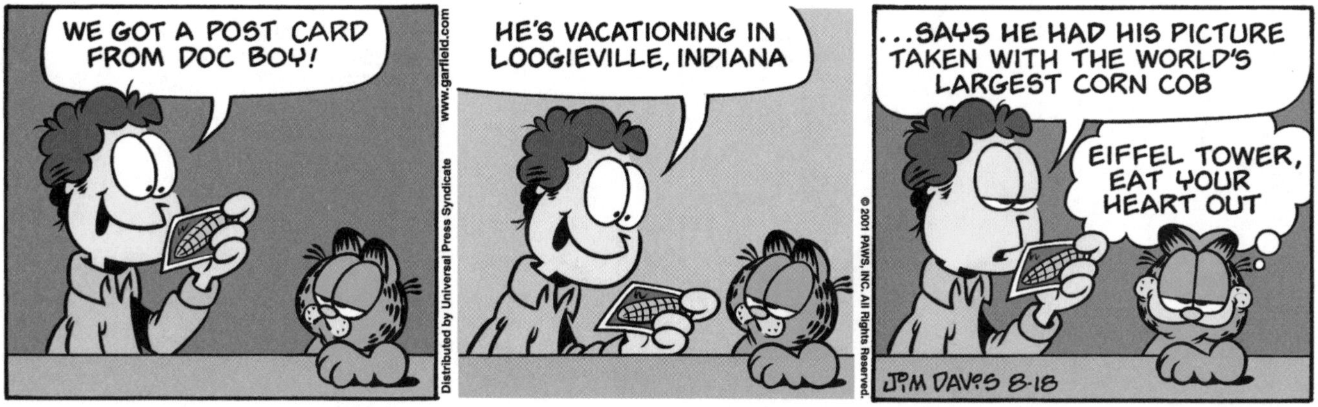
WE GOT A POST CARD FROM DOC BOY!
www.garfield.com
Distributed by Universal Press Syndicate
HE'S VACATIONING IN LOOGIEVILLE, INDIANA
© 2001 PAWS, INC. All Rights Reserved.
...SAYS HE HAD HIS PICTURE TAKEN WITH THE WORLD'S LARGEST CORN COB
EIFFEL TOWER, EAT YOUR HEART OUT
JIM DAVIS 8-18

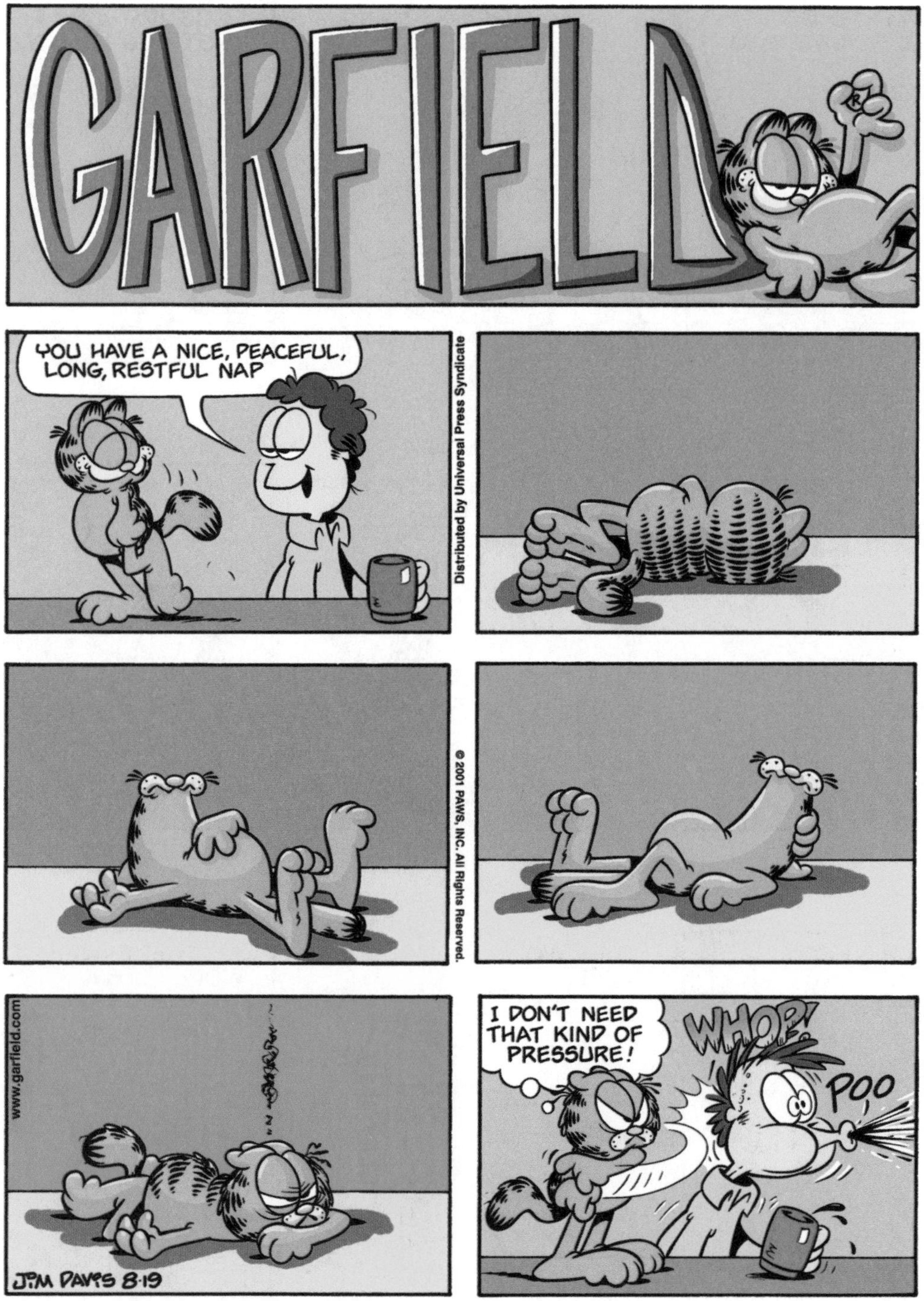
GARFIELD
YOU HAVE A NICE, PEACEFUL, LONG, RESTFUL NAP
Distributed by Universal Press Syndicate
© 2001 PAWS, INC. All Rights Reserved.
www.garfield.com
JIM DAVIS 8·19
I DON'T NEED THAT KIND OF PRESSURE!
WHOP!
POO

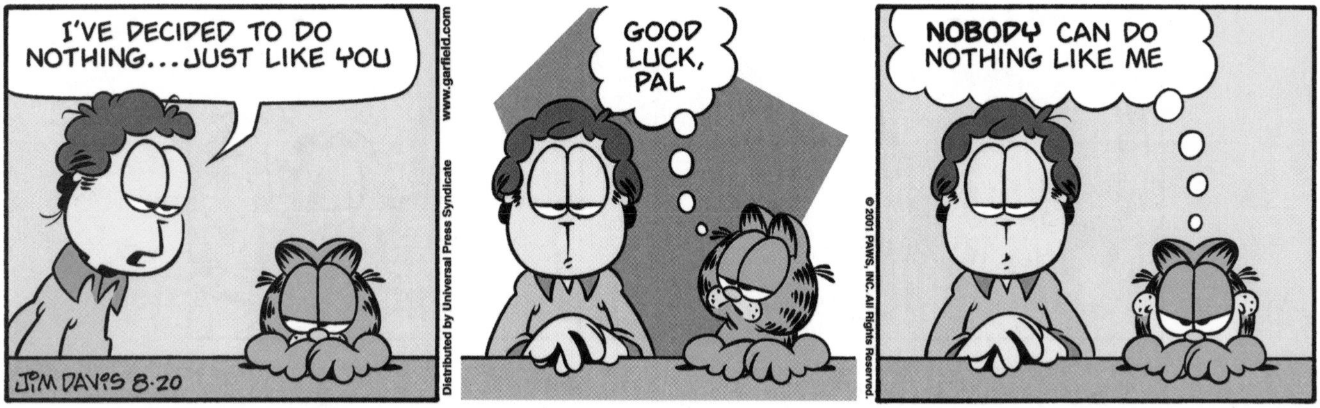
I'VE DECIDED TO DO NOTHING... JUST LIKE YOU
JIM DAVIS 8-20
www.garfield.com
Distributed by Universal Press Syndicate
GOOD LUCK, PAL
© 2001 PAWS, INC. All Rights Reserved.
NOBODY CAN DO NOTHING LIKE ME

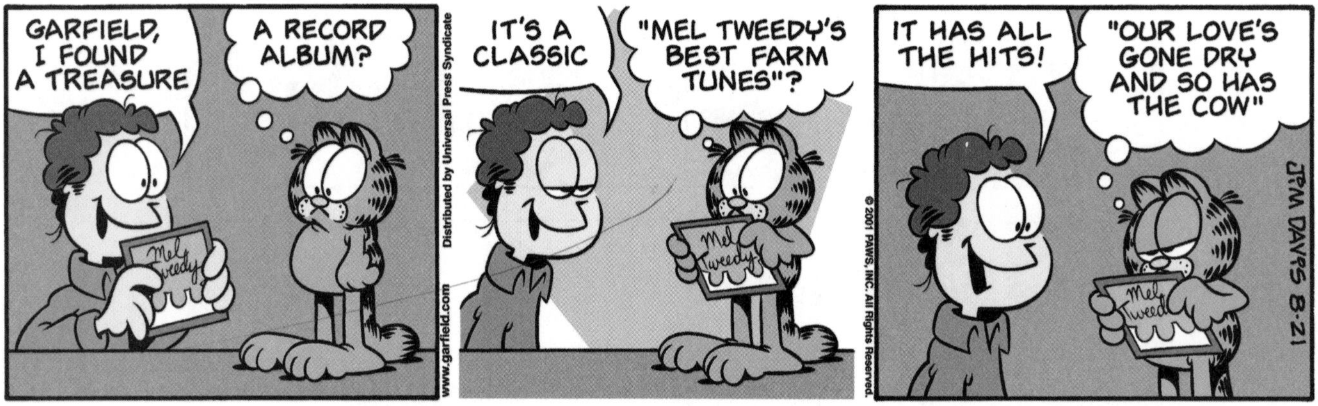
GARFIELD, I FOUND A TREASURE
A RECORD ALBUM?
Mel Tweedy
Distributed by Universal Press Syndicate
www.garfield.com
IT'S A CLASSIC
"MEL TWEEDY'S BEST FARM TUNES"?
© 2001 PAWS, INC. All Rights Reserved.
IT HAS ALL THE HITS!
"OUR LOVE'S GONE DRY AND SO HAS THE COW"
JIM DAVIS 8-21

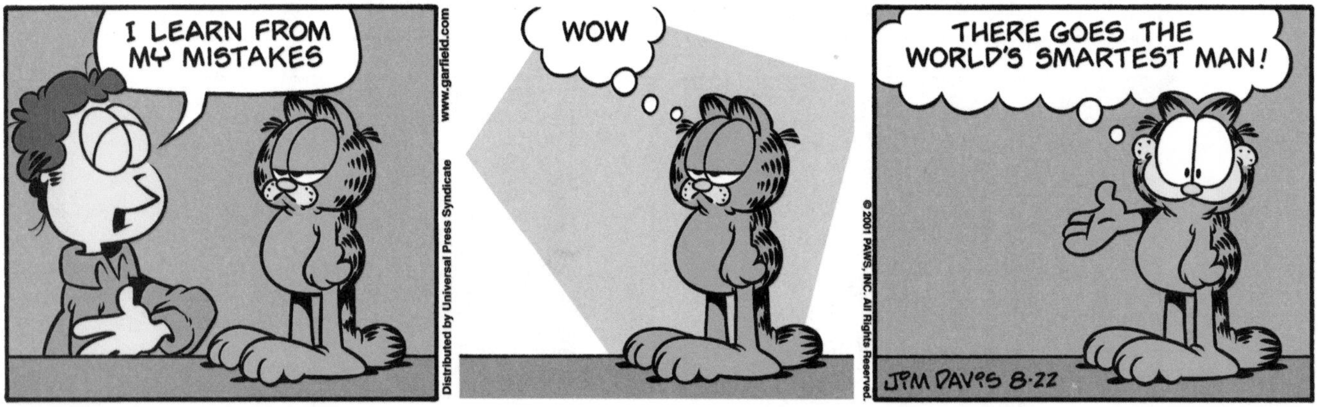
I LEARN FROM MY MISTAKES
www.garfield.com
Distributed by Universal Press Syndicate
WOW
© 2001 PAWS, INC. All Rights Reserved.
THERE GOES THE WORLD'S SMARTEST MAN!
JIM DAVIS 8-22

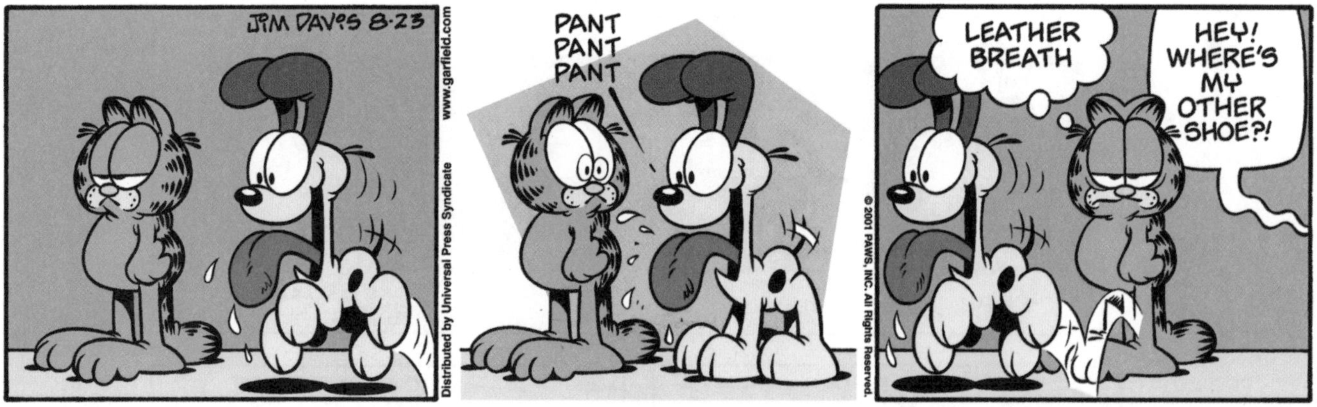
JIM DAVIS 8-23
www.garfield.com
Distributed by Universal Press Syndicate
PANT PANT PANT
© 2001 PAWS, INC. All Rights Reserved.
LEATHER BREATH
HEY! WHERE'S MY OTHER SHOE?!

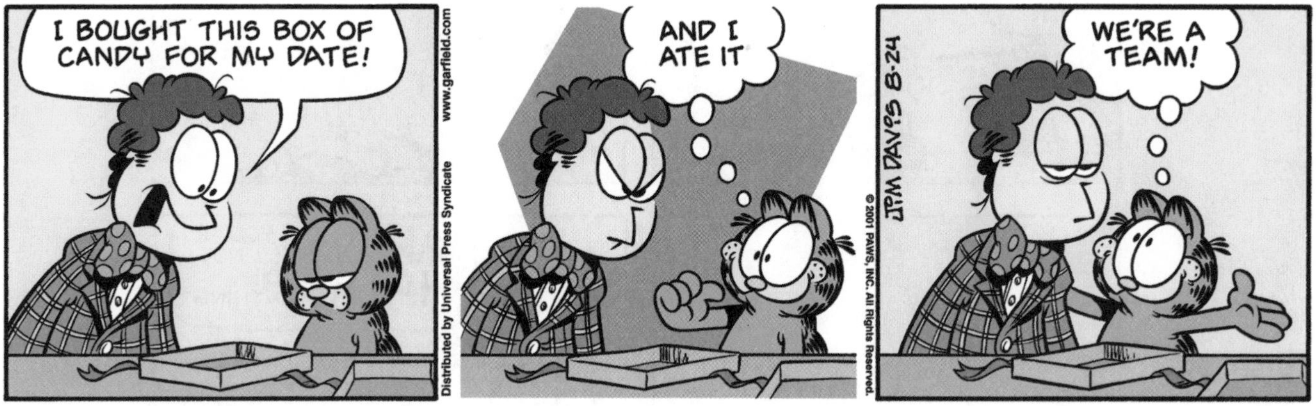
I BOUGHT THIS BOX OF CANDY FOR MY DATE!
www.garfield.com
Distributed by Universal Press Syndicate
AND I ATE IT
© 2001 PAWS, INC. All Rights Reserved.
JIM DAVIS 8-24
WE'RE A TEAM!

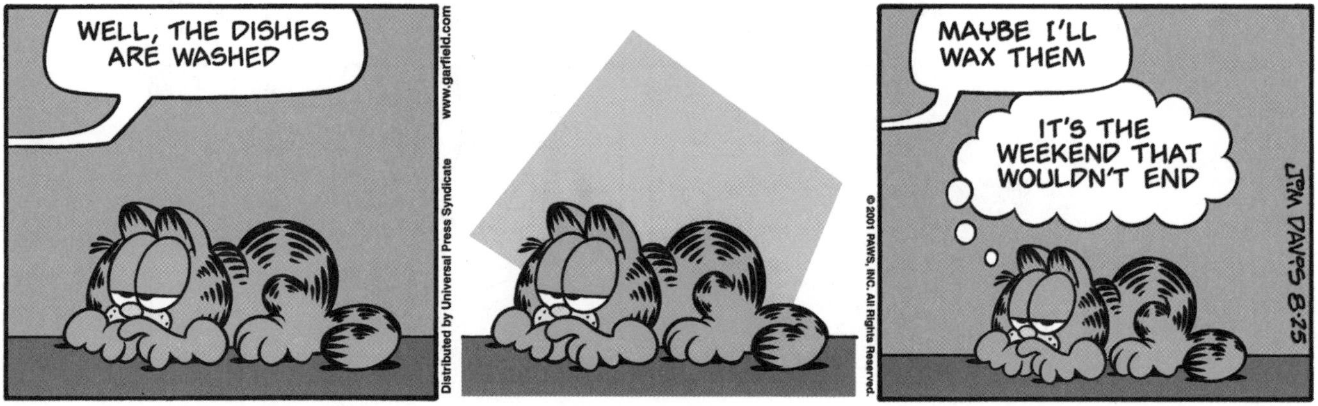
WELL, THE DISHES ARE WASHED
www.garfield.com
Distributed by Universal Press Syndicate
© 2001 PAWS, INC. All Rights Reserved.
MAYBE I'LL WAX THEM
IT'S THE WEEKEND THAT WOULDN'T END
JIM DAVIS 8-25

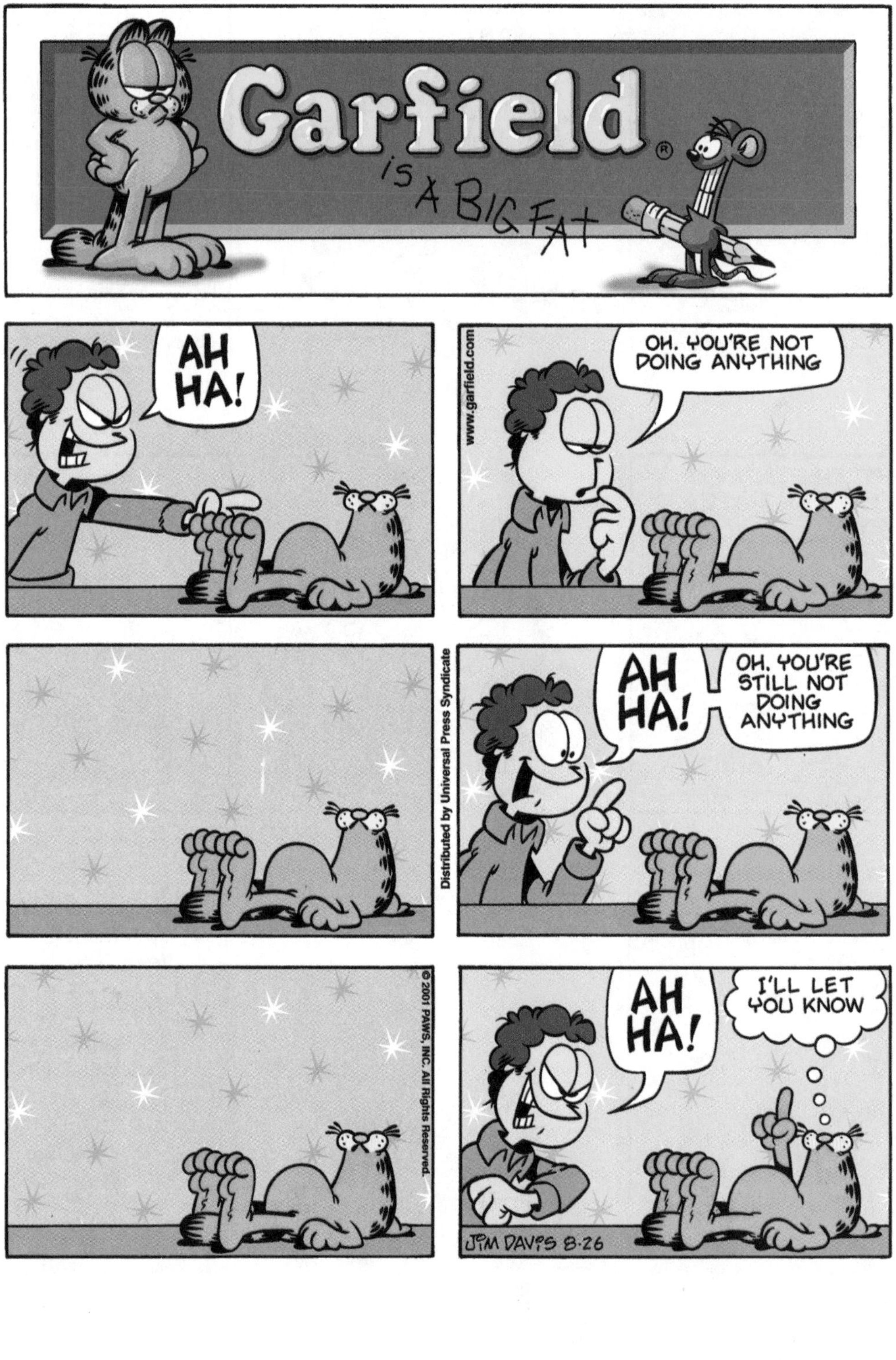
Garfield
IS A BIG FAT
AH HA!
OH. YOU'RE NOT DOING ANYTHING
www.garfield.com
Distributed by Universal Press Syndicate
AH HA!
OH. YOU'RE STILL NOT DOING ANYTHING
© 2001 PAWS, INC. All Rights Reserved.
AH HA!
I'LL LET YOU KNOW
JIM DAVIS 8-26

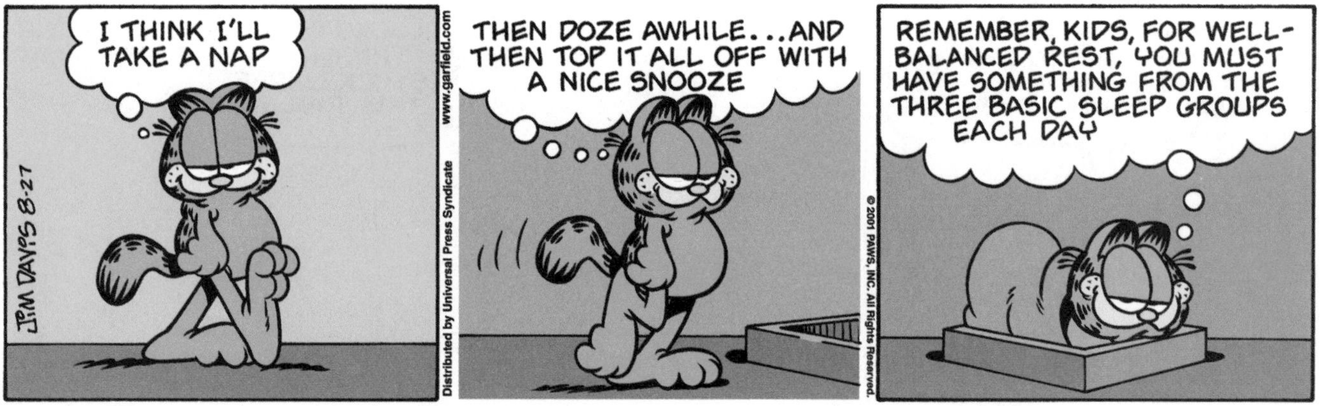
I THINK I'LL TAKE A NAP
THEN DOZE AWHILE...AND THEN TOP IT ALL OFF WITH A NICE SNOOZE
REMEMBER, KIDS, FOR WELL-BALANCED REST, YOU MUST HAVE SOMETHING FROM THE THREE BASIC SLEEP GROUPS EACH DAY
JIM DAVIS 8-27
Distributed by Universal Press Syndicate www.garfield.com
© 2001 PAWS, INC. All Rights Reserved.

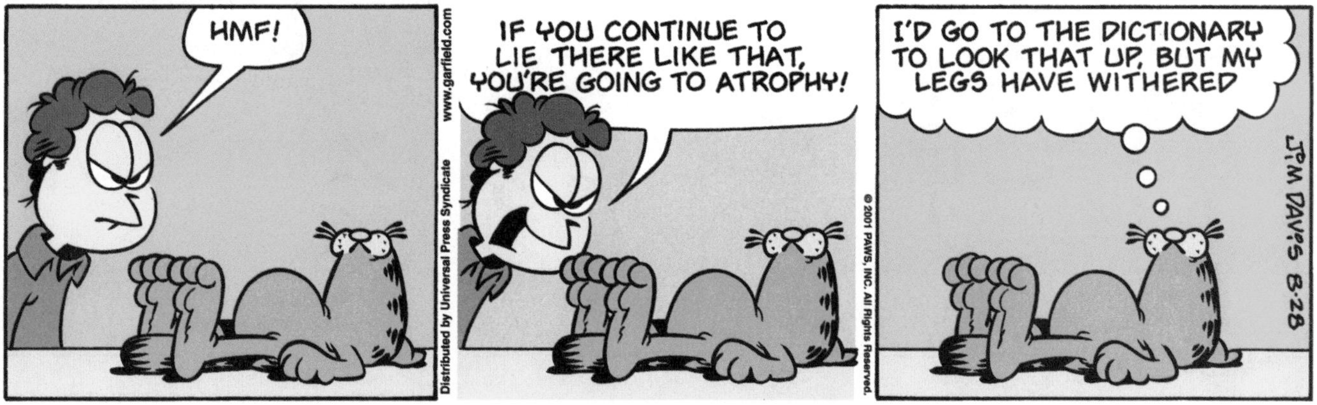
HMF!
IF YOU CONTINUE TO LIE THERE LIKE THAT, YOU'RE GOING TO ATROPHY!
I'D GO TO THE DICTIONARY TO LOOK THAT UP, BUT MY LEGS HAVE WITHERED
JIM DAVIS 8-28
Distributed by Universal Press Syndicate www.garfield.com
© 2001 PAWS, INC. All Rights Reserved.

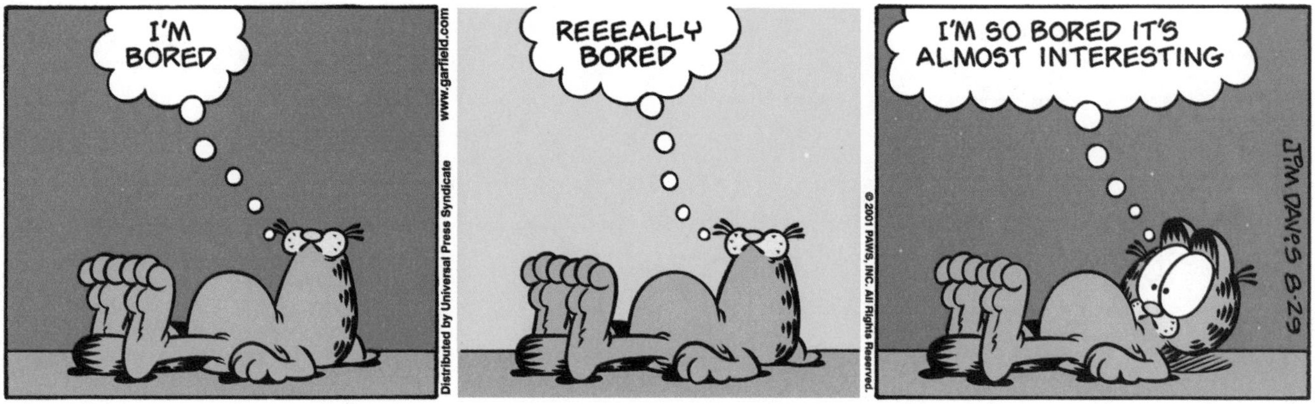
I'M BORED
REEEALLY BORED
I'M SO BORED IT'S ALMOST INTERESTING
JIM DAVIS 8-29
Distributed by Universal Press Syndicate www.garfield.com
© 2001 PAWS, INC. All Rights Reserved.

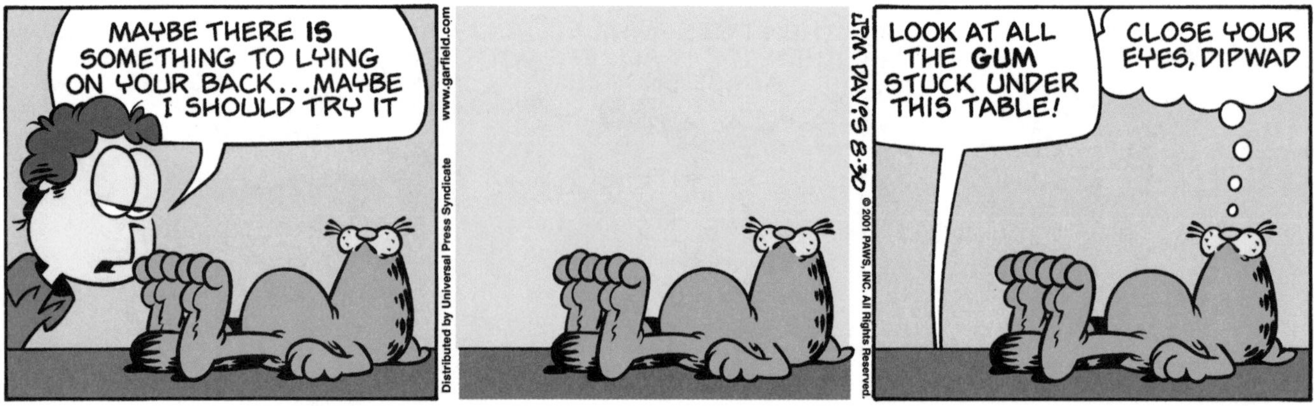
MAYBE THERE **IS** SOMETHING TO LYING ON YOUR BACK...MAYBE I SHOULD TRY IT
www.garfield.com
Distributed by Universal Press Syndicate
JIM DAVIS 8-30
© 2001 PAWS, INC. All Rights Reserved.
LOOK AT ALL THE **GUM** STUCK UNDER THIS TABLE!
CLOSE YOUR EYES, DIPWAD

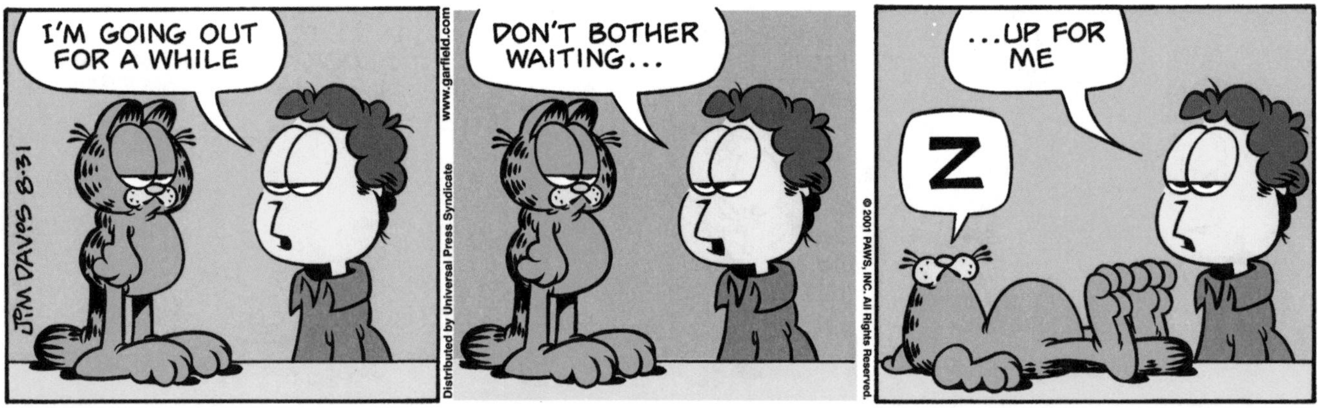
I'M GOING OUT FOR A WHILE
JIM DAVIS 8-31
www.garfield.com
Distributed by Universal Press Syndicate
DON'T BOTHER WAITING...
© 2001 PAWS, INC. All Rights Reserved.
Z
...UP FOR ME

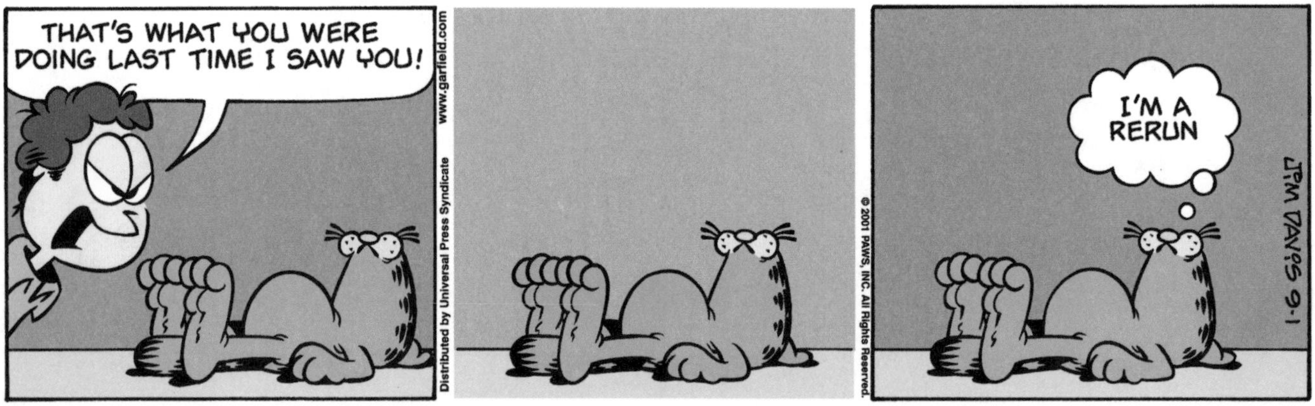
THAT'S WHAT YOU WERE DOING LAST TIME I SAW YOU!
www.garfield.com
Distributed by Universal Press Syndicate
© 2001 PAWS, INC. All Rights Reserved.
I'M A RERUN
JIM DAVIS 9-1

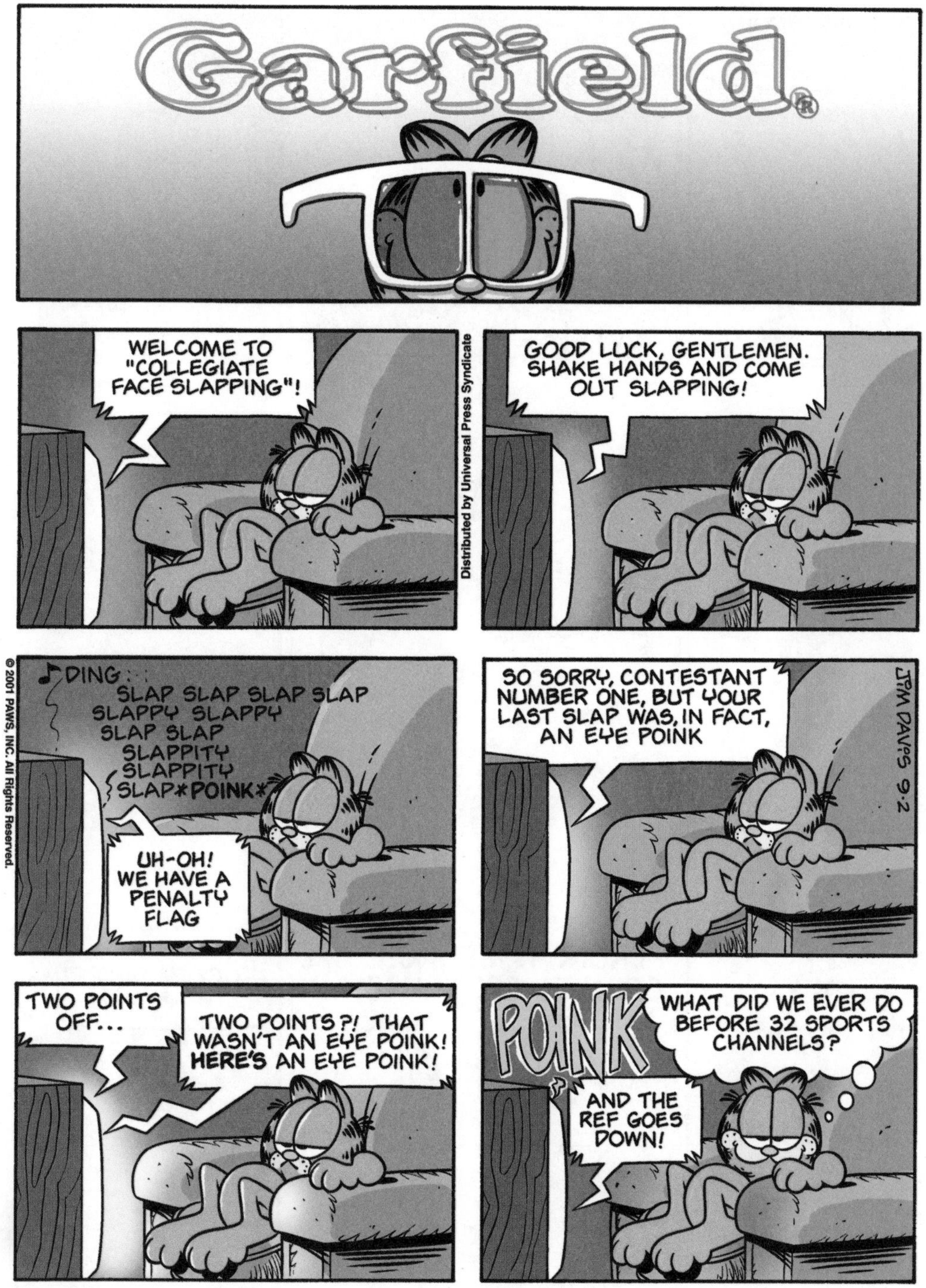

Garfield®
WELCOME TO "COLLEGIATE FACE SLAPPING"!
Distributed by Universal Press Syndicate
GOOD LUCK, GENTLEMEN. SHAKE HANDS AND COME OUT SLAPPING!
DING
SLAP SLAP SLAP SLAP SLAPPY SLAPPY SLAP SLAP SLAPPITY SLAPPITY SLAP*POINK*
UH-OH! WE HAVE A PENALTY FLAG
© 2001 PAWS, INC. All Rights Reserved.
SO SORRY, CONTESTANT NUMBER ONE, BUT YOUR LAST SLAP WAS, IN FACT, AN EYE POINK
JPM DAVIS 9-2
TWO POINTS OFF...
TWO POINTS?! THAT WASN'T AN EYE POINK! HERE'S AN EYE POINK!
POINK
AND THE REF GOES DOWN!
WHAT DID WE EVER DO BEFORE 32 SPORTS CHANNELS?

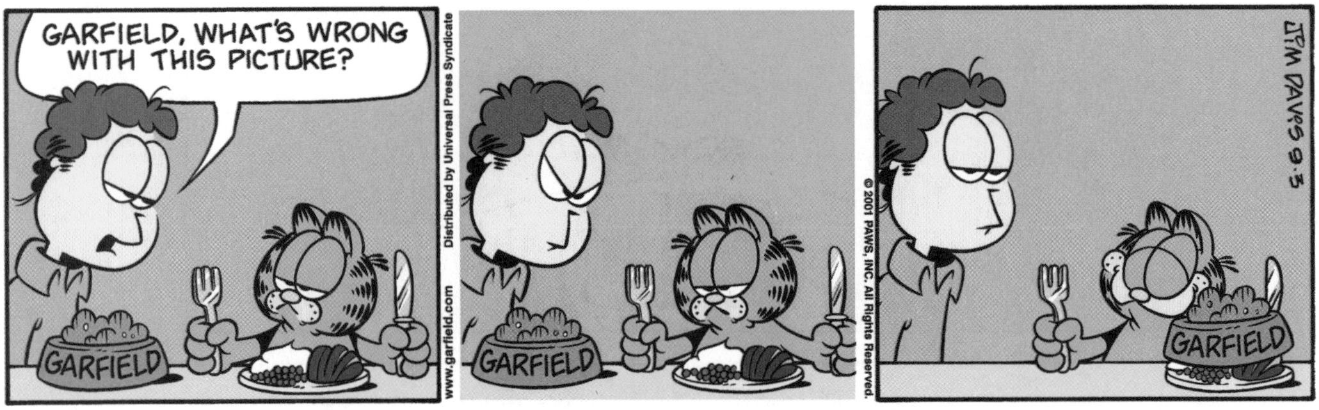
GARFIELD, WHAT'S WRONG WITH THIS PICTURE?
GARFIELD
www.garfield.com Distributed by Universal Press Syndicate
© 2001 PAWS, INC. All Rights Reserved.
JIM DAVIS 9-3

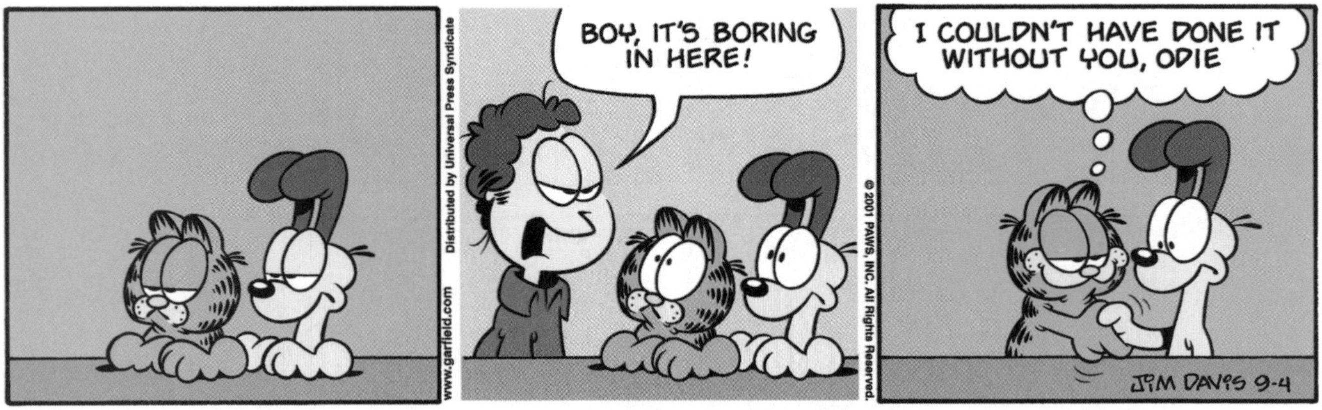
www.garfield.com Distributed by Universal Press Syndicate
BOY, IT'S BORING IN HERE!
© 2001 PAWS, INC. All Rights Reserved.
I COULDN'T HAVE DONE IT WITHOUT YOU, ODIE
JIM DAVIS 9-4

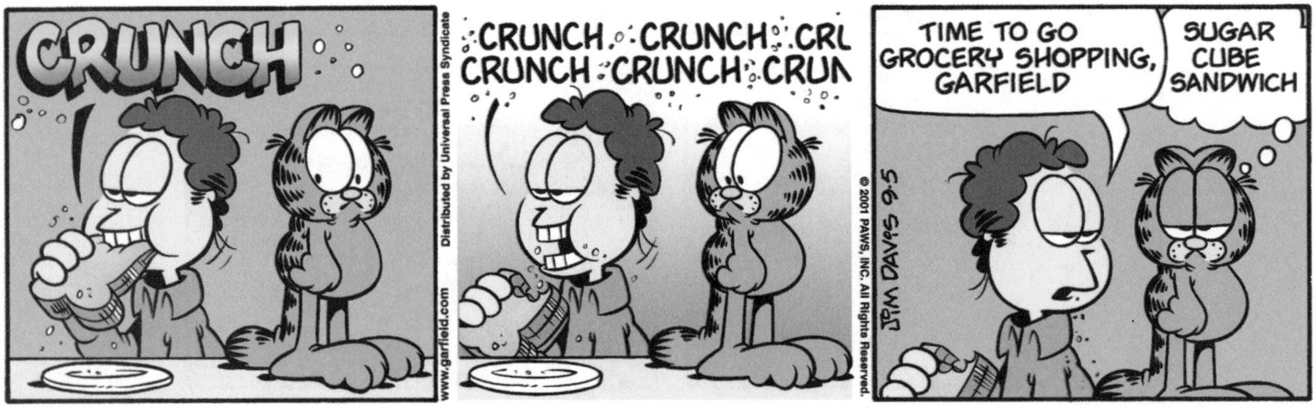
CRUNCH
www.garfield.com Distributed by Universal Press Syndicate
CRUNCH CRUNCH CRU
CRUNCH CRUNCH CRUN
© 2001 PAWS, INC. All Rights Reserved.
JIM DAVIS 9-5
TIME TO GO GROCERY SHOPPING, GARFIELD
SUGAR CUBE SANDWICH

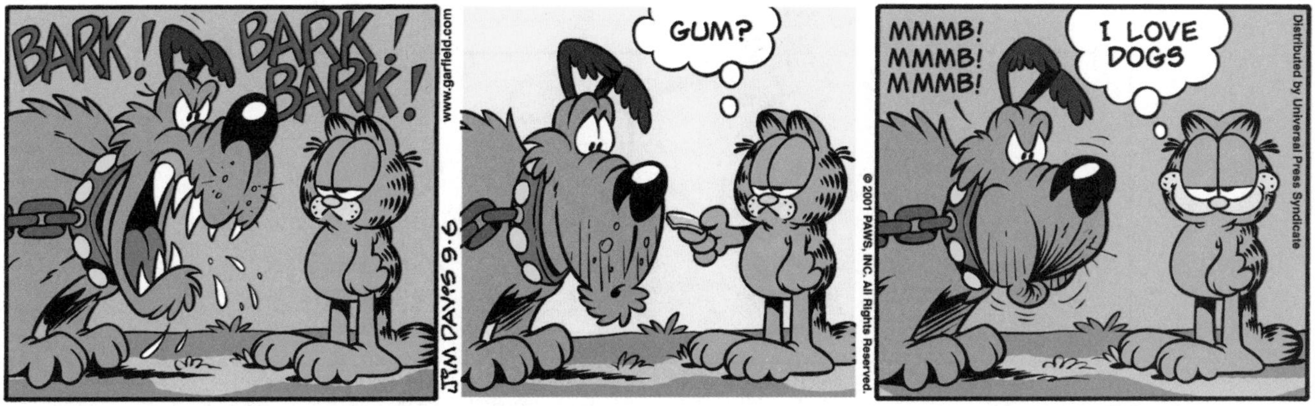
BARK! BARK! BARK!
www.garfield.com
JIM DAVIS 9·6
GUM?
© 2001 PAWS, INC. All Rights Reserved.
MMMB! MMMB! MMMB!
I LOVE DOGS
Distributed by Universal Press Syndicate

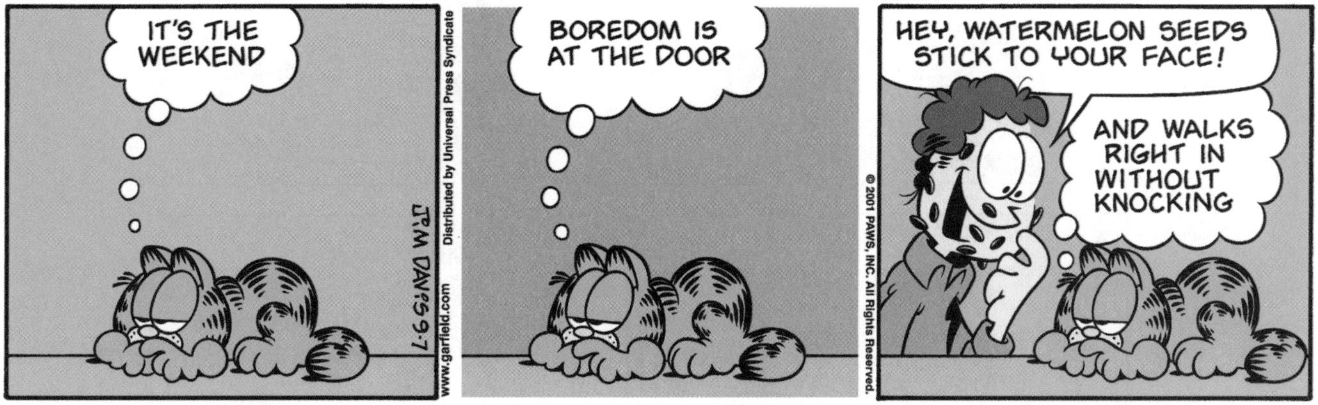
IT'S THE WEEKEND
JIM DAVIS 9·7
Distributed by Universal Press Syndicate
www.garfield.com
BOREDOM IS AT THE DOOR
© 2001 PAWS, INC. All Rights Reserved.
HEY, WATERMELON SEEDS STICK TO YOUR FACE!
AND WALKS RIGHT IN WITHOUT KNOCKING

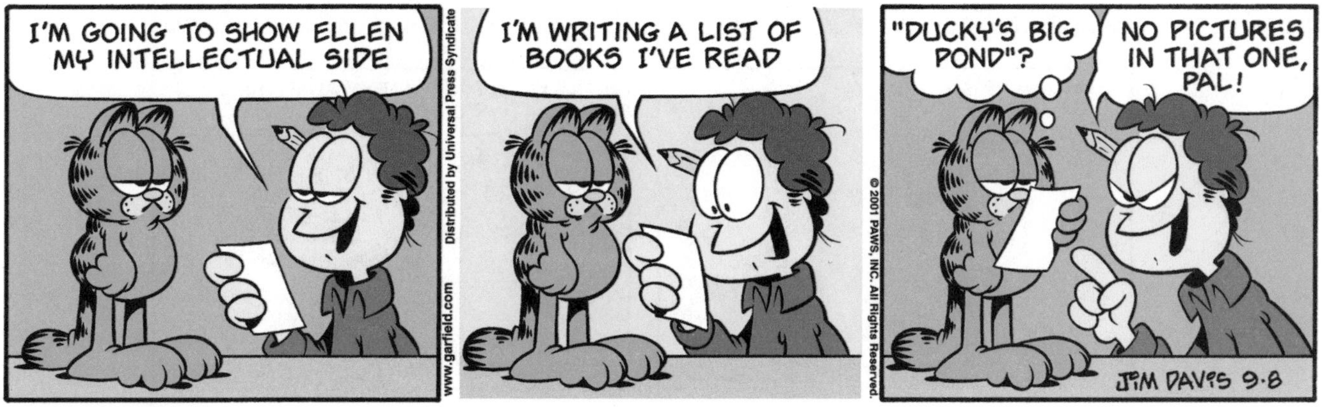
I'M GOING TO SHOW ELLEN MY INTELLECTUAL SIDE
Distributed by Universal Press Syndicate
www.garfield.com
I'M WRITING A LIST OF BOOKS I'VE READ
© 2001 PAWS, INC. All Rights Reserved.
"DUCKY'S BIG POND"?
NO PICTURES IN THAT ONE, PAL!
JIM DAVIS 9·8

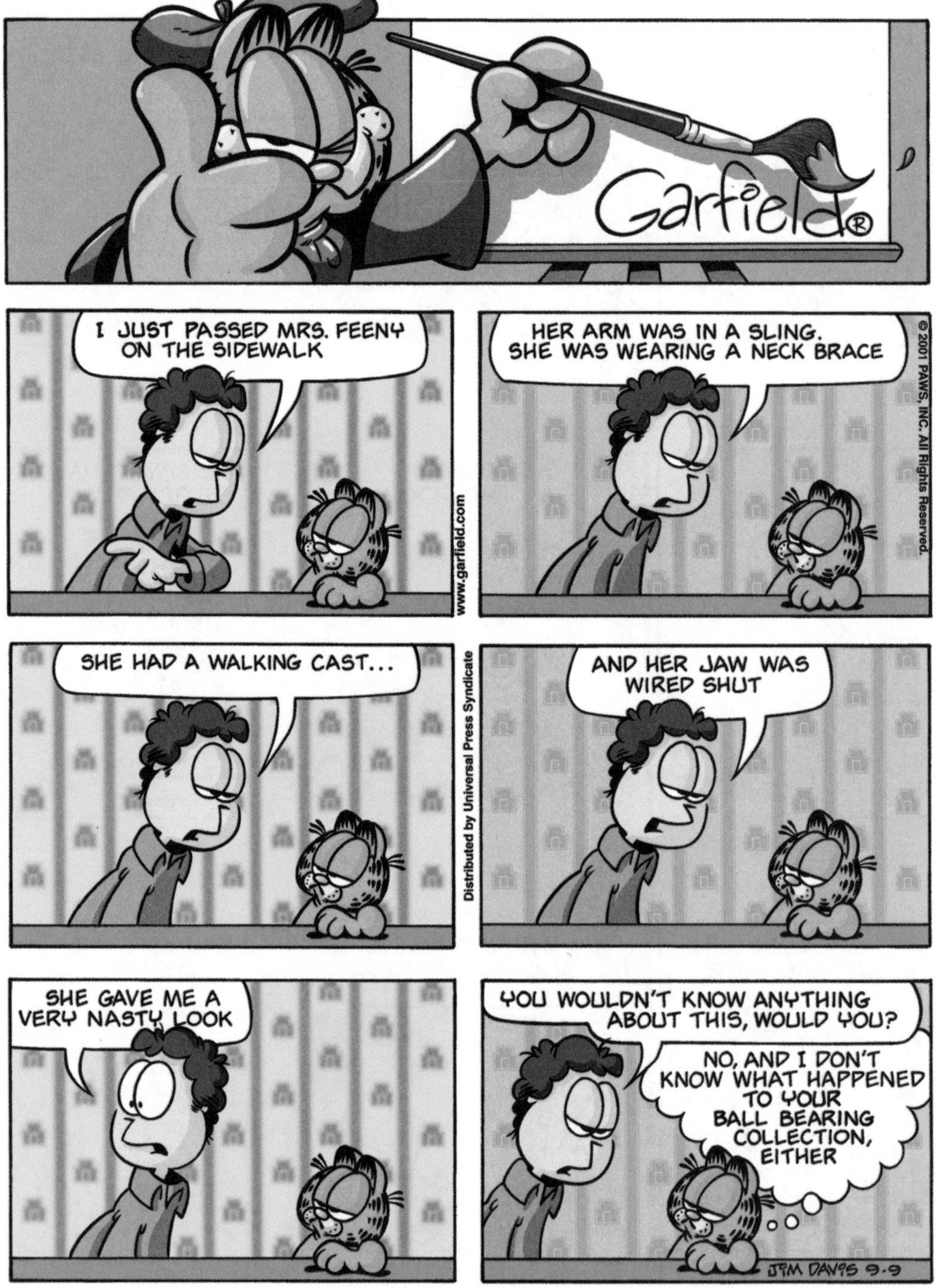
Garfield®
I JUST PASSED MRS. FEENY ON THE SIDEWALK
HER ARM WAS IN A SLING. SHE WAS WEARING A NECK BRACE
SHE HAD A WALKING CAST...
AND HER JAW WAS WIRED SHUT
SHE GAVE ME A VERY NASTY LOOK
YOU WOULDN'T KNOW ANYTHING ABOUT THIS, WOULD YOU?
NO, AND I DON'T KNOW WHAT HAPPENED TO YOUR BALL BEARING COLLECTION, EITHER
JIM DAVIS 9-9
www.garfield.com
© 2001 PAWS, INC. All Rights Reserved.
Distributed by Universal Press Syndicate

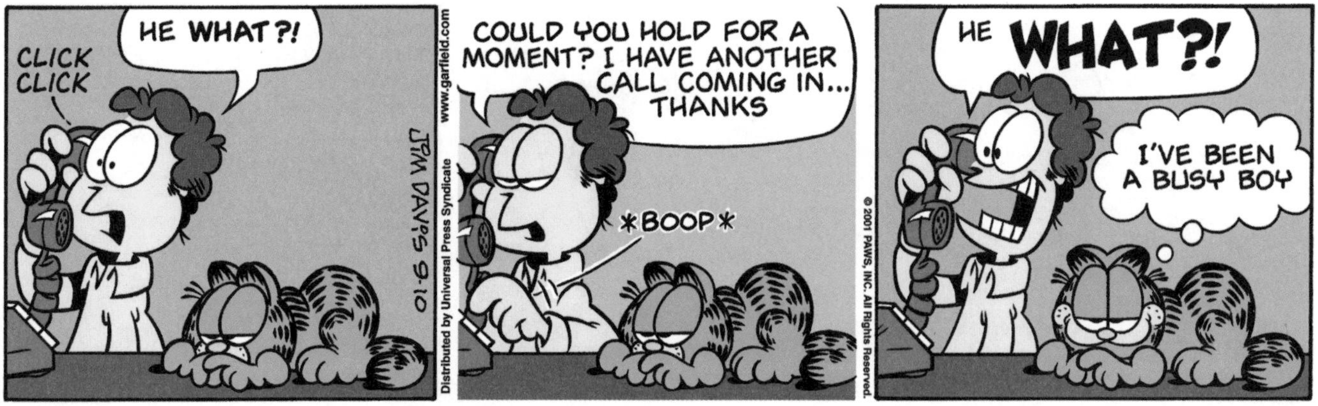
CLICK CLICK
HE WHAT?!
JIM DAVIS 9-10
Distributed by Universal Press Syndicate www.garfield.com
COULD YOU HOLD FOR A MOMENT? I HAVE ANOTHER CALL COMING IN... THANKS
BOOP
© 2001 PAWS, INC. All Rights Reserved.
HE WHAT?!
I'VE BEEN A BUSY BOY

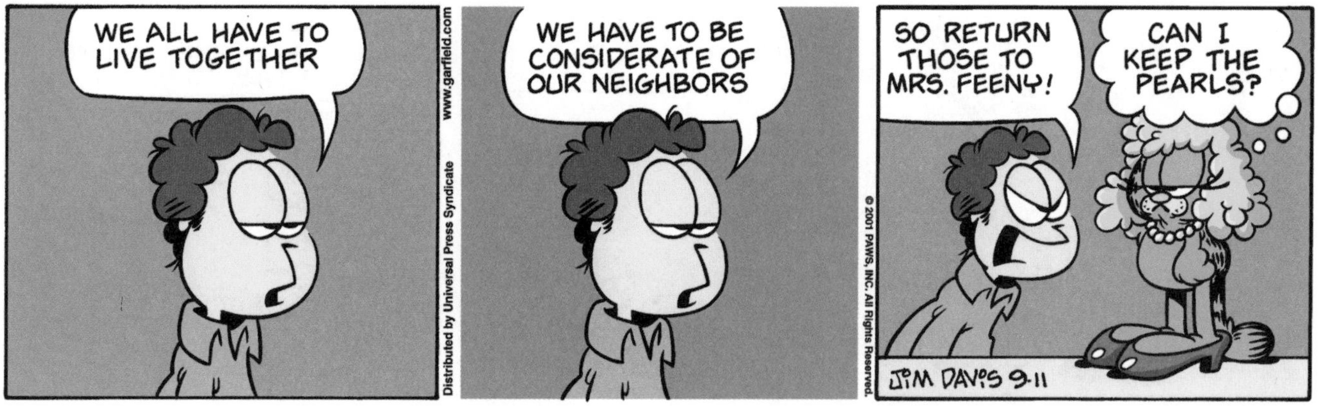
WE ALL HAVE TO LIVE TOGETHER
Distributed by Universal Press Syndicate www.garfield.com
WE HAVE TO BE CONSIDERATE OF OUR NEIGHBORS
© 2001 PAWS, INC. All Rights Reserved.
SO RETURN THOSE TO MRS. FEENY!
CAN I KEEP THE PEARLS?
JIM DAVIS 9-11

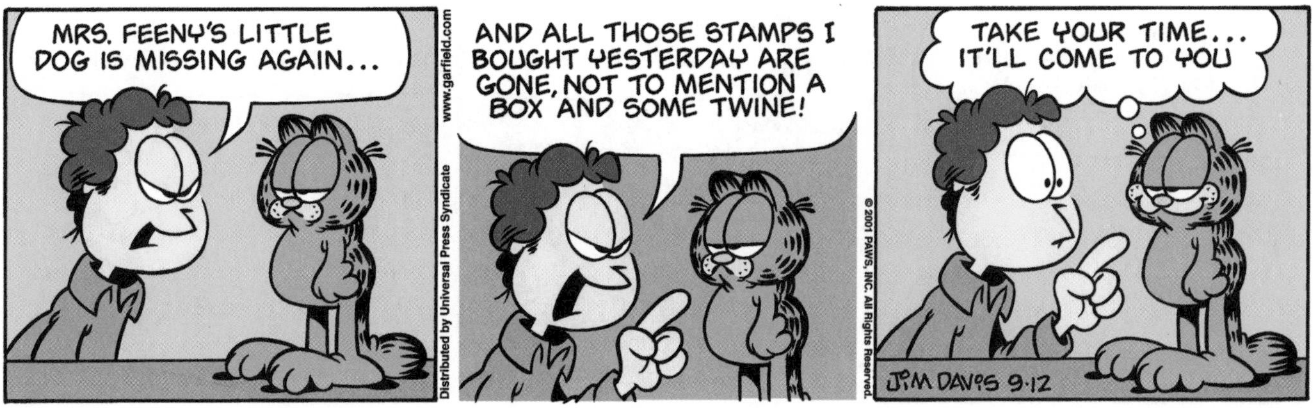
MRS. FEENY'S LITTLE DOG IS MISSING AGAIN...
Distributed by Universal Press Syndicate www.garfield.com
AND ALL THOSE STAMPS I BOUGHT YESTERDAY ARE GONE, NOT TO MENTION A BOX AND SOME TWINE!
© 2001 PAWS, INC. All Rights Reserved.
TAKE YOUR TIME... IT'LL COME TO YOU
JIM DAVIS 9-12

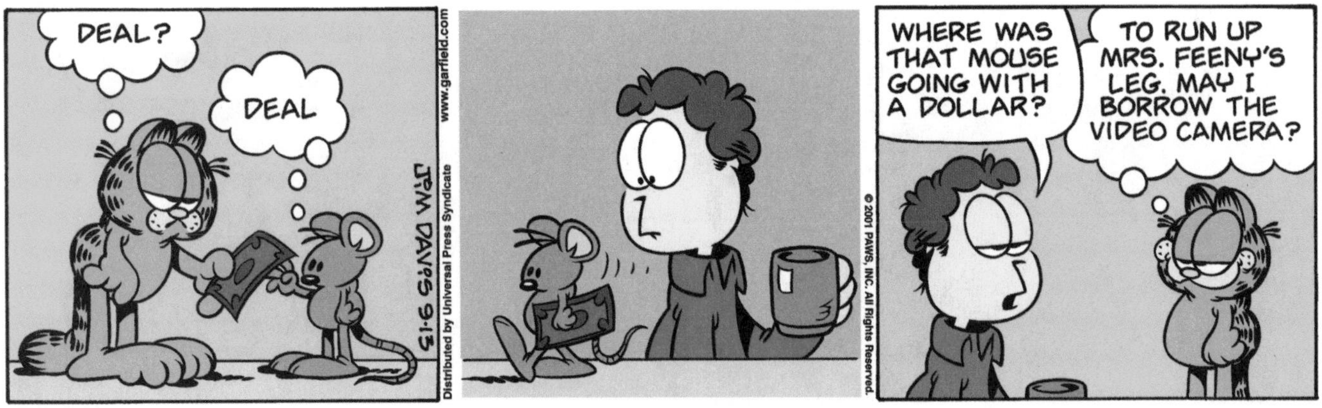
DEAL?
DEAL
JIM DAVIS 9-13
Distributed by Universal Press Syndicate
www.garfield.com
© 2001 PAWS, INC. All Rights Reserved.
WHERE WAS THAT MOUSE GOING WITH A DOLLAR?
TO RUN UP MRS. FEENY'S LEG. MAY I BORROW THE VIDEO CAMERA?

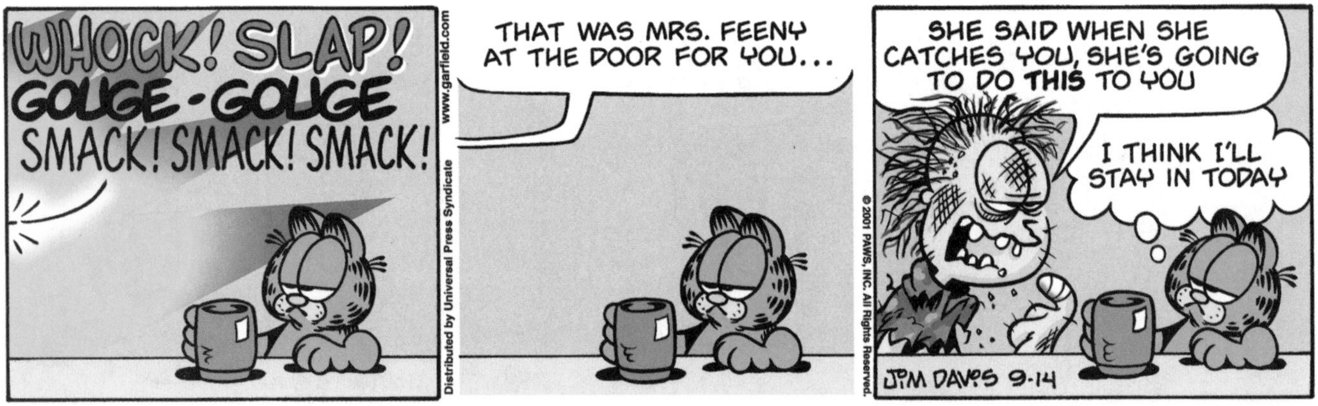
WHOCK! SLAP!
GOUGE - GOUGE
SMACK! SMACK! SMACK!
Distributed by Universal Press Syndicate
www.garfield.com
THAT WAS MRS. FEENY AT THE DOOR FOR YOU...
© 2001 PAWS, INC. All Rights Reserved.
SHE SAID WHEN SHE CATCHES YOU, SHE'S GOING TO DO **THIS** TO YOU
I THINK I'LL STAY IN TODAY
JIM DAVIS 9-14

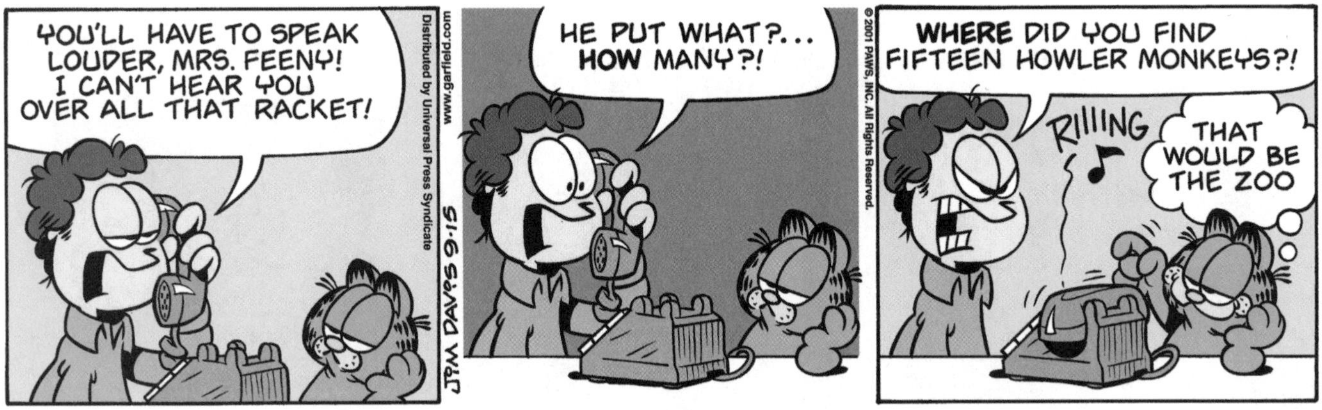
YOU'LL HAVE TO SPEAK LOUDER, MRS. FEENY! I CAN'T HEAR YOU OVER ALL THAT RACKET!
Distributed by Universal Press Syndicate
www.garfield.com
JIM DAVIS 9-15
HE PUT WHAT?... **HOW** MANY?!
© 2001 PAWS, INC. All Rights Reserved.
WHERE DID YOU FIND FIFTEEN HOWLER MONKEYS?!
RIIIING
THAT WOULD BE THE ZOO

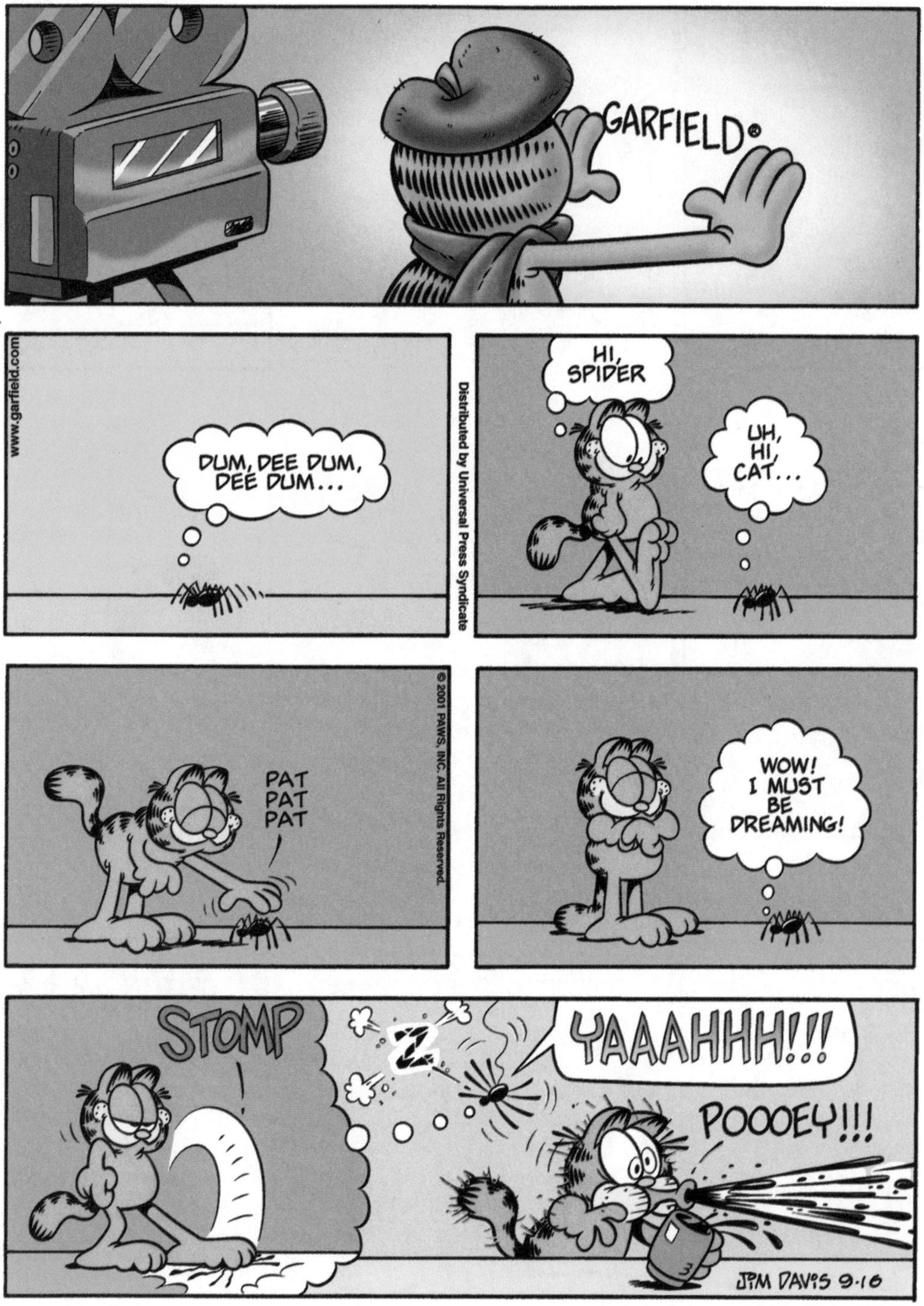
GARFIELD®
www.garfield.com
DUM, DEE DUM, DEE DUM...
Distributed by Universal Press Syndicate
HI, SPIDER
UH, HI, CAT...
© 2001 PAWS, INC. All Rights Reserved.
PAT PAT PAT
WOW! I MUST BE DREAMING!
STOMP
YAAAHHH!!!
POOOEY!!!
JIM DAVIS 9-16

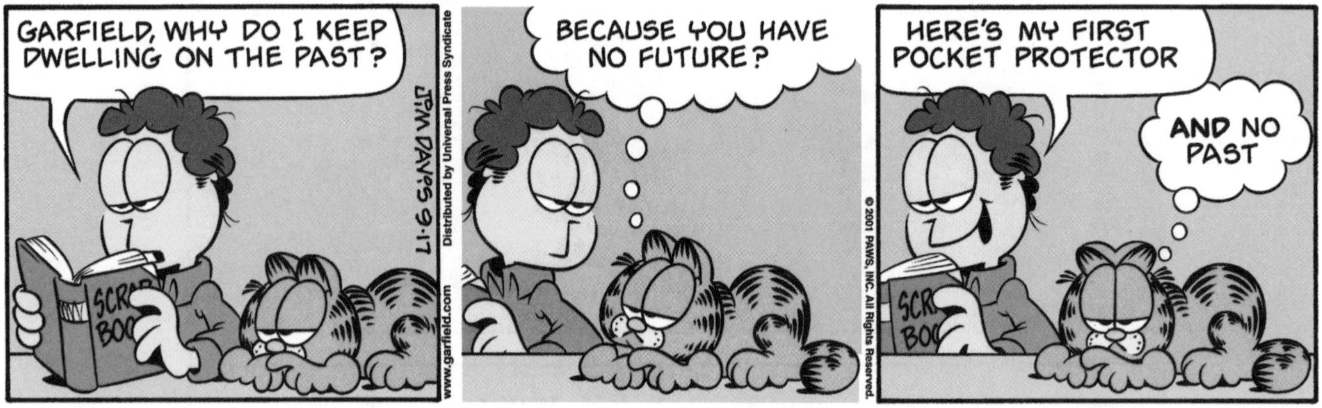
GARFIELD, WHY DO I KEEP DWELLING ON THE PAST?
JIM DAVIS 9-17
Distributed by Universal Press Syndicate
www.garfield.com
BECAUSE YOU HAVE NO FUTURE?
© 2001 PAWS, INC. All Rights Reserved.
HERE'S MY FIRST POCKET PROTECTOR
AND NO PAST

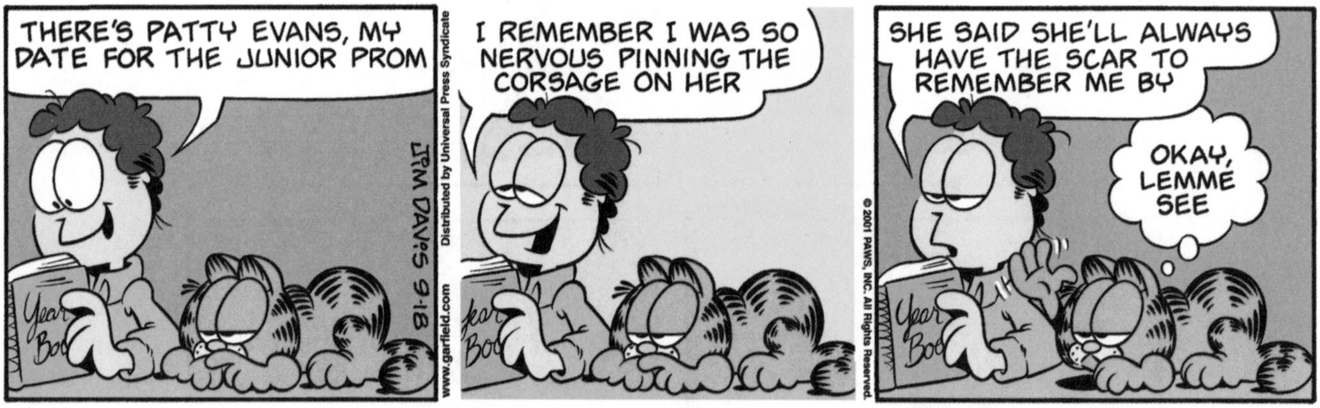
THERE'S PATTY EVANS, MY DATE FOR THE JUNIOR PROM
Year Book
JIM DAVIS 9-18
Distributed by Universal Press Syndicate
www.garfield.com
I REMEMBER I WAS SO NERVOUS PINNING THE CORSAGE ON HER
© 2001 PAWS, INC. All Rights Reserved.
SHE SAID SHE'LL ALWAYS HAVE THE SCAR TO REMEMBER ME BY
OKAY, LEMME SEE

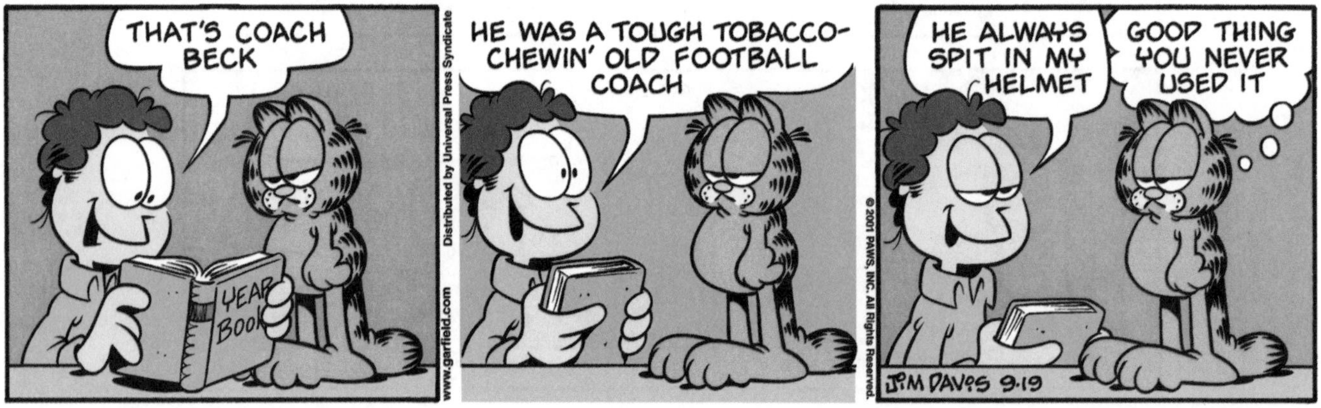
THAT'S COACH BECK
YEAR Book
Distributed by Universal Press Syndicate
www.garfield.com
HE WAS A TOUGH TOBACCO-CHEWIN' OLD FOOTBALL COACH
© 2001 PAWS, INC. All Rights Reserved.
HE ALWAYS SPIT IN MY HELMET
GOOD THING YOU NEVER USED IT
JIM DAVIS 9-19

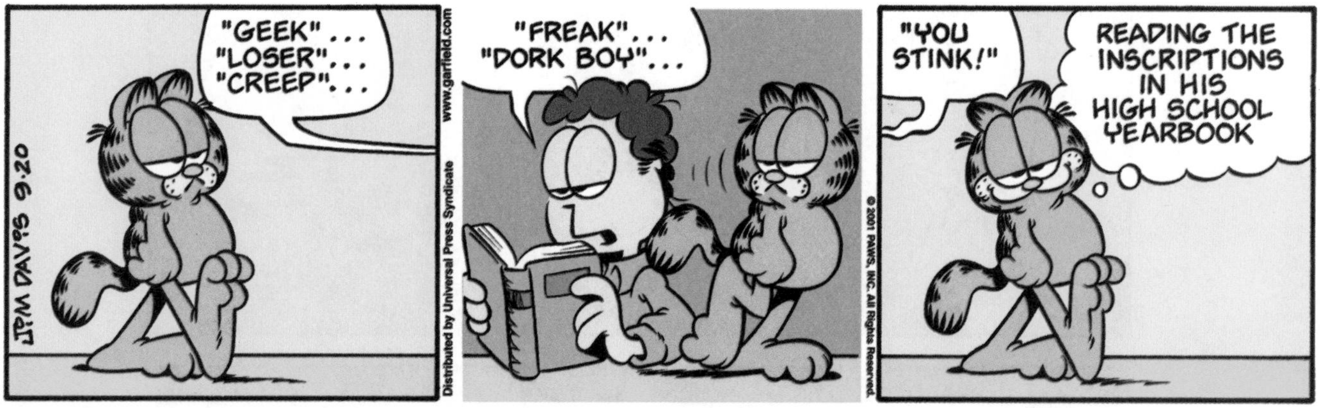
JIM DAVIS 9-20
"GEEK"... "LOSER"... "CREEP"...
www.garfield.com
Distributed by Universal Press Syndicate
"FREAK"... "DORK BOY"...
© 2001 PAWS, INC. All Rights Reserved.
"YOU STINK!"
READING THE INSCRIPTIONS IN HIS HIGH SCHOOL YEARBOOK

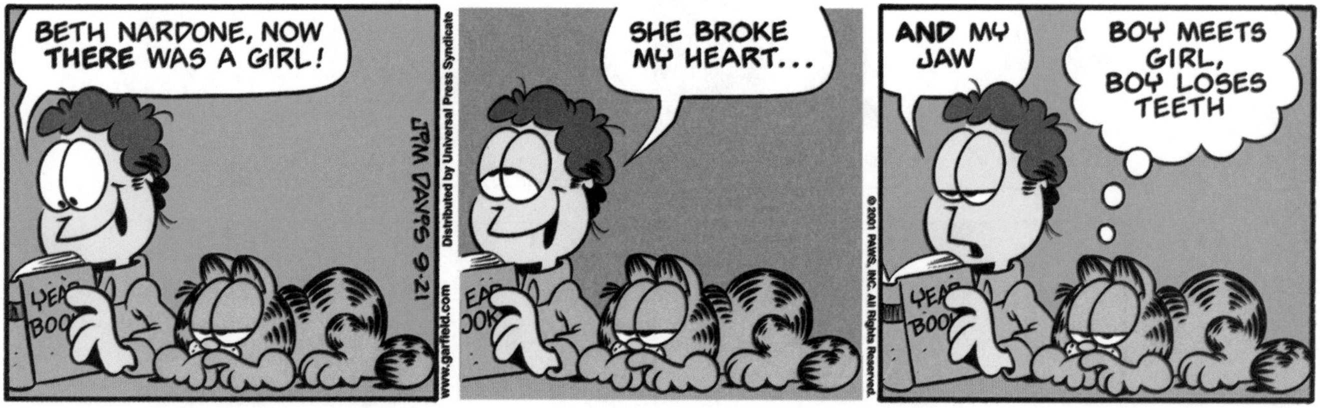
BETH NARDONE, NOW THERE WAS A GIRL!
JIM DAVIS 9-21
Distributed by Universal Press Syndicate
www.garfield.com
SHE BROKE MY HEART...
© 2001 PAWS, INC. All Rights Reserved.
AND MY JAW
BOY MEETS GIRL, BOY LOSES TEETH

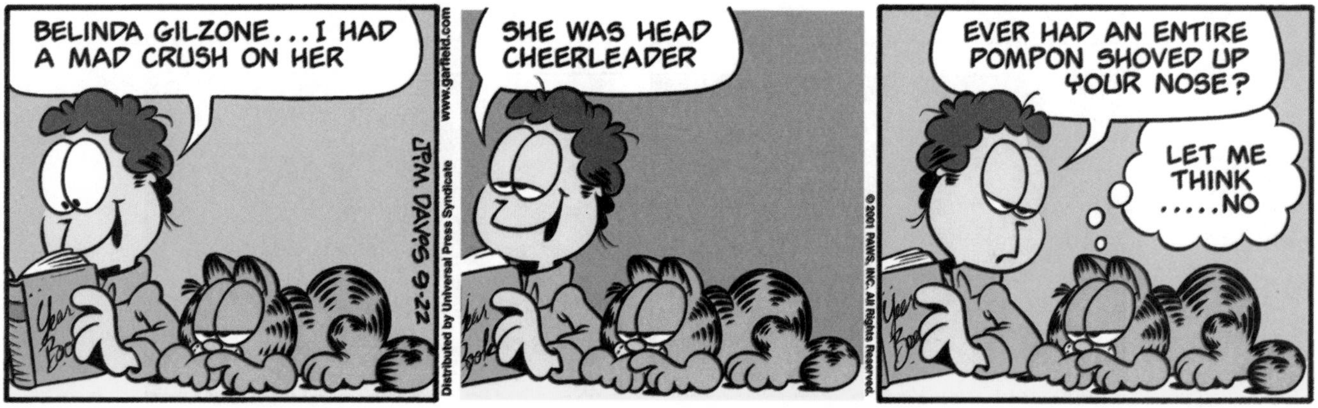
BELINDA GILZONE...I HAD A MAD CRUSH ON HER
JIM DAVIS 9-22
www.garfield.com
Distributed by Universal Press Syndicate
SHE WAS HEAD CHEERLEADER
© 2001 PAWS, INC. All Rights Reserved.
EVER HAD AN ENTIRE POMPON SHOVED UP YOUR NOSE?
LET ME THINK .....NO

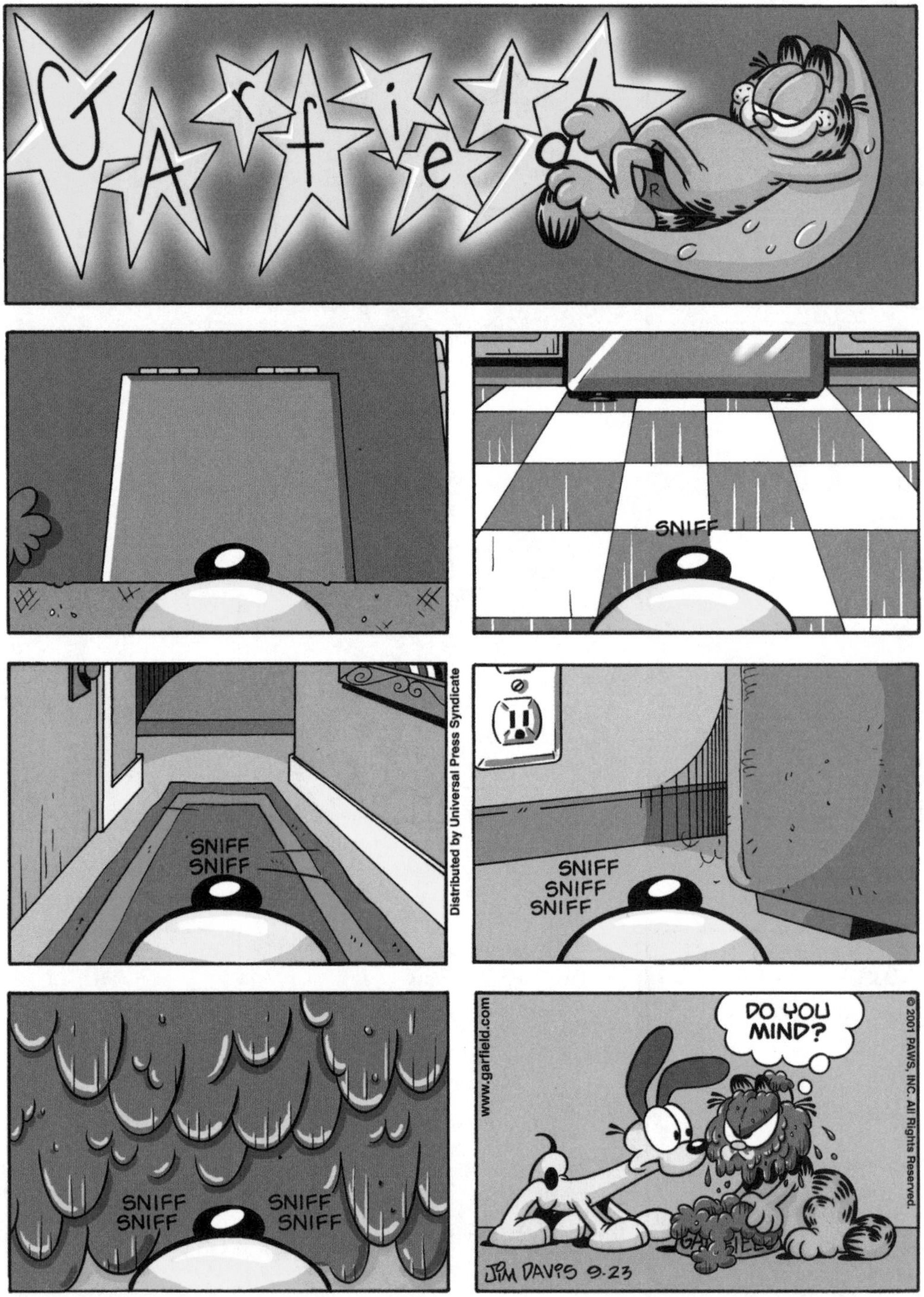
Garfield
SNIFF
SNIFF
SNIFF
SNIFF
SNIFF
SNIFF
SNIFF
SNIFF
SNIFF
SNIFF
DO YOU MIND?
Distributed by Universal Press Syndicate
www.garfield.com
© 2001 PAWS, INC. All Rights Reserved.
JIM DAVIS 9-23

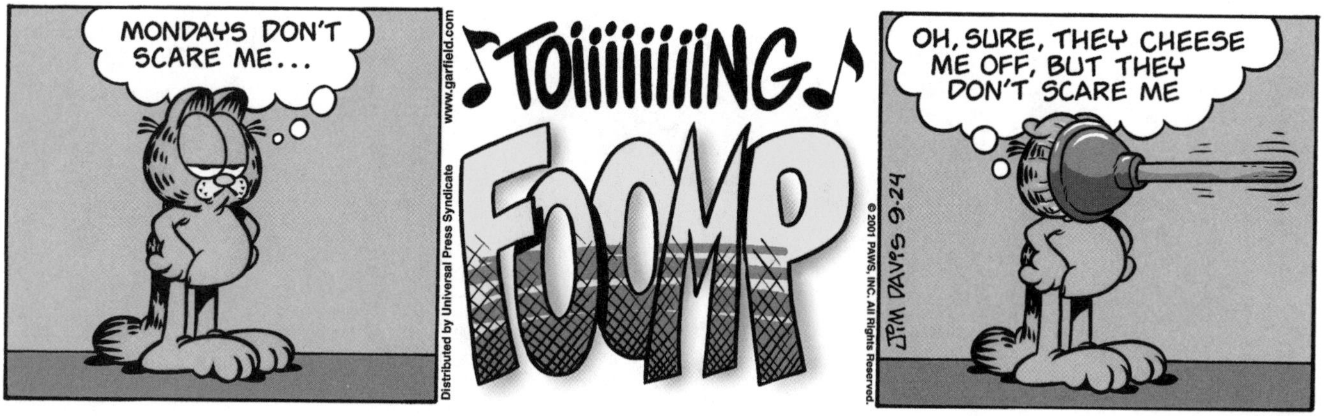
MONDAYS DON'T SCARE ME...
TOiiiiiiiiNG
FOOMP
OH, SURE, THEY CHEESE ME OFF, BUT THEY DON'T SCARE ME
Distributed by Universal Press Syndicate www.garfield.com
© 2001 PAWS, INC. All Rights Reserved.
JIM DAVIS 9-24

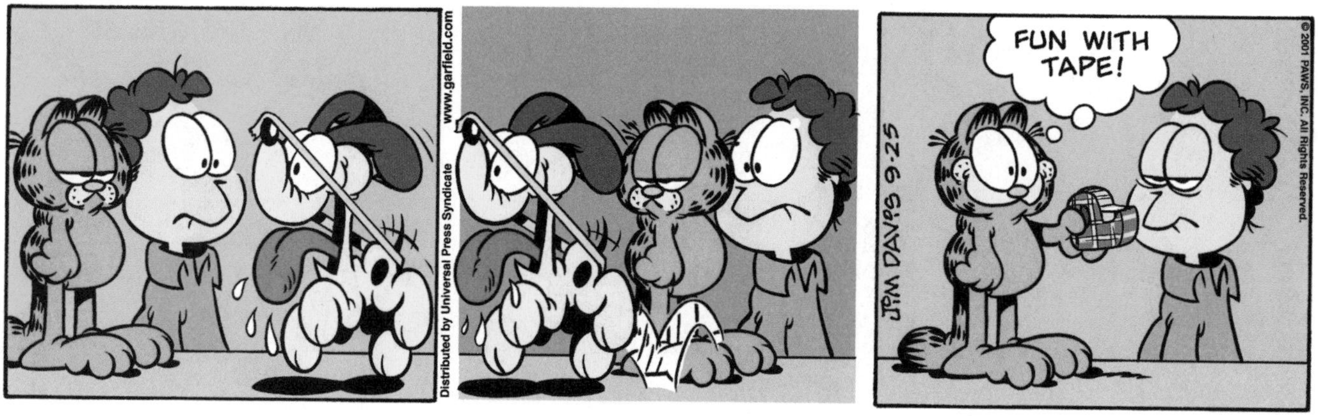
FUN WITH TAPE!
Distributed by Universal Press Syndicate www.garfield.com
© 2001 PAWS, INC. All Rights Reserved.
JIM DAVIS 9-25

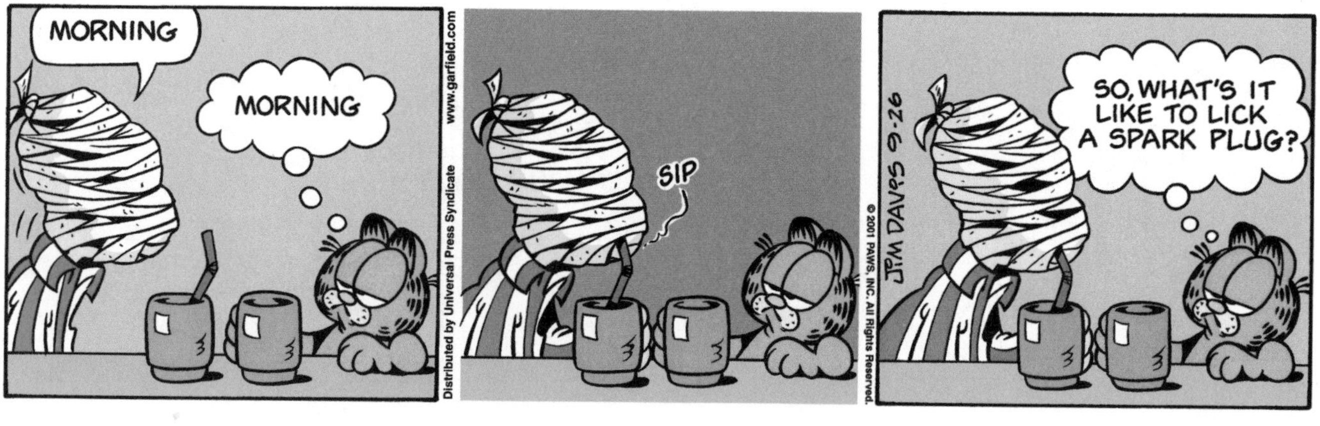
MORNING
MORNING
SIP
SO, WHAT'S IT LIKE TO LICK A SPARK PLUG?
Distributed by Universal Press Syndicate www.garfield.com
© 2001 PAWS, INC. All Rights Reserved.
JIM DAVIS 9-26

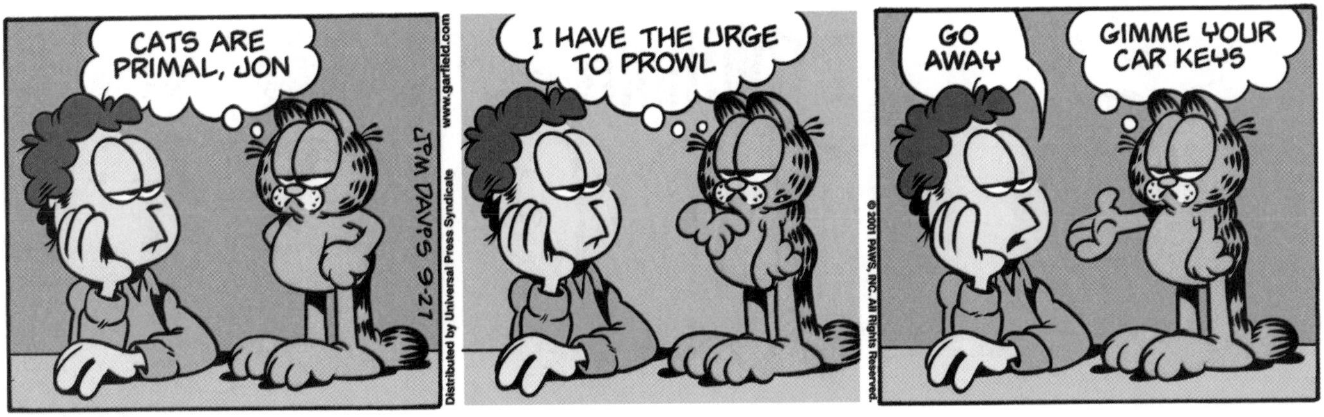
CATS ARE PRIMAL, JON
I HAVE THE URGE TO PROWL
GO AWAY
GIMME YOUR CAR KEYS
JIM DAVIS 9-21
www.garfield.com
Distributed by Universal Press Syndicate
© 2001 PAWS, INC. All Rights Reserved.

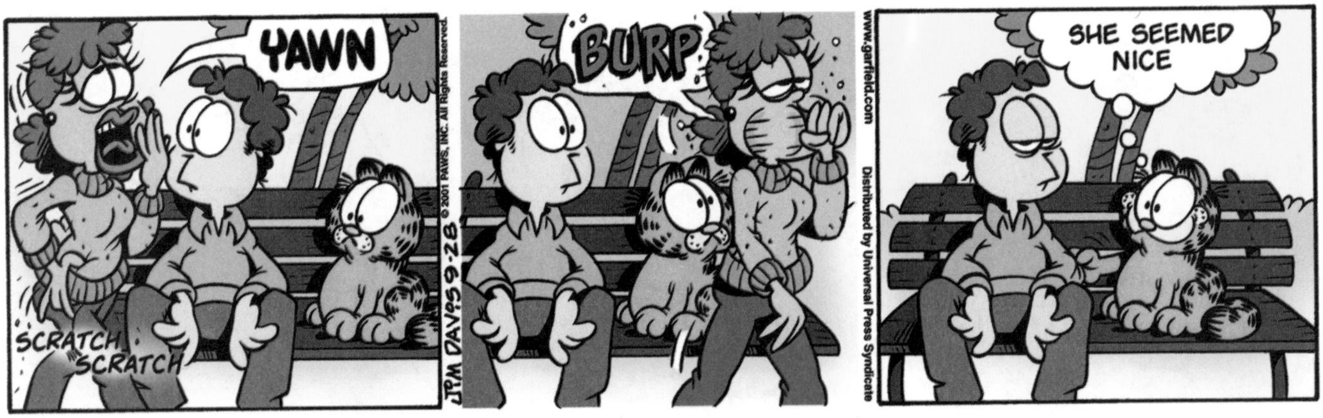
YAWN
SCRATCH SCRATCH
BURP
SHE SEEMED NICE
JIM DAVIS 9-28
© 2001 PAWS, INC. All Rights Reserved.
www.garfield.com
Distributed by Universal Press Syndicate

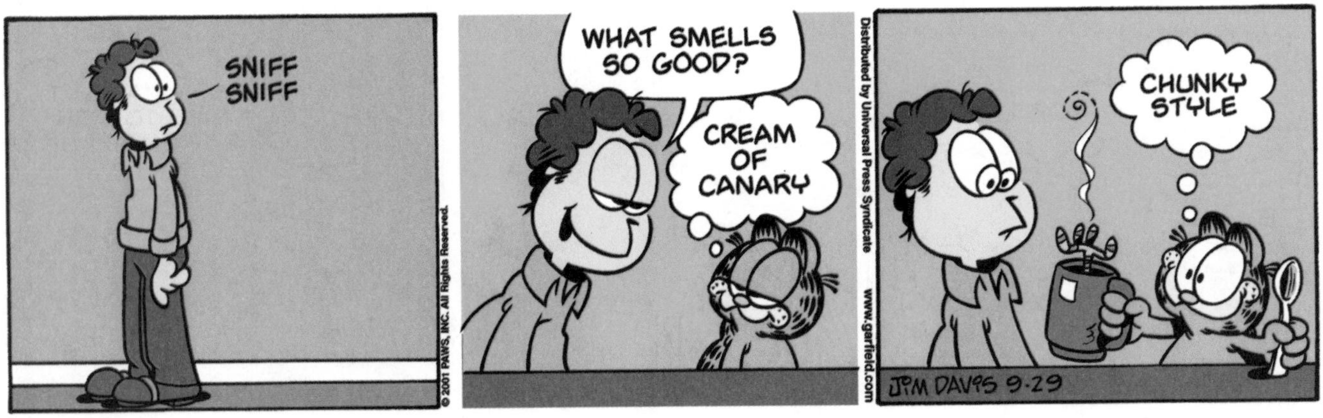
SNIFF SNIFF
WHAT SMELLS SO GOOD?
CREAM OF CANARY
CHUNKY STYLE
JIM DAVIS 9-29
© 2001 PAWS, INC. All Rights Reserved.
Distributed by Universal Press Syndicate
www.garfield.com

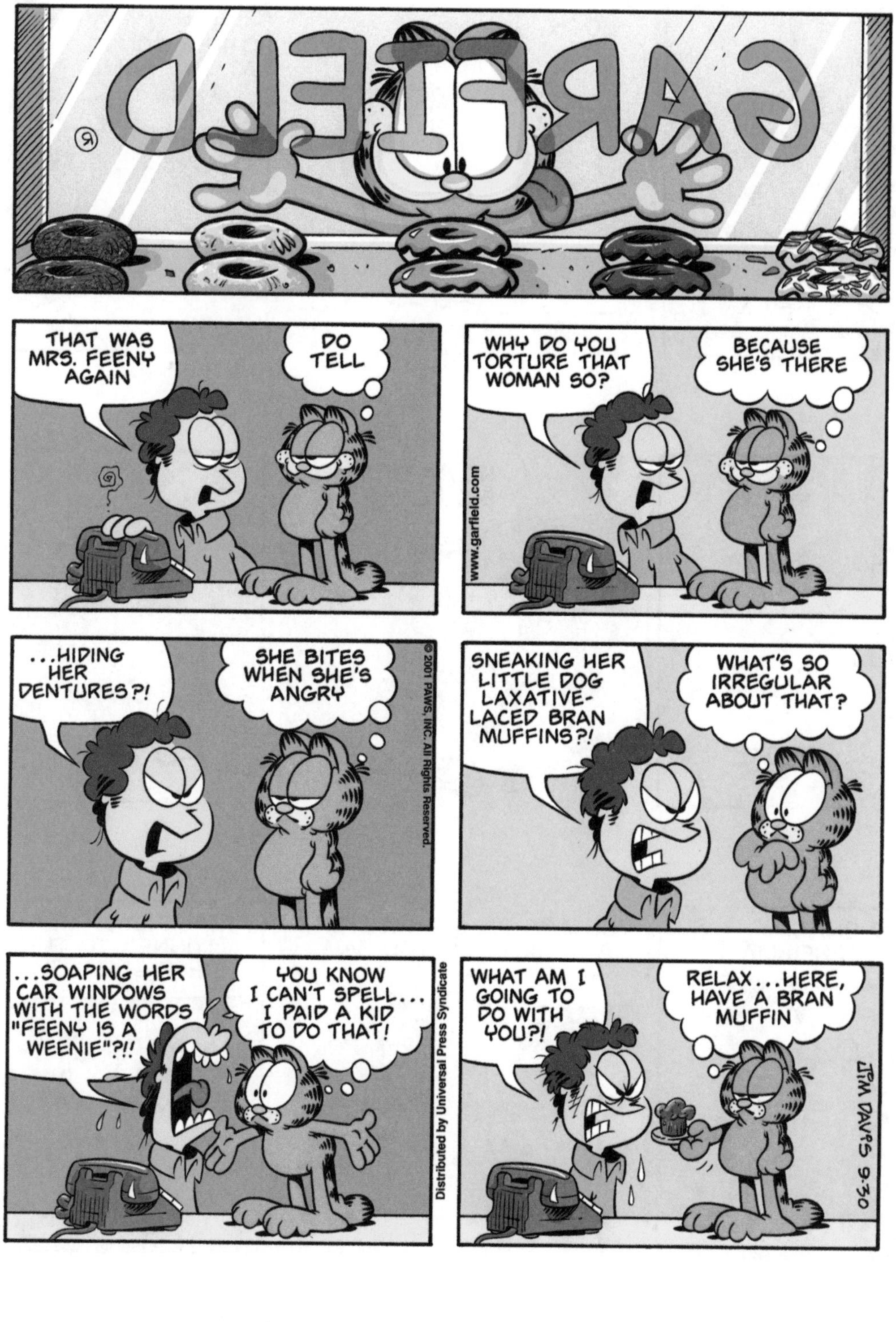
GARFIELD ®
THAT WAS MRS. FEENY AGAIN
DO TELL
WHY DO YOU TORTURE THAT WOMAN SO?
BECAUSE SHE'S THERE
www.garfield.com
...HIDING HER DENTURES?!
SHE BITES WHEN SHE'S ANGRY
© 2001 PAWS, INC. All Rights Reserved.
SNEAKING HER LITTLE DOG LAXATIVE-LACED BRAN MUFFINS?!
WHAT'S SO IRREGULAR ABOUT THAT?
...SOAPING HER CAR WINDOWS WITH THE WORDS "FEENY IS A WEENIE"?!!
YOU KNOW I CAN'T SPELL... I PAID A KID TO DO THAT!
Distributed by Universal Press Syndicate
WHAT AM I GOING TO DO WITH YOU?!
RELAX...HERE, HAVE A BRAN MUFFIN
JIM DAVIS 9-30

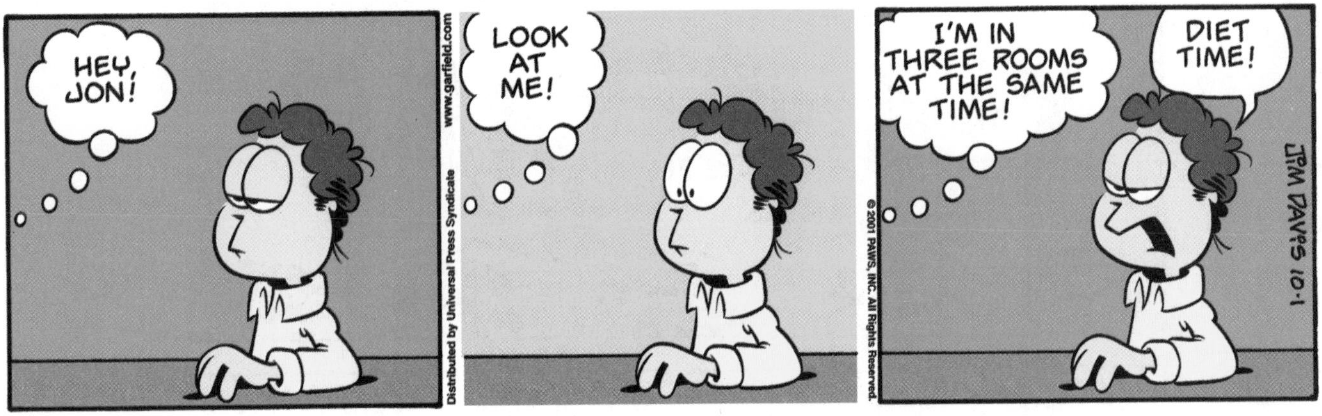
HEY, JON!
LOOK AT ME!
I'M IN THREE ROOMS AT THE SAME TIME!
DIET TIME!
JIM DAVIS 10-1
www.garfield.com
Distributed by Universal Press Syndicate
© 2001 PAWS, INC. All Rights Reserved.

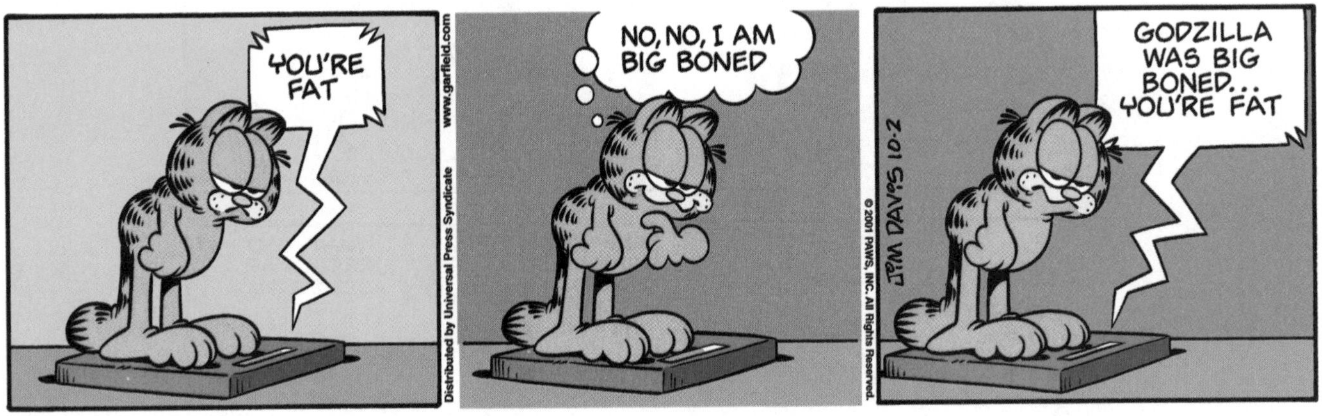
YOU'RE FAT
NO, NO, I AM BIG BONED
GODZILLA WAS BIG BONED... YOU'RE FAT
JIM DAVIS 10-2
www.garfield.com
Distributed by Universal Press Syndicate
© 2001 PAWS, INC. All Rights Reserved.

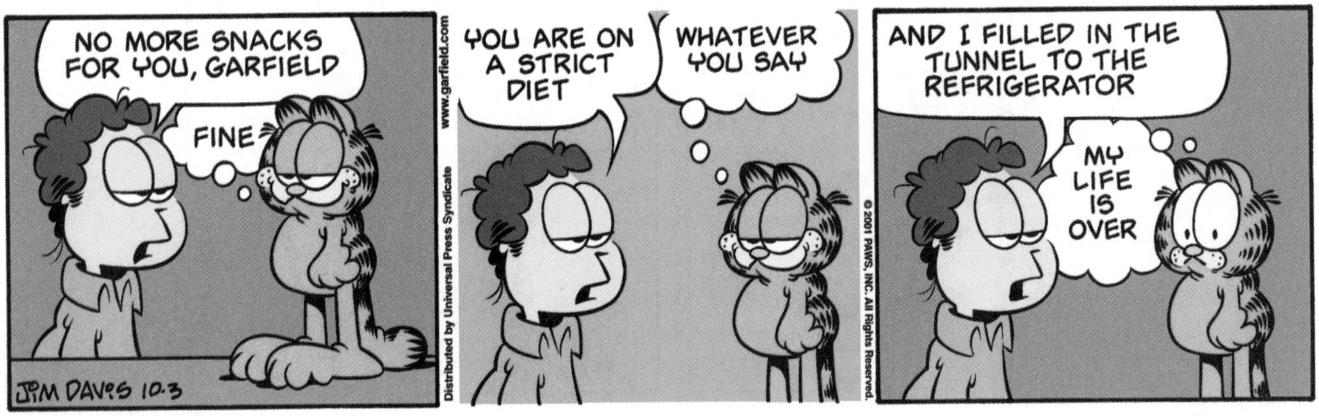
NO MORE SNACKS FOR YOU, GARFIELD
FINE
YOU ARE ON A STRICT DIET
WHATEVER YOU SAY
AND I FILLED IN THE TUNNEL TO THE REFRIGERATOR
MY LIFE IS OVER
JIM DAVIS 10-3
www.garfield.com
Distributed by Universal Press Syndicate
© 2001 PAWS, INC. All Rights Reserved.

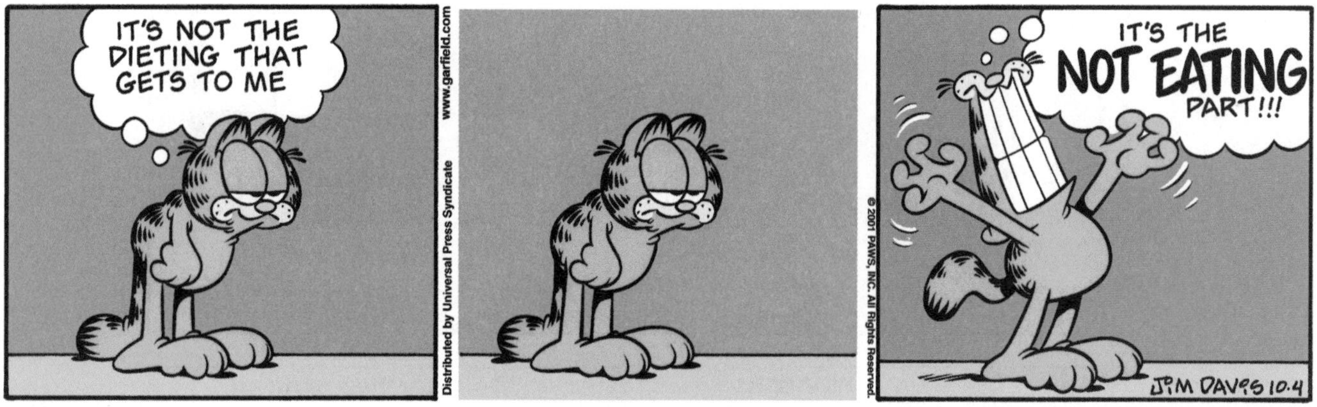
IT'S NOT THE DIETING THAT GETS TO ME
IT'S THE NOT EATING PART!!!
www.garfield.com
Distributed by Universal Press Syndicate
© 2001 PAWS, INC. All Rights Reserved.
JIM DAVIS 10-4

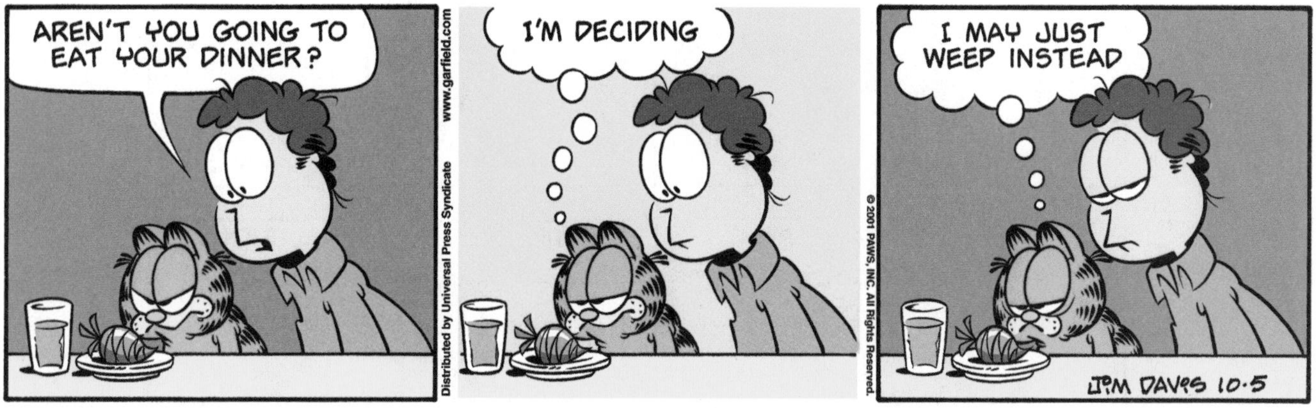
AREN'T YOU GOING TO EAT YOUR DINNER?
I'M DECIDING
I MAY JUST WEEP INSTEAD
www.garfield.com
Distributed by Universal Press Syndicate
© 2001 PAWS, INC. All Rights Reserved.
JIM DAVIS 10-5

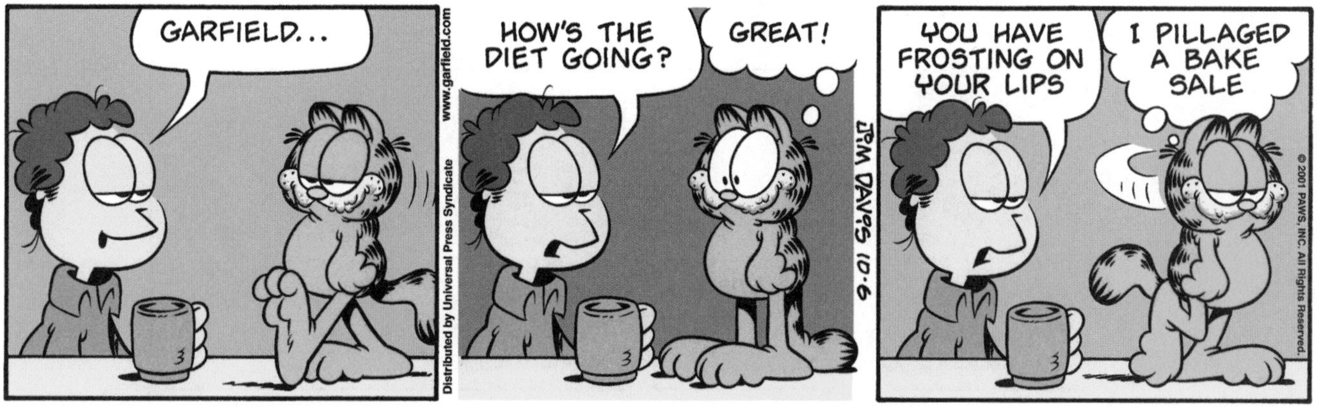
GARFIELD...
HOW'S THE DIET GOING?
GREAT!
YOU HAVE FROSTING ON YOUR LIPS
I PILLAGED A BAKE SALE
www.garfield.com
Distributed by Universal Press Syndicate
JIM DAVIS 10-6
© 2001 PAWS, INC. All Rights Reserved.

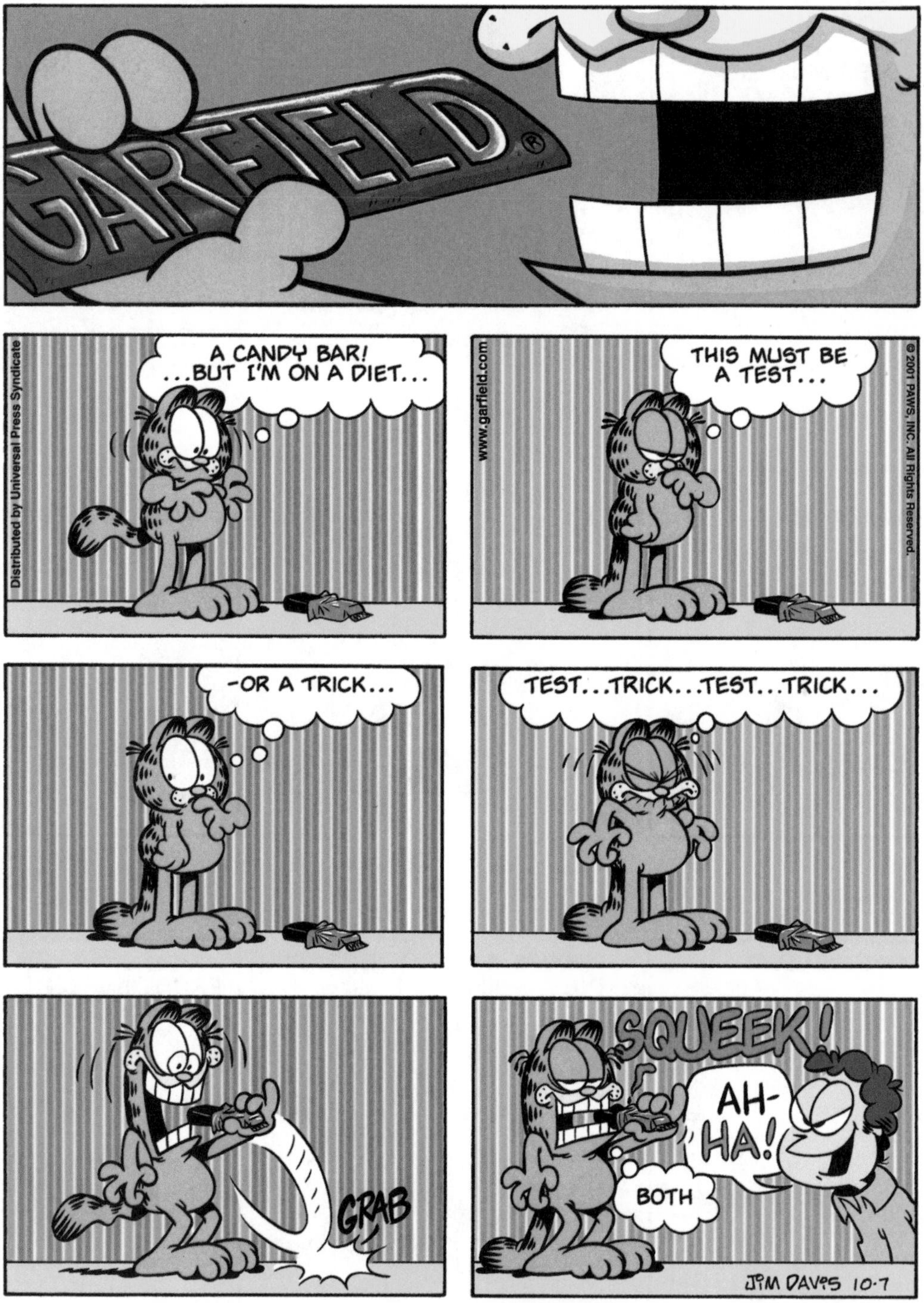
GARFIELD®
A CANDY BAR! ...BUT I'M ON A DIET...
THIS MUST BE A TEST...
-OR A TRICK...
TEST...TRICK...TEST...TRICK...
GRAB
SQUEEK!
AH-HA!
BOTH
JIM DAVIS 10-7

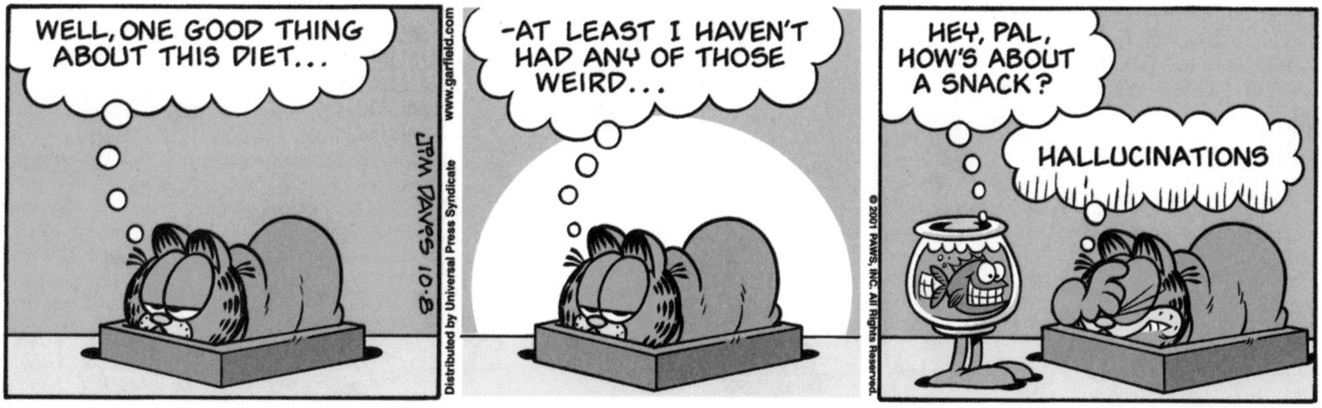
WELL, ONE GOOD THING ABOUT THIS DIET...
-AT LEAST I HAVEN'T HAD ANY OF THOSE WEIRD...
HEY, PAL, HOW'S ABOUT A SNACK?
HALLUCINATIONS
JIM DAVIS 10-8
Distributed by Universal Press Syndicate www.garfield.com
© 2001 PAWS, INC. All Rights Reserved.

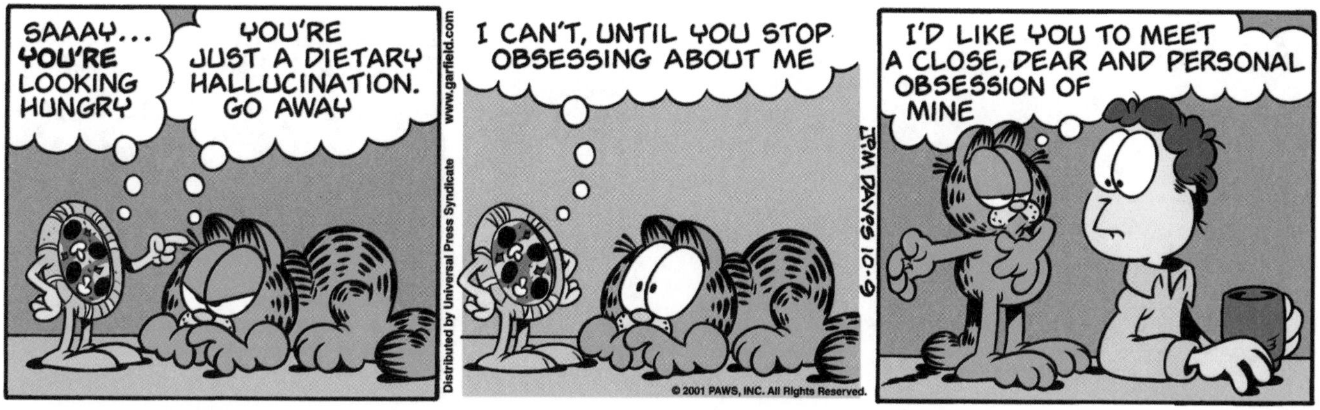
SAAAY... **YOU'RE** LOOKING HUNGRY
YOU'RE JUST A DIETARY HALLUCINATION. GO AWAY
I CAN'T, UNTIL YOU STOP OBSESSING ABOUT ME
I'D LIKE YOU TO MEET A CLOSE, DEAR AND PERSONAL OBSESSION OF MINE
JIM DAVIS 10-9
Distributed by Universal Press Syndicate www.garfield.com
© 2001 PAWS, INC. All Rights Reserved.

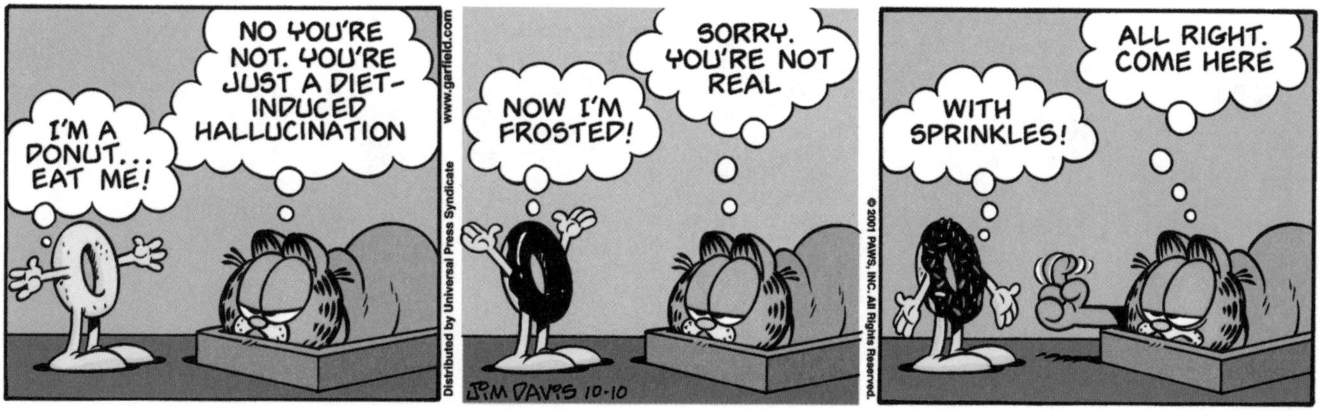
I'M A DONUT... EAT ME!
NO YOU'RE NOT. YOU'RE JUST A DIET-INDUCED HALLUCINATION
NOW I'M FROSTED!
SORRY. YOU'RE NOT REAL
WITH SPRINKLES!
ALL RIGHT. COME HERE
JIM DAVIS 10-10
Distributed by Universal Press Syndicate www.garfield.com
© 2001 PAWS, INC. All Rights Reserved.

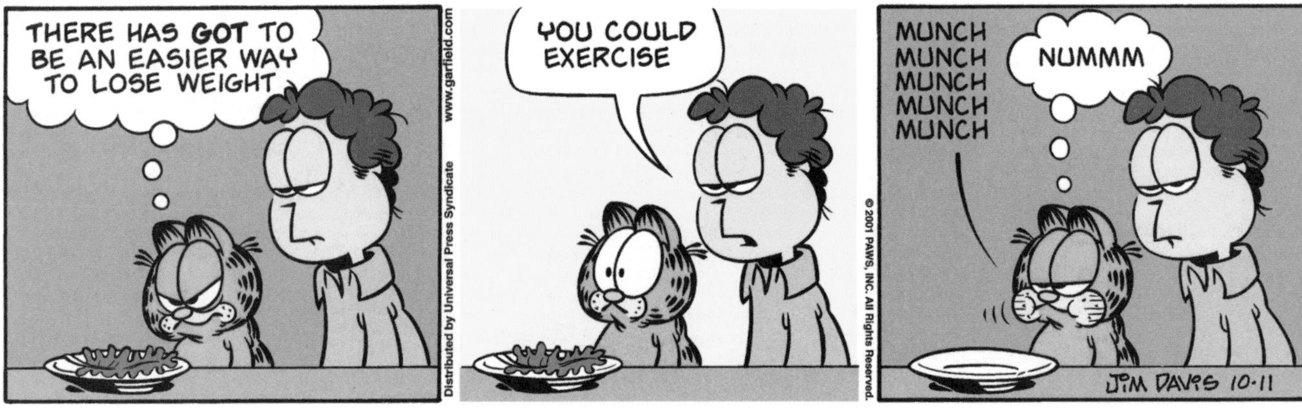
THERE HAS GOT TO BE AN EASIER WAY TO LOSE WEIGHT
YOU COULD EXERCISE
MUNCH MUNCH MUNCH MUNCH MUNCH
NUMMM
JIM DAVIS 10-11
Distributed by Universal Press Syndicate www.garfield.com
© 2001 PAWS, INC. All Rights Reserved.

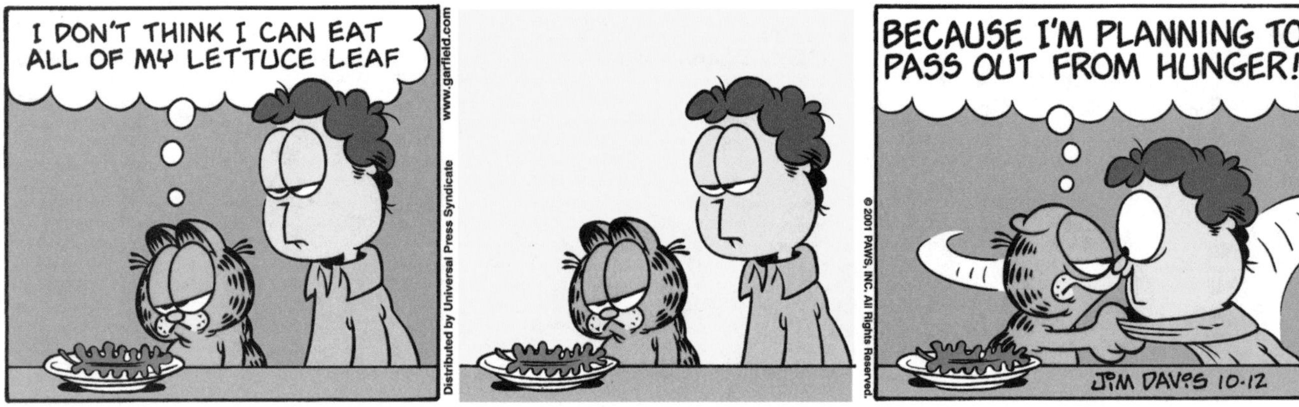
I DON'T THINK I CAN EAT ALL OF MY LETTUCE LEAF
BECAUSE I'M PLANNING TO PASS OUT FROM HUNGER!
JIM DAVIS 10-12
Distributed by Universal Press Syndicate www.garfield.com
© 2001 PAWS, INC. All Rights Reserved.

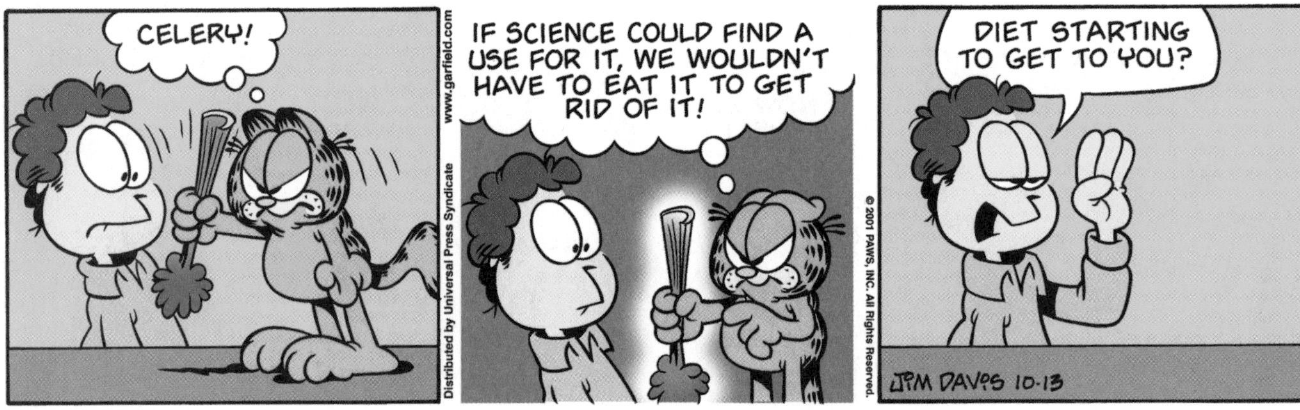
CELERY!
IF SCIENCE COULD FIND A USE FOR IT, WE WOULDN'T HAVE TO EAT IT TO GET RID OF IT!
DIET STARTING TO GET TO YOU?
JIM DAVIS 10-13
Distributed by Universal Press Syndicate www.garfield.com
© 2001 PAWS, INC. All Rights Reserved.

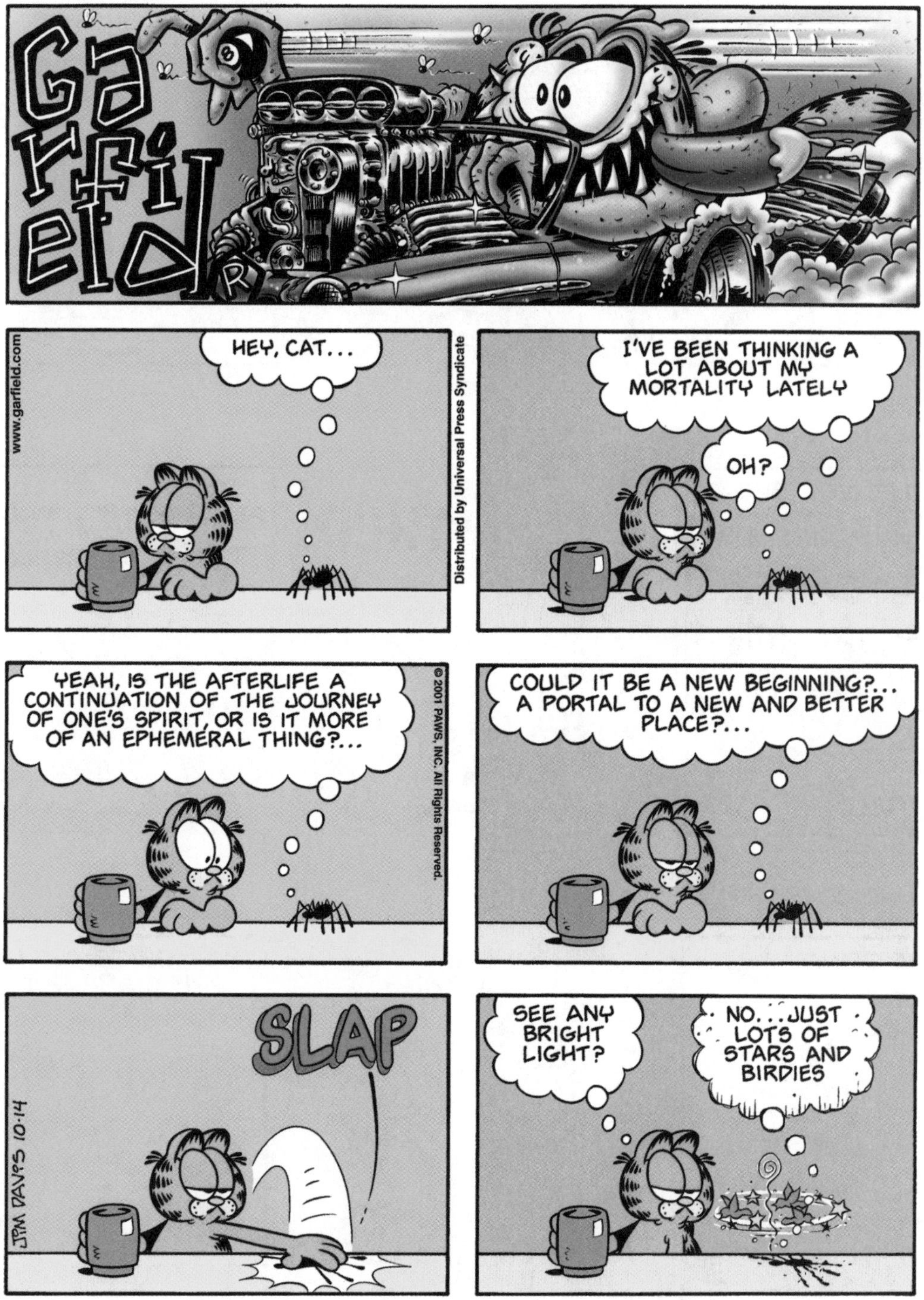

GARFIELD
www.garfield.com
HEY, CAT...
Distributed by Universal Press Syndicate
I'VE BEEN THINKING A LOT ABOUT MY MORTALITY LATELY
OH?
YEAH, IS THE AFTERLIFE A CONTINUATION OF THE JOURNEY OF ONE'S SPIRIT, OR IS IT MORE OF AN EPHEMERAL THING?...
© 2001 PAWS, INC. All Rights Reserved.
COULD IT BE A NEW BEGINNING?... A PORTAL TO A NEW AND BETTER PLACE?...
JIM DAVIS 10-14
SLAP
SEE ANY BRIGHT LIGHT?
NO...JUST LOTS OF STARS AND BIRDIES

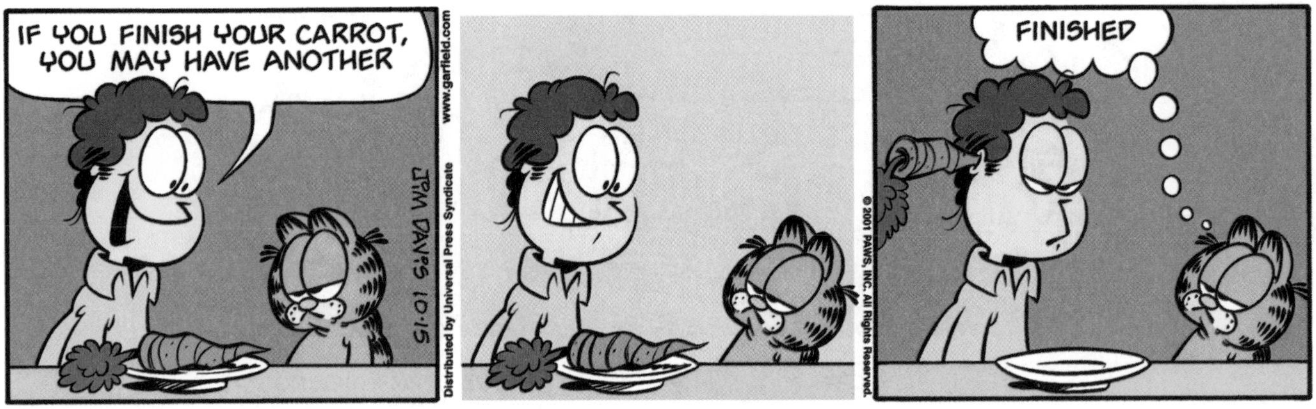
IF YOU FINISH YOUR CARROT, YOU MAY HAVE ANOTHER
JIM DAVIS 10-15
www.garfield.com
Distributed by Universal Press Syndicate
© 2001 PAWS, INC. All Rights Reserved.
FINISHED

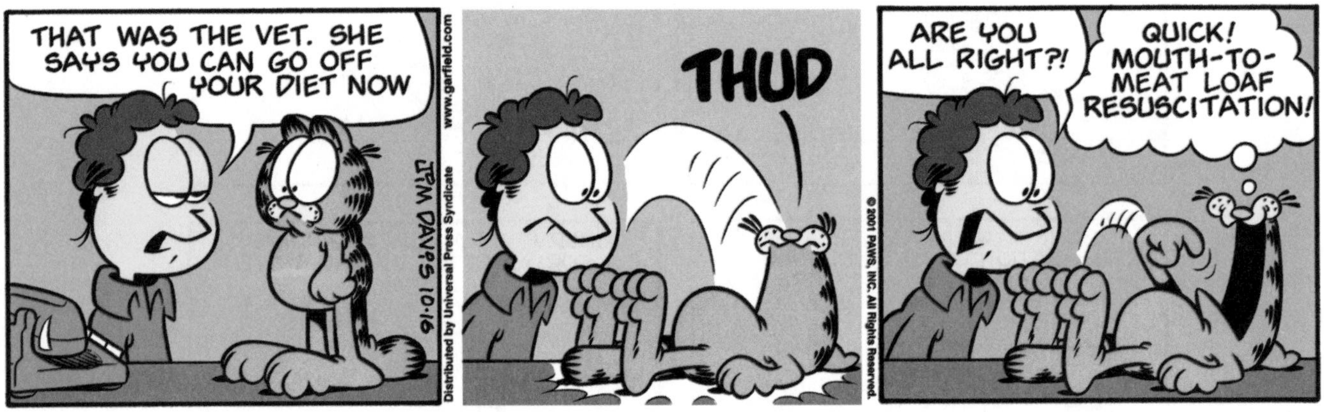
THAT WAS THE VET. SHE SAYS YOU CAN GO OFF YOUR DIET NOW
JIM DAVIS 10-16
www.garfield.com
Distributed by Universal Press Syndicate
THUD
© 2001 PAWS, INC. All Rights Reserved.
ARE YOU ALL RIGHT?!
QUICK! MOUTH-TO-MEAT LOAF RESUSCITATION!

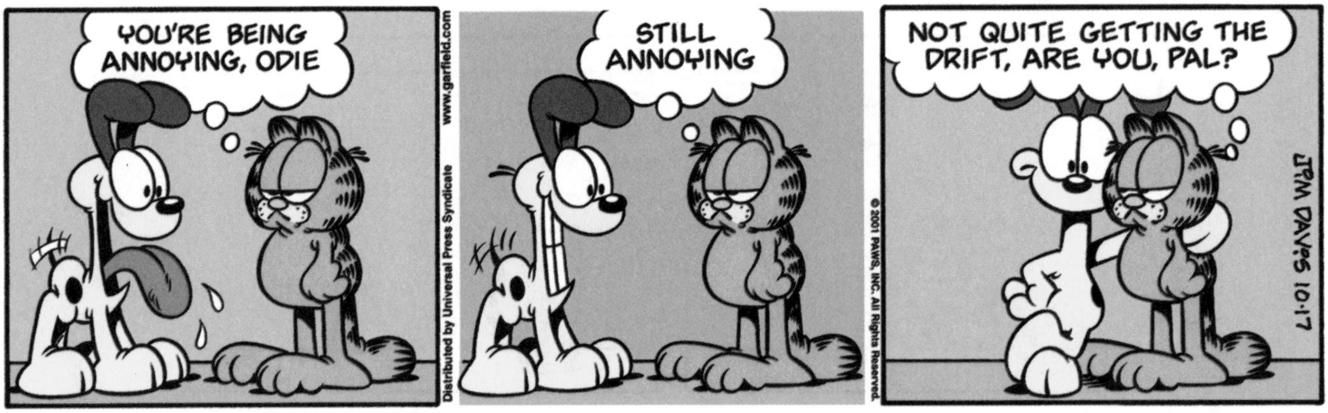
YOU'RE BEING ANNOYING, ODIE
www.garfield.com
Distributed by Universal Press Syndicate
STILL ANNOYING
© 2001 PAWS, INC. All Rights Reserved.
NOT QUITE GETTING THE DRIFT, ARE YOU, PAL?
JIM DAVIS 10-17

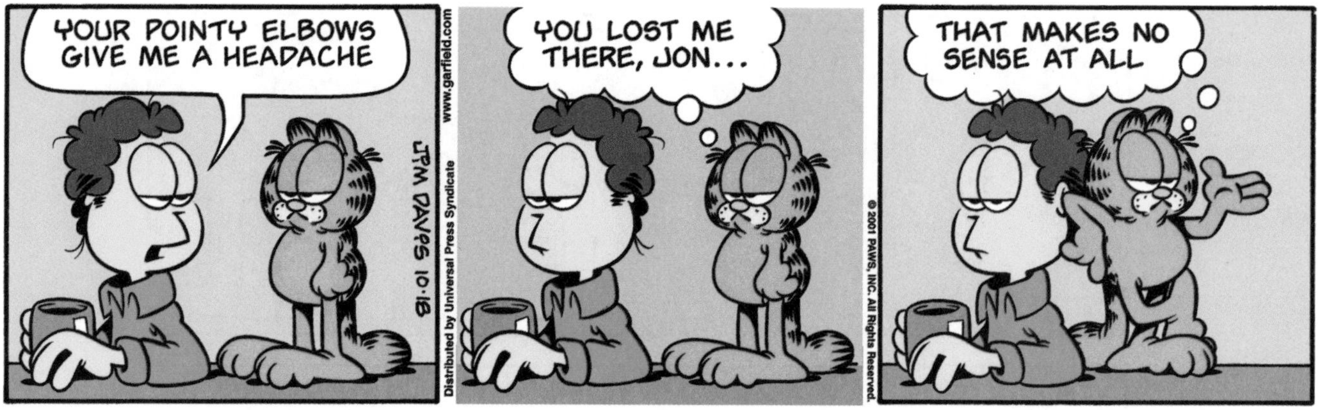
YOUR POINTY ELBOWS GIVE ME A HEADACHE
JIM DAVIS 10-18
Distributed by Universal Press Syndicate www.garfield.com
YOU LOST ME THERE, JON...
THAT MAKES NO SENSE AT ALL
© 2001 PAWS, INC. All Rights Reserved.

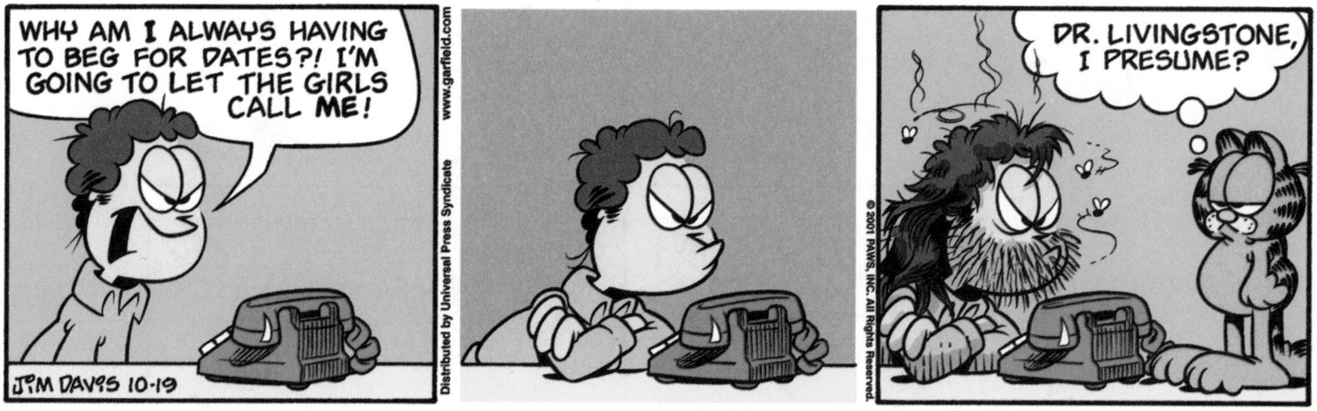
WHY AM I ALWAYS HAVING TO BEG FOR DATES?! I'M GOING TO LET THE GIRLS CALL ME!
JIM DAVIS 10-19
Distributed by Universal Press Syndicate www.garfield.com
DR. LIVINGSTONE, I PRESUME?
© 2001 PAWS, INC. All Rights Reserved.

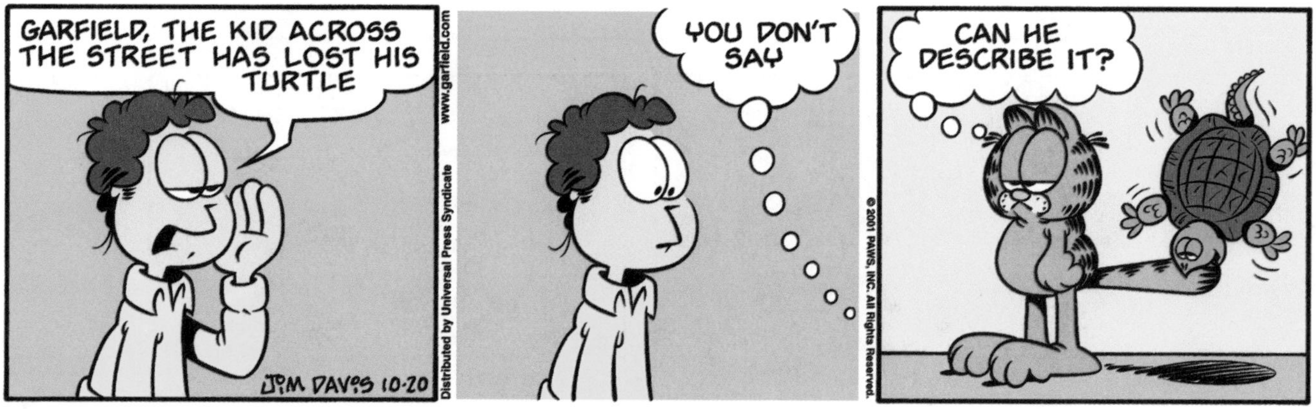
GARFIELD, THE KID ACROSS THE STREET HAS LOST HIS TURTLE
JIM DAVIS 10-20
Distributed by Universal Press Syndicate www.garfield.com
YOU DON'T SAY
CAN HE DESCRIBE IT?
© 2001 PAWS, INC. All Rights Reserved.

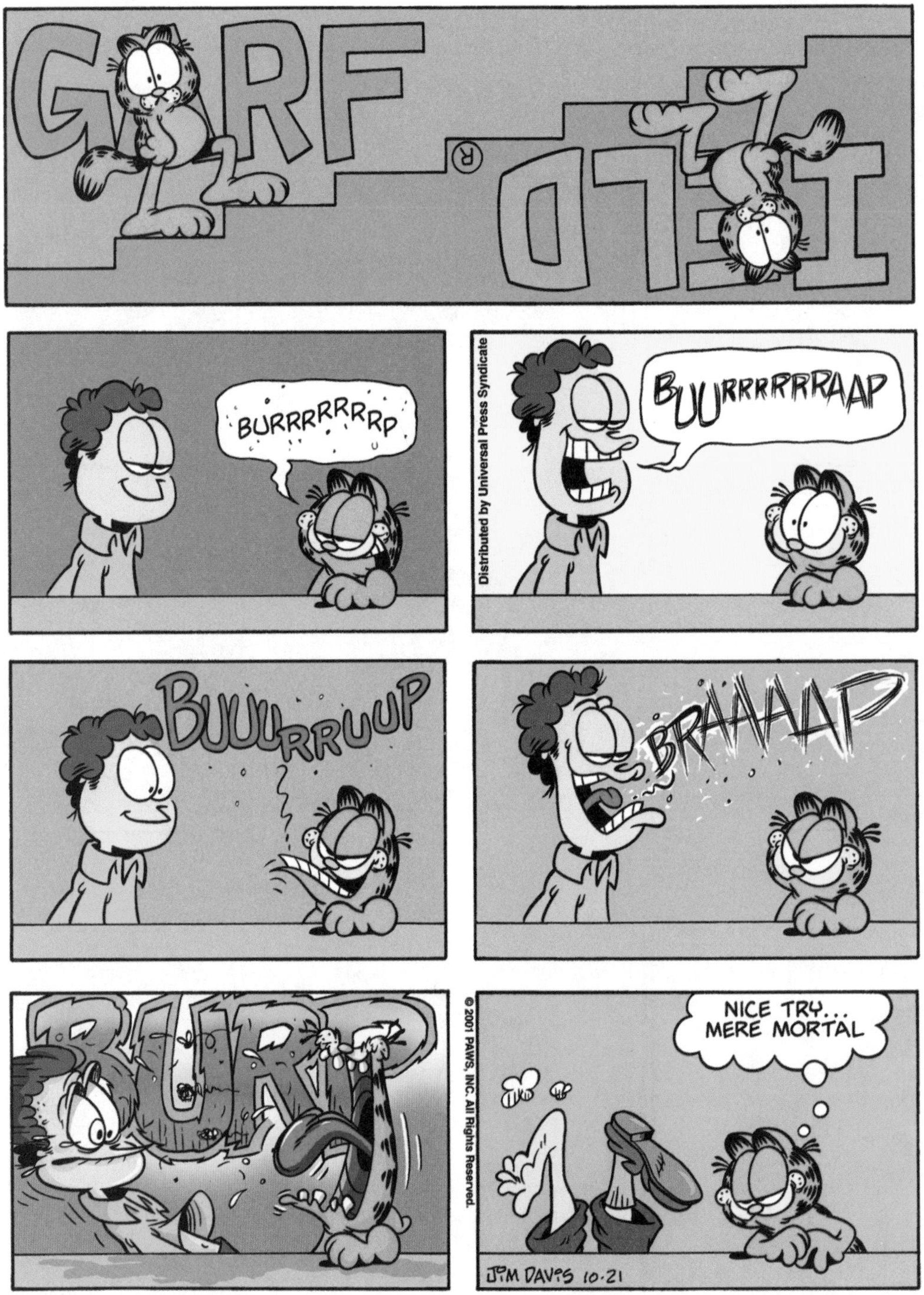
GARFIELD®
BURRRRRRRP
BUURRRRRRAAP
Distributed by Universal Press Syndicate
BUUURRUUP
BRAAAAP
BURP
© 2001 PAWS, INC. All Rights Reserved.
NICE TRY... MERE MORTAL
JIM DAVIS 10-21

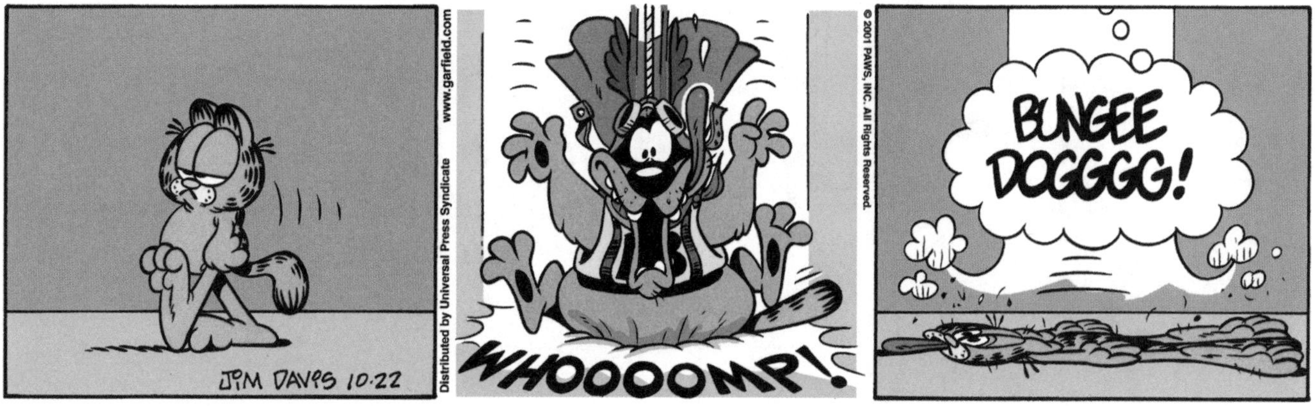

JIM DAVIS 10-22
Distributed by Universal Press Syndicate www.garfield.com
WHOOOOMP!
© 2001 PAWS, INC. All Rights Reserved.
BUNGEE DOGGGG!

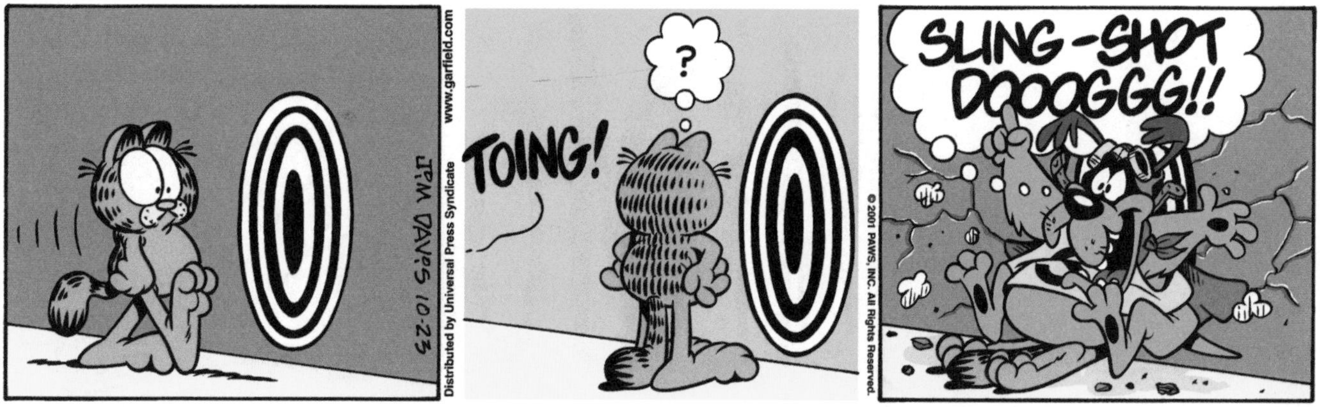

JIM DAVIS 10-23
Distributed by Universal Press Syndicate www.garfield.com
?
TOING!
© 2001 PAWS, INC. All Rights Reserved.
SLING-SHOT DOOOGGG!!

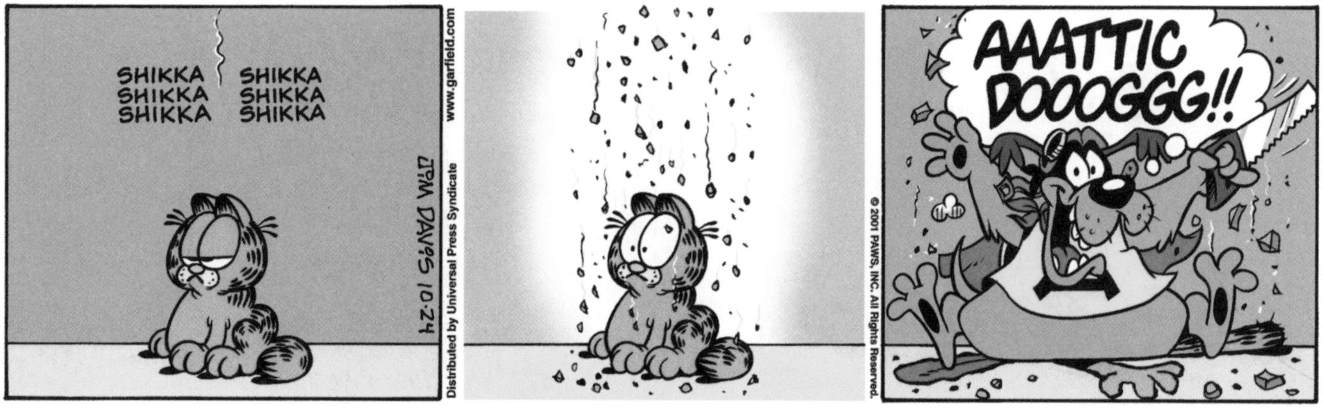

SHIKKA SHIKKA SHIKKA
SHIKKA SHIKKA SHIKKA
JIM DAVIS 10-24
Distributed by Universal Press Syndicate www.garfield.com
© 2001 PAWS, INC. All Rights Reserved.
AAATTIC DOOOGGG!!

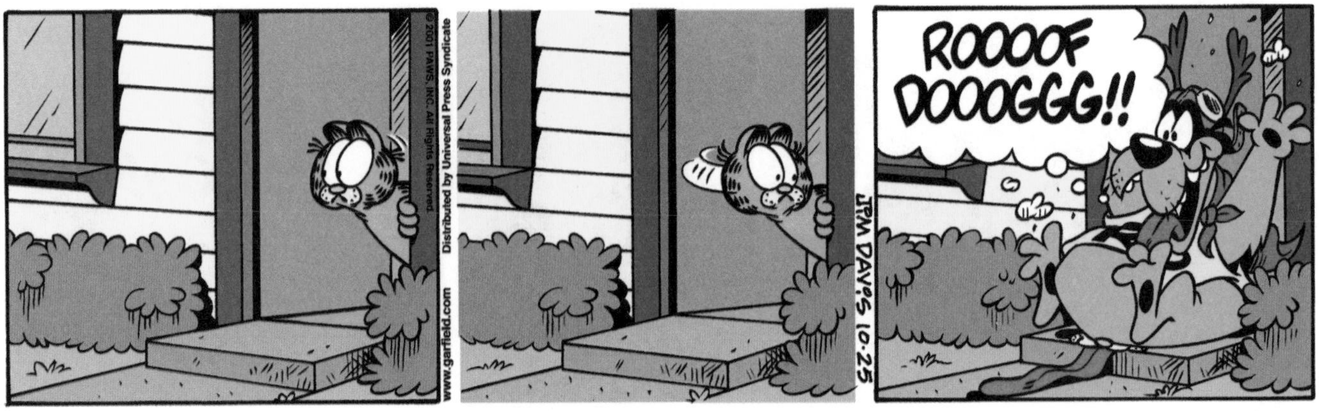
© 2001 PAWS, INC. All Rights Reserved.
Distributed by Universal Press Syndicate
www.garfield.com
JIM DAVIS 10-25
ROOOOF DOOOGGG!!

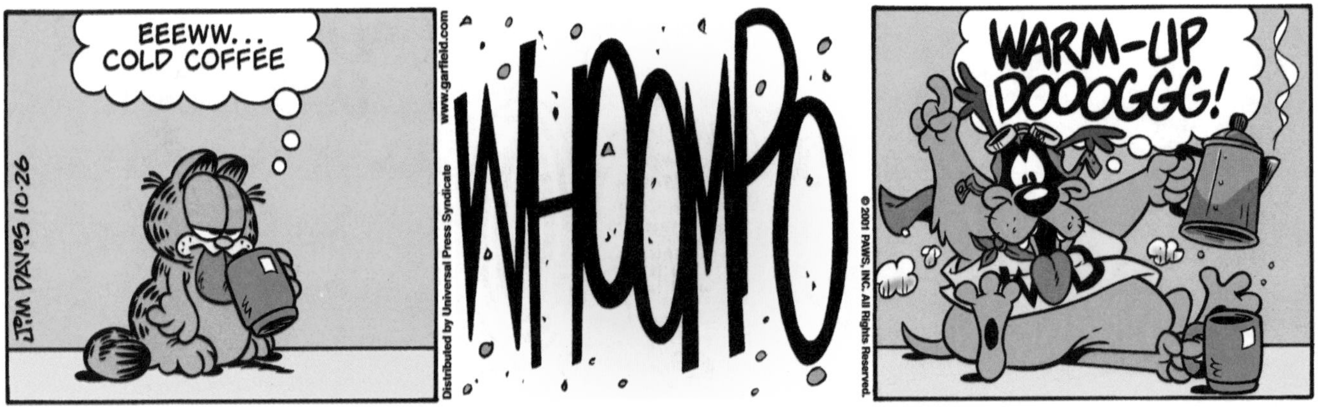
EEEWW... COLD COFFEE
JIM DAVIS 10-26
www.garfield.com
Distributed by Universal Press Syndicate
WHOOMPO
© 2001 PAWS, INC. All Rights Reserved.
WARM-UP DOOOGGG!

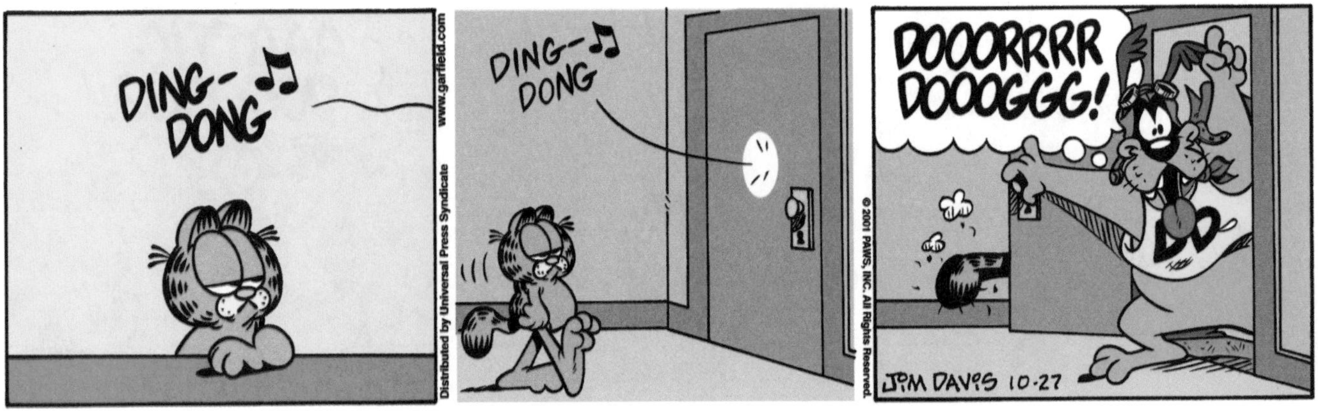
DING-DONG
www.garfield.com
Distributed by Universal Press Syndicate
DING-DONG
© 2001 PAWS, INC. All Rights Reserved.
DOOORRRR DOOOGGG!
JIM DAVIS 10-27

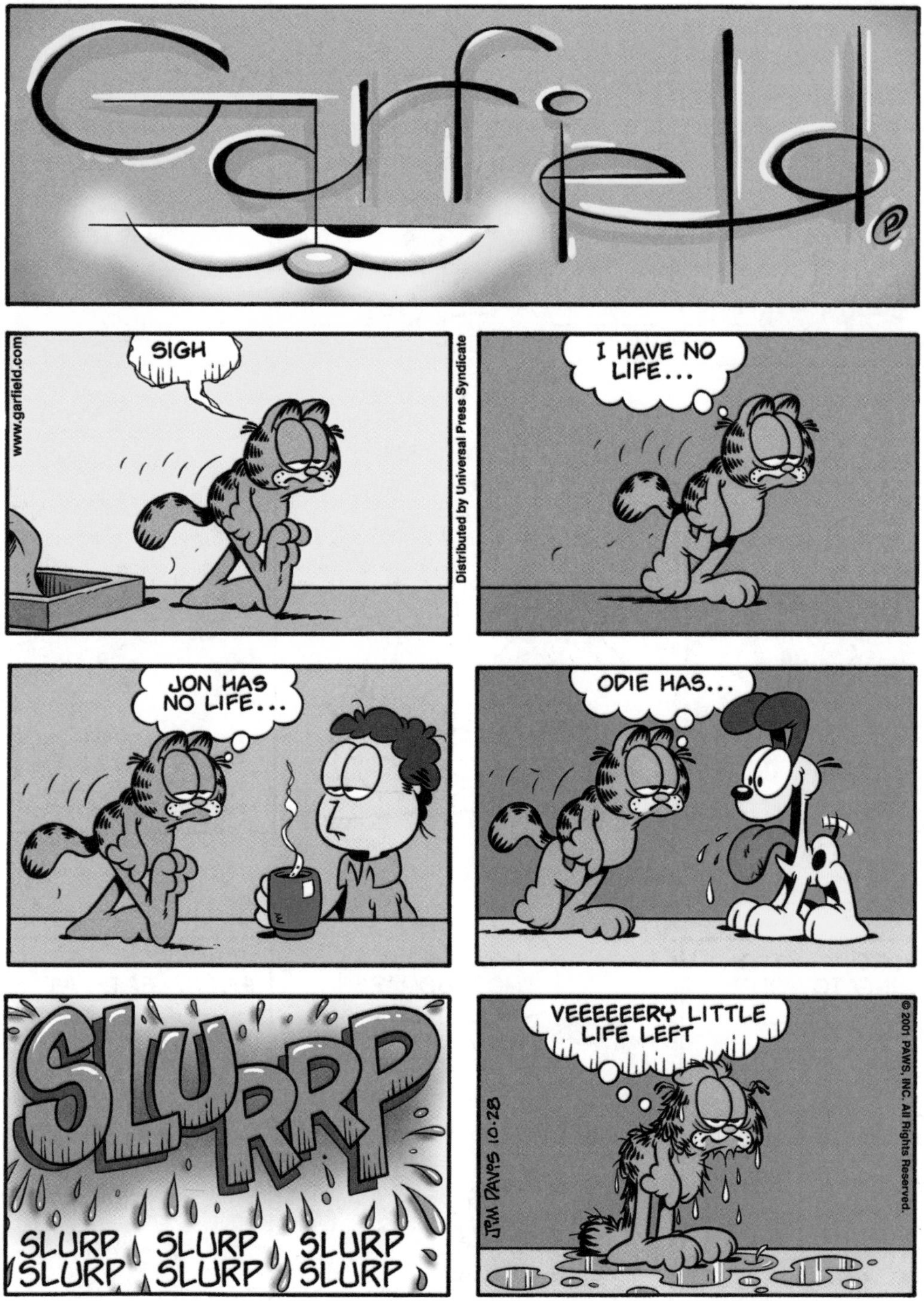
Garfield
www.garfield.com
SIGH
Distributed by Universal Press Syndicate
I HAVE NO LIFE...
JON HAS NO LIFE...
ODIE HAS...
SLURRP
SLURP SLURP SLURP
SLURP SLURP SLURP
JIM DAVIS 10-28
VEEEEEERY LITTLE LIFE LEFT
© 2001 PAWS, INC. All Rights Reserved.

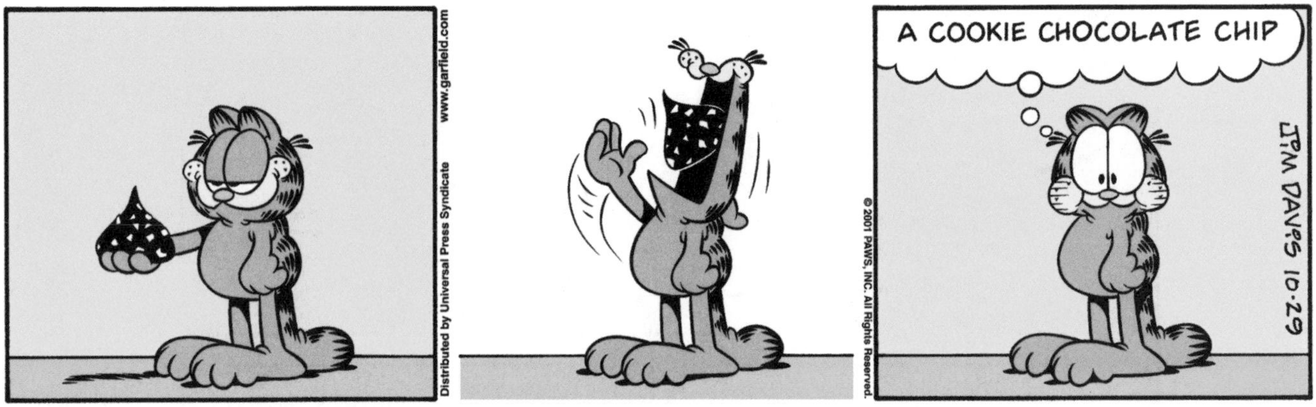
A COOKIE CHOCOLATE CHIP
JIM DAVIS 10-29
www.garfield.com
Distributed by Universal Press Syndicate
© 2001 PAWS, INC. All Rights Reserved.

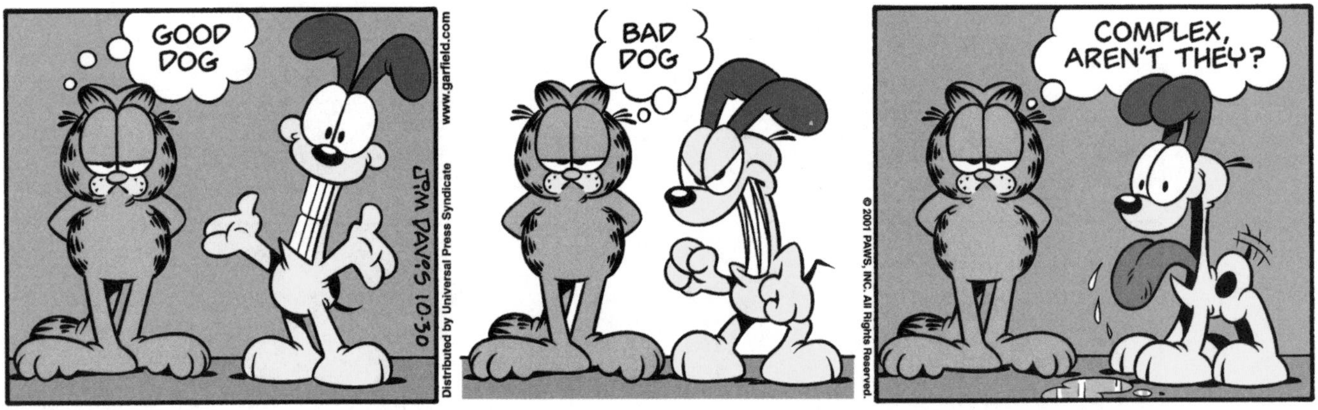
GOOD DOG
JIM DAVIS 10-30
BAD DOG
COMPLEX, AREN'T THEY?
www.garfield.com
Distributed by Universal Press Syndicate
© 2001 PAWS, INC. All Rights Reserved.

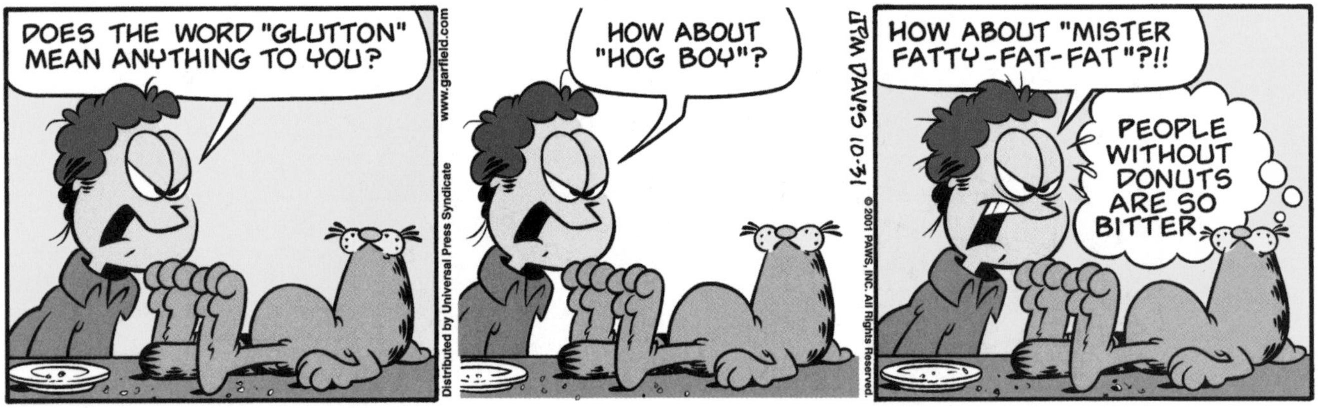
DOES THE WORD "GLUTTON" MEAN ANYTHING TO YOU?
HOW ABOUT "HOG BOY"?
JIM DAVIS 10-31
HOW ABOUT "MISTER FATTY-FAT-FAT"?!!
PEOPLE WITHOUT DONUTS ARE SO BITTER
www.garfield.com
Distributed by Universal Press Syndicate
© 2001 PAWS, INC. All Rights Reserved.

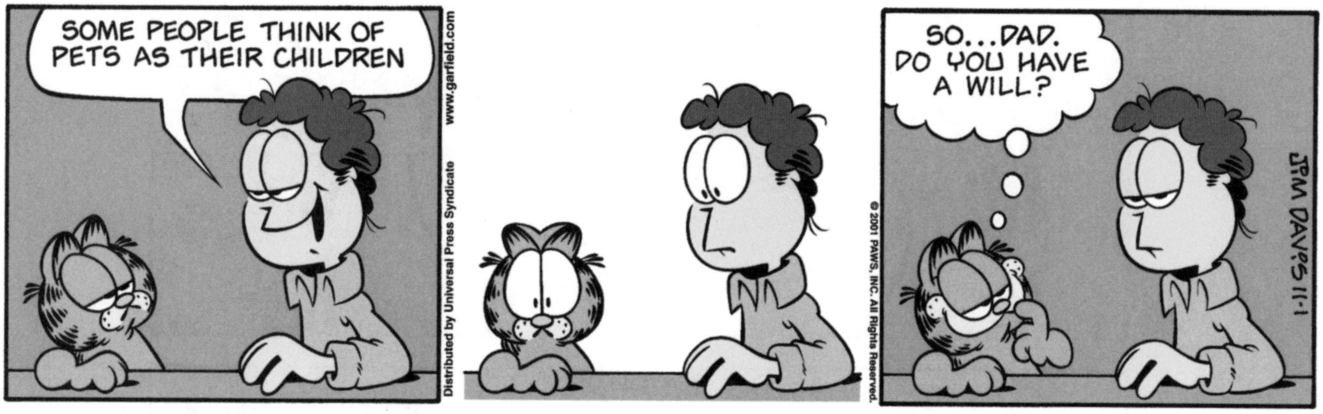
SOME PEOPLE THINK OF PETS AS THEIR CHILDREN
SO...DAD. DO YOU HAVE A WILL?
JIM DAVIS 11-1
www.garfield.com
Distributed by Universal Press Syndicate
© 2001 PAWS, INC. All Rights Reserved.

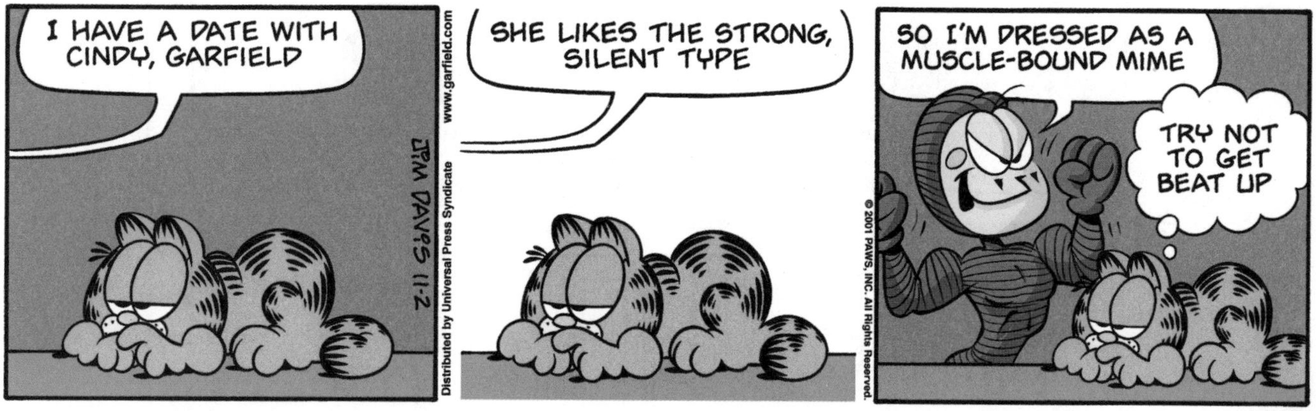
I HAVE A DATE WITH CINDY, GARFIELD
SHE LIKES THE STRONG, SILENT TYPE
SO I'M DRESSED AS A MUSCLE-BOUND MIME
TRY NOT TO GET BEAT UP
JIM DAVIS 11-2
www.garfield.com
Distributed by Universal Press Syndicate
© 2001 PAWS, INC. All Rights Reserved.

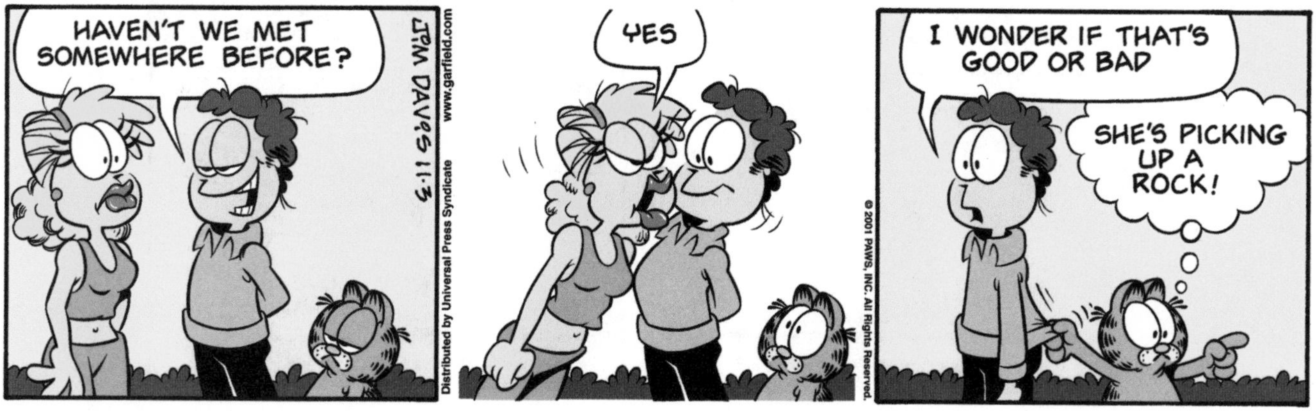
HAVEN'T WE MET SOMEWHERE BEFORE?
YES
I WONDER IF THAT'S GOOD OR BAD
SHE'S PICKING UP A ROCK!
JIM DAVIS 11-3
www.garfield.com
Distributed by Universal Press Syndicate
© 2001 PAWS, INC. All Rights Reserved.

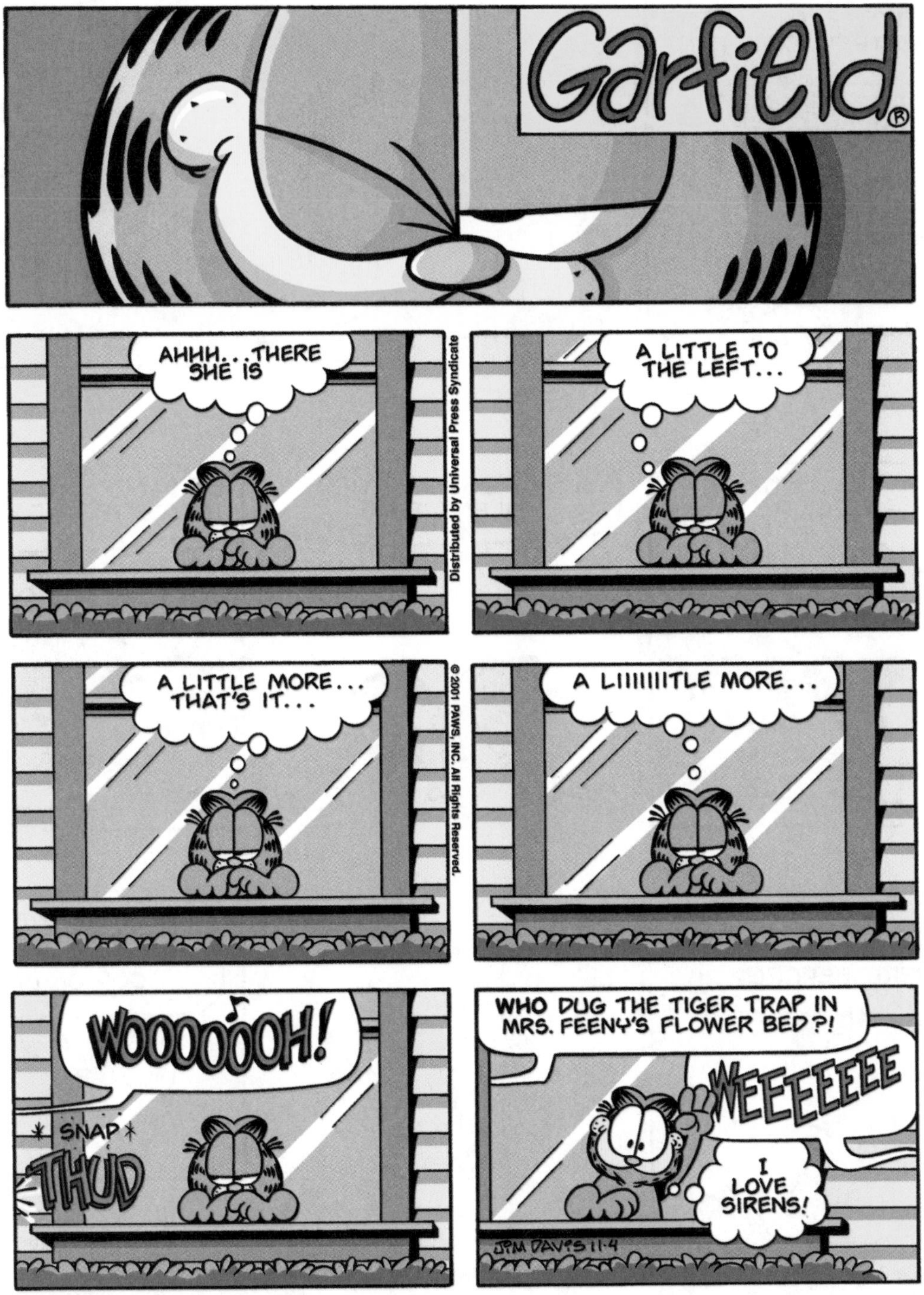
Garfield®
AHHH... THERE SHE IS
A LITTLE TO THE LEFT...
A LITTLE MORE... THAT'S IT...
A LIIIIIIITLE MORE...
WOOOOOOOH!
* SNAP *
THUD
WHO DUG THE TIGER TRAP IN MRS. FEENY'S FLOWER BED?!
WEEEEEEE
I LOVE SIRENS!
JPM DAVIS 11·4
Distributed by Universal Press Syndicate
© 2001 PAWS, INC. All Rights Reserved.

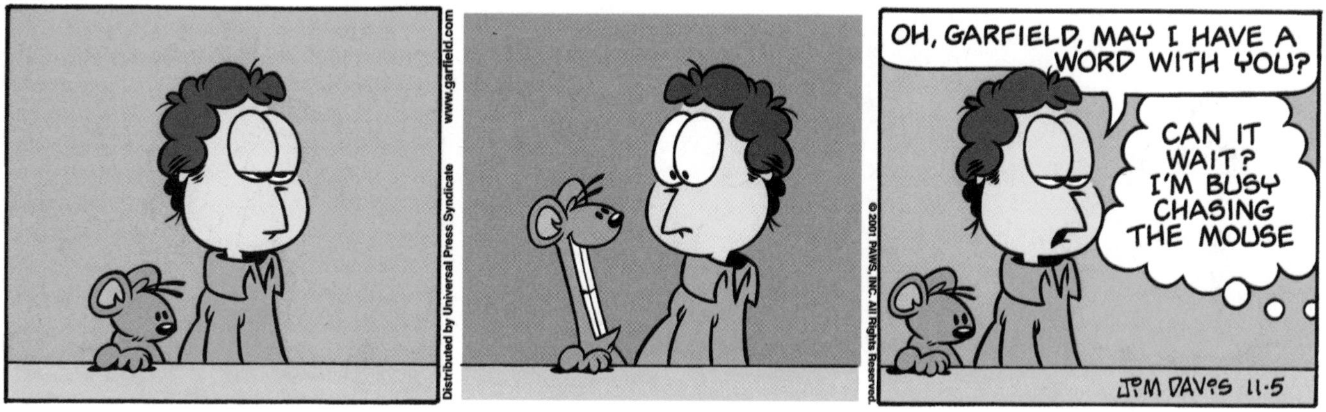
Distributed by Universal Press Syndicate www.garfield.com
© 2001 PAWS, INC. All Rights Reserved.
OH, GARFIELD, MAY I HAVE A WORD WITH YOU?
CAN IT WAIT? I'M BUSY CHASING THE MOUSE
JIM DAVIS 11-5

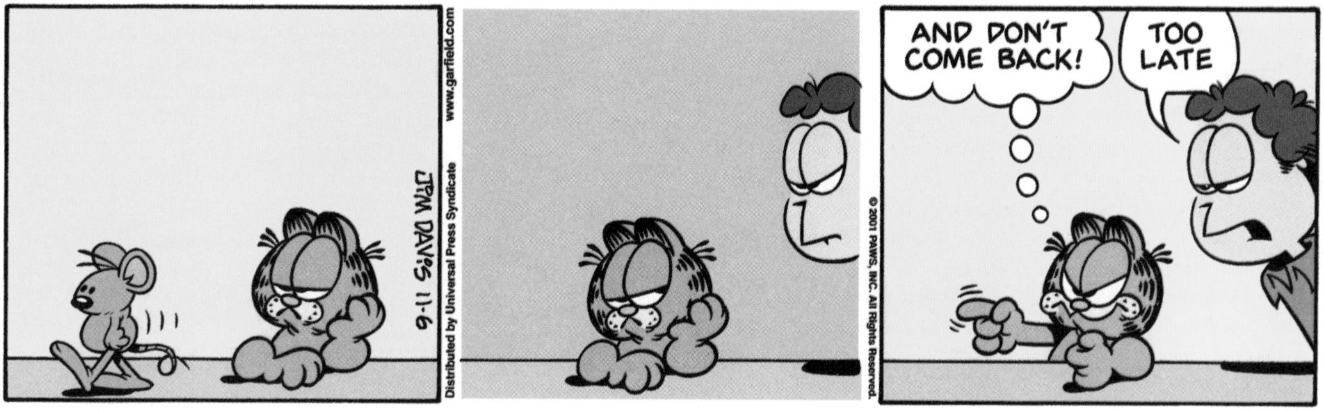
JIM DAVIS 11-6
Distributed by Universal Press Syndicate www.garfield.com
© 2001 PAWS, INC. All Rights Reserved.
AND DON'T COME BACK!
TOO LATE

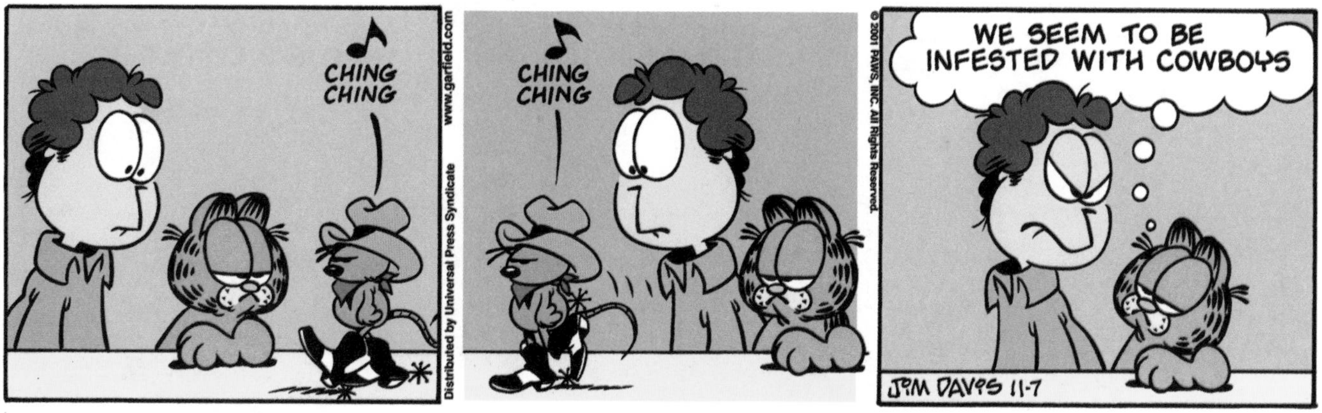
CHING CHING
Distributed by Universal Press Syndicate www.garfield.com
CHING CHING
© 2001 PAWS, INC. All Rights Reserved.
WE SEEM TO BE INFESTED WITH COWBOYS
JIM DAVIS 11-7

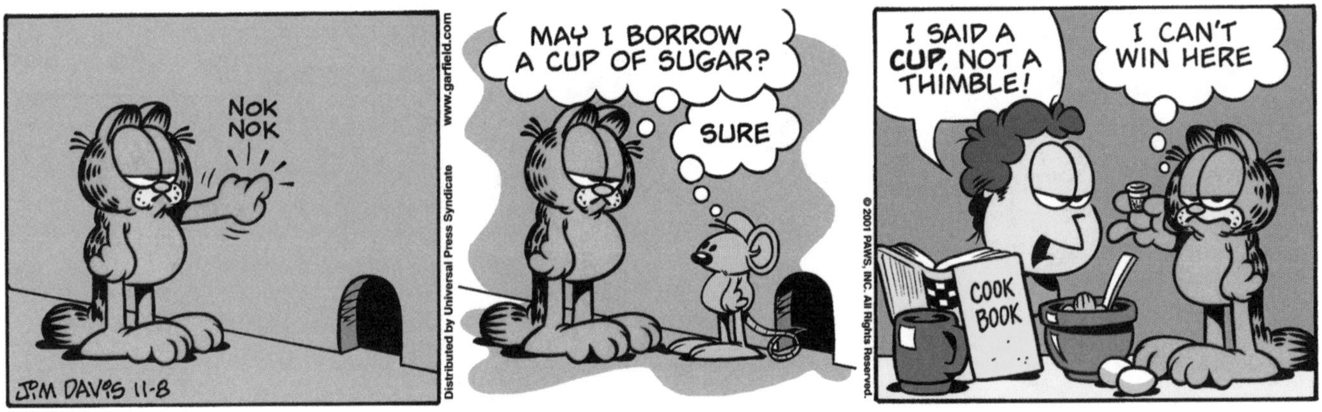
NOK NOK
JIM DAVIS 11-8
MAY I BORROW A CUP OF SUGAR?
SURE
I SAID A **CUP**, NOT A THIMBLE!
COOK BOOK
I CAN'T WIN HERE

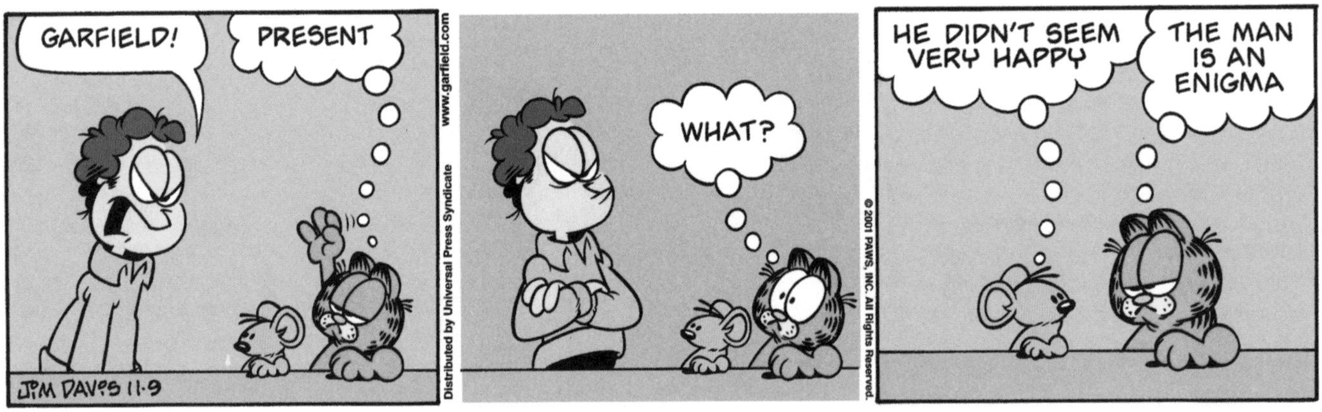
GARFIELD!
PRESENT
JIM DAVIS 11-9
WHAT?
HE DIDN'T SEEM VERY HAPPY
THE MAN IS AN ENIGMA

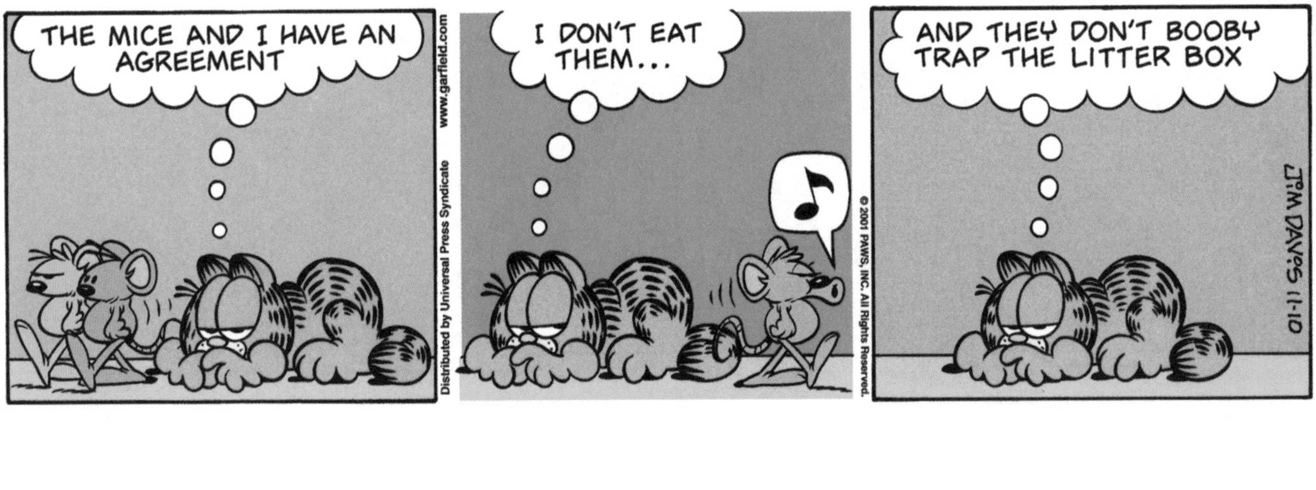
THE MICE AND I HAVE AN AGREEMENT
I DON'T EAT THEM...
AND THEY DON'T BOOBY TRAP THE LITTER BOX
JIM DAVIS 11-10

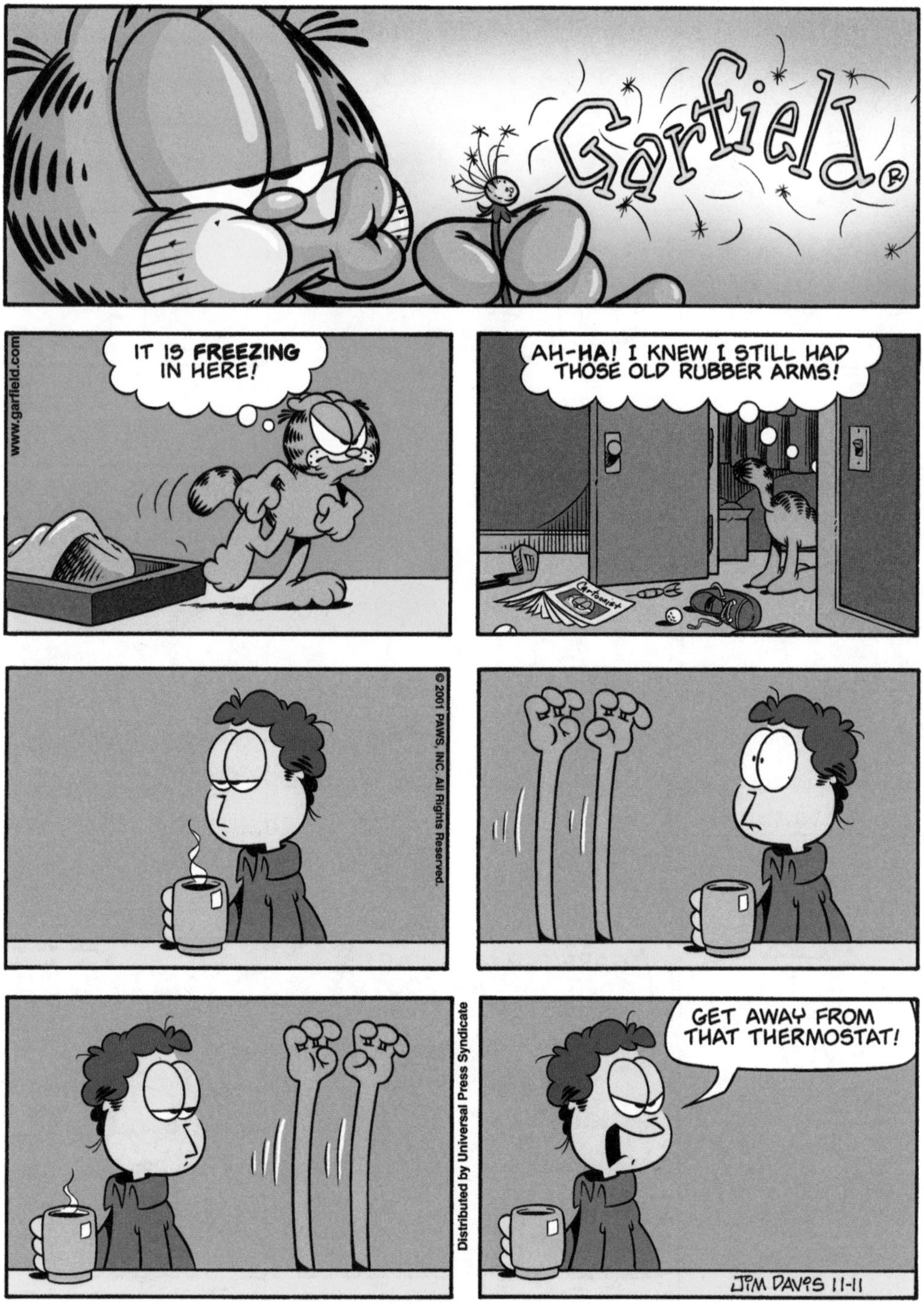
Garfield®
www.garfield.com
IT IS FREEZING IN HERE!
AH-HA! I KNEW I STILL HAD THOSE OLD RUBBER ARMS!
© 2001 PAWS, INC. All Rights Reserved.
Distributed by Universal Press Syndicate
GET AWAY FROM THAT THERMOSTAT!
JIM DAVIS 11-11

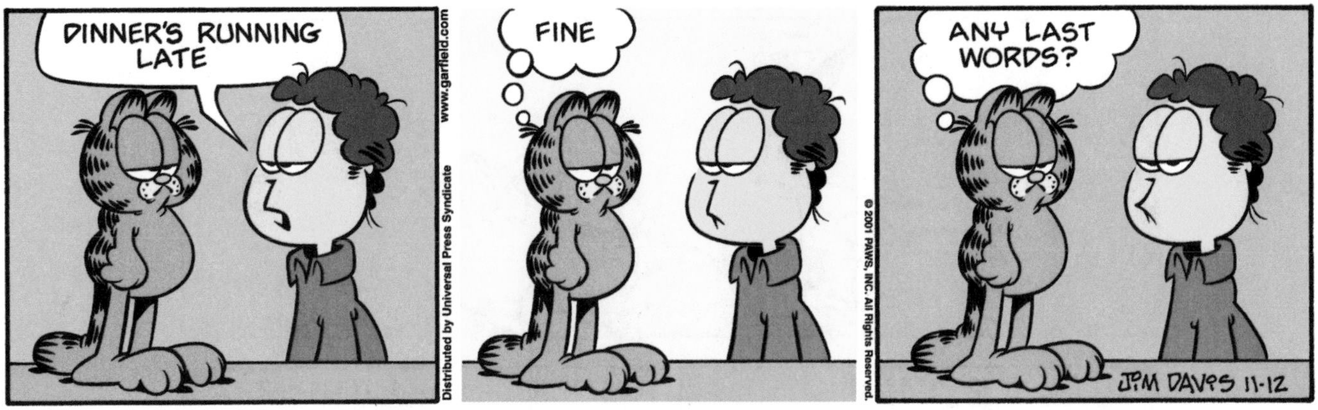
DINNER'S RUNNING LATE
Distributed by Universal Press Syndicate www.garfield.com
FINE
© 2001 PAWS, INC. All Rights Reserved.
ANY LAST WORDS?
JIM DAVIS 11-12

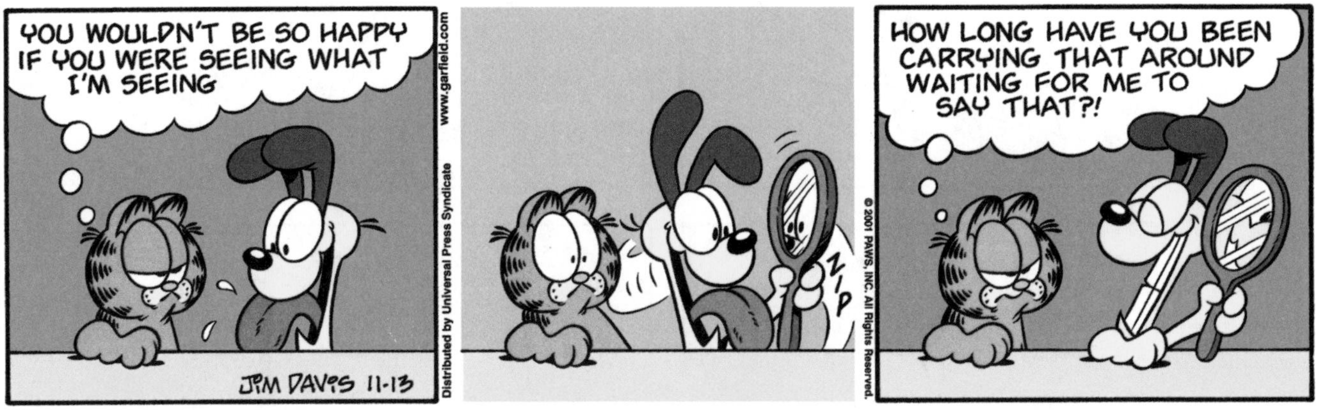
YOU WOULDN'T BE SO HAPPY IF YOU WERE SEEING WHAT I'M SEEING
JIM DAVIS 11-13
Distributed by Universal Press Syndicate www.garfield.com
ZIP
© 2001 PAWS, INC. All Rights Reserved.
HOW LONG HAVE YOU BEEN CARRYING THAT AROUND WAITING FOR ME TO SAY THAT?!

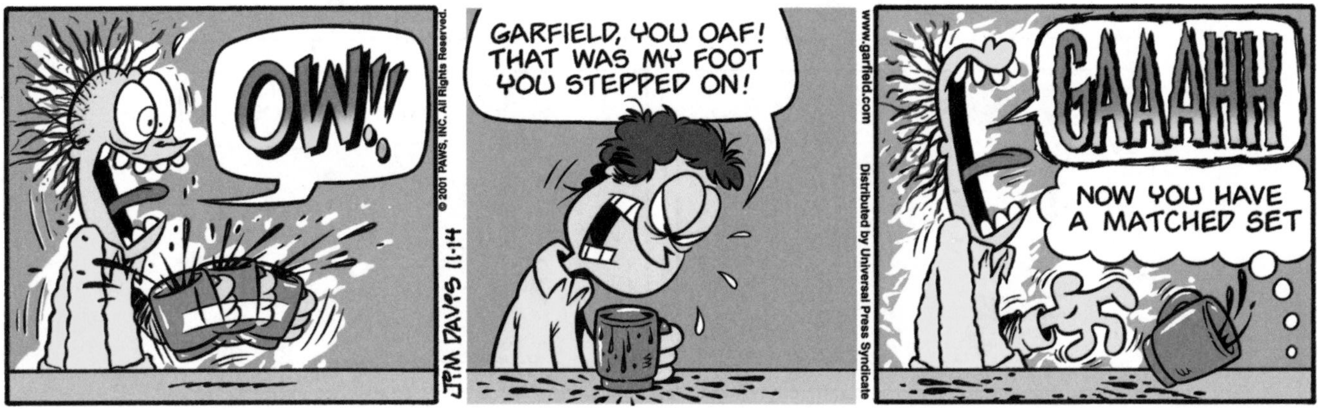
OW!!
© 2001 PAWS, INC. All Rights Reserved.
JIM DAVIS 11-14
GARFIELD, YOU OAF! THAT WAS MY FOOT YOU STEPPED ON!
www.garfield.com Distributed by Universal Press Syndicate
GAAAHH
NOW YOU HAVE A MATCHED SET

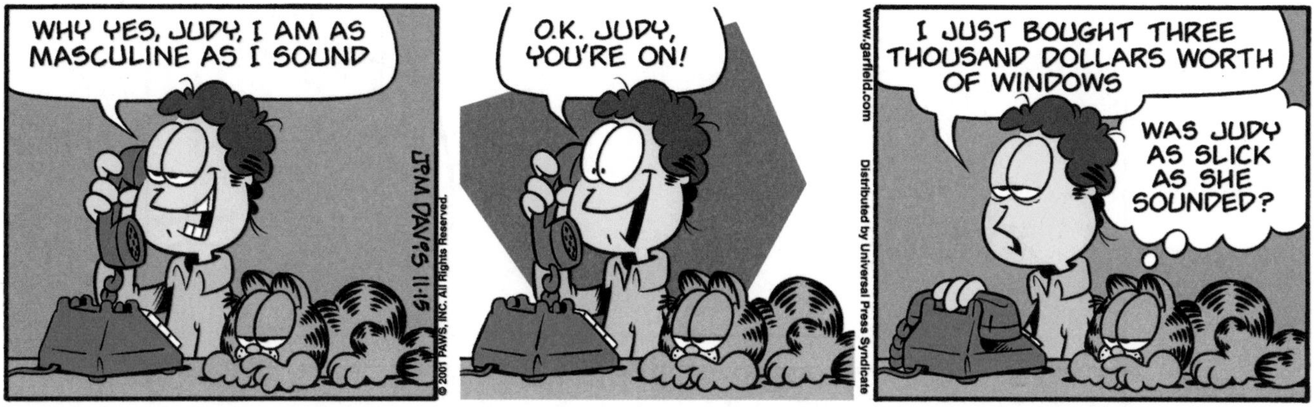
WHY YES, JUDY, I AM AS MASCULINE AS I SOUND
JIM DAVIS 11-15
© 2001 PAWS, INC. All Rights Reserved.
O.K. JUDY, YOU'RE ON!
www.garfield.com
Distributed by Universal Press Syndicate
I JUST BOUGHT THREE THOUSAND DOLLARS WORTH OF WINDOWS
WAS JUDY AS SLICK AS SHE SOUNDED?

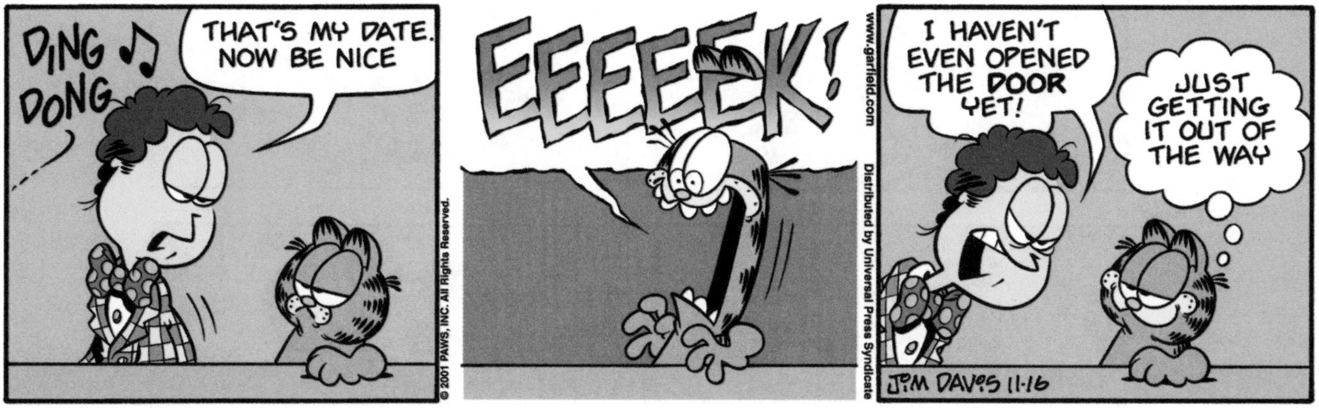
DING DONG
THAT'S MY DATE. NOW BE NICE
© 2001 PAWS, INC. All Rights Reserved.
EEEEEEK!
www.garfield.com
Distributed by Universal Press Syndicate
I HAVEN'T EVEN OPENED THE DOOR YET!
JUST GETTING IT OUT OF THE WAY
JIM DAVIS 11-16

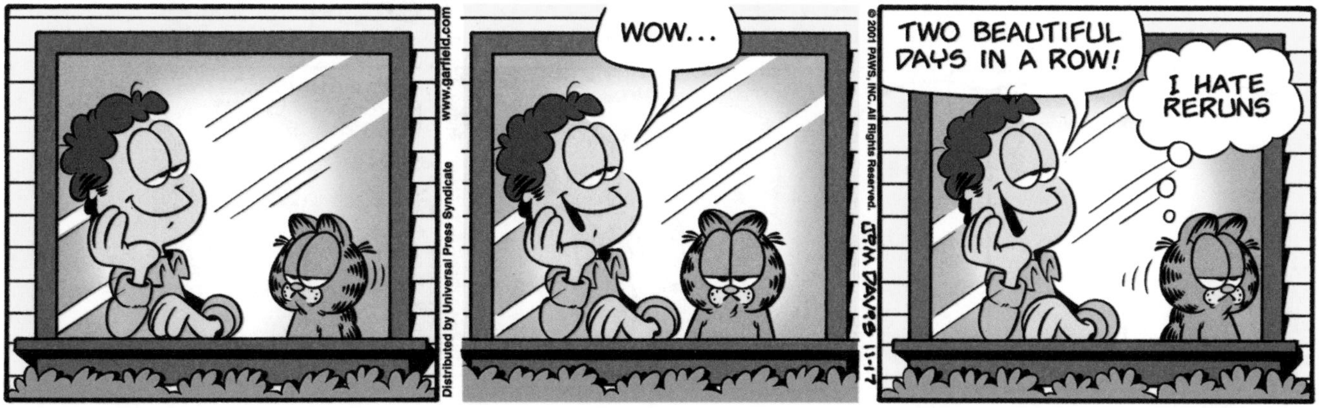
www.garfield.com
Distributed by Universal Press Syndicate
WOW...
© 2001 PAWS, INC. All Rights Reserved.
JIM DAVIS 11-17
TWO BEAUTIFUL DAYS IN A ROW!
I HATE RERUNS

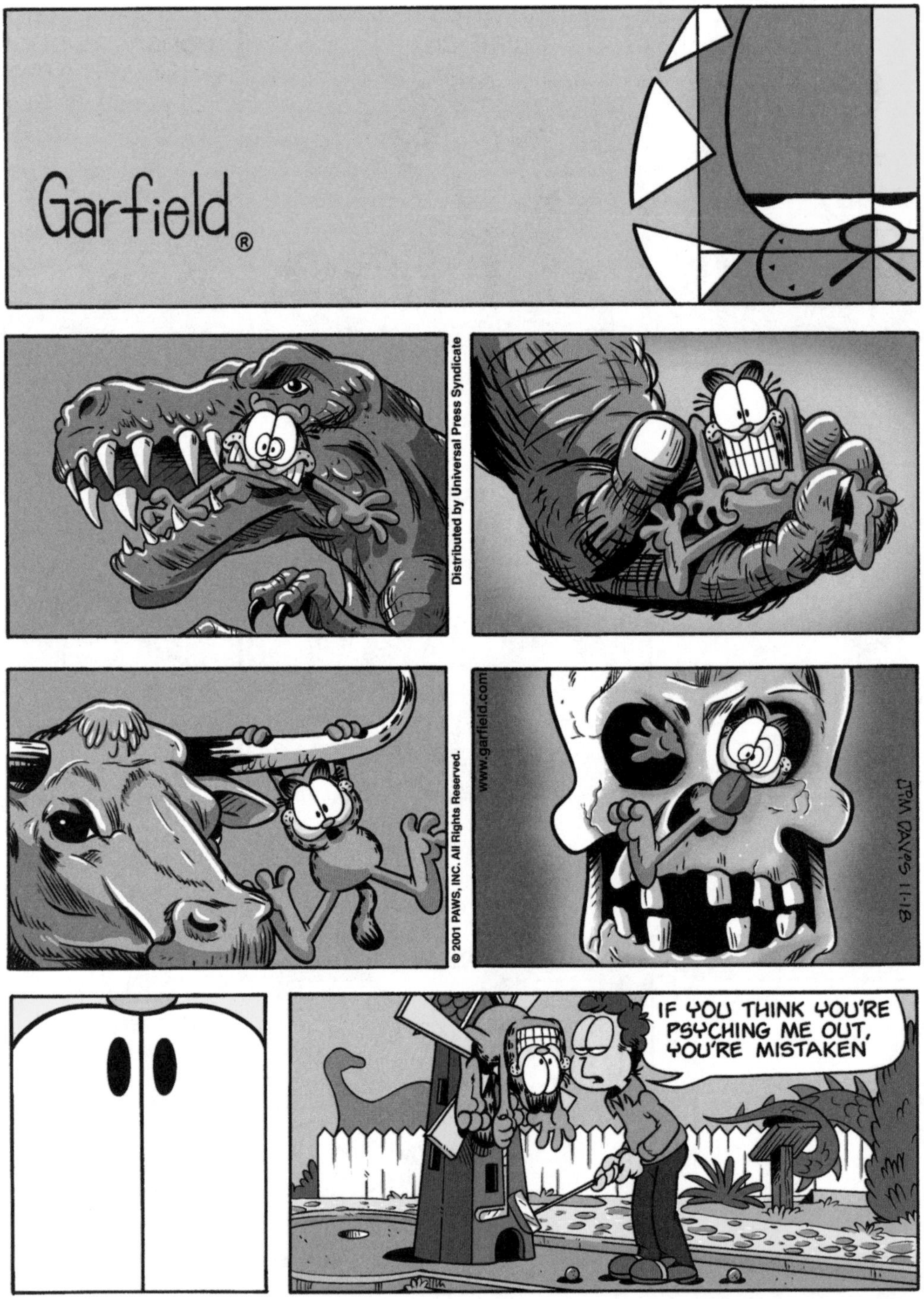
Garfield®
Distributed by Universal Press Syndicate
© 2001 PAWS, INC. All Rights Reserved.
www.garfield.com
JIM DAVIS 11-18
IF YOU THINK YOU'RE PSYCHING ME OUT, YOU'RE MISTAKEN

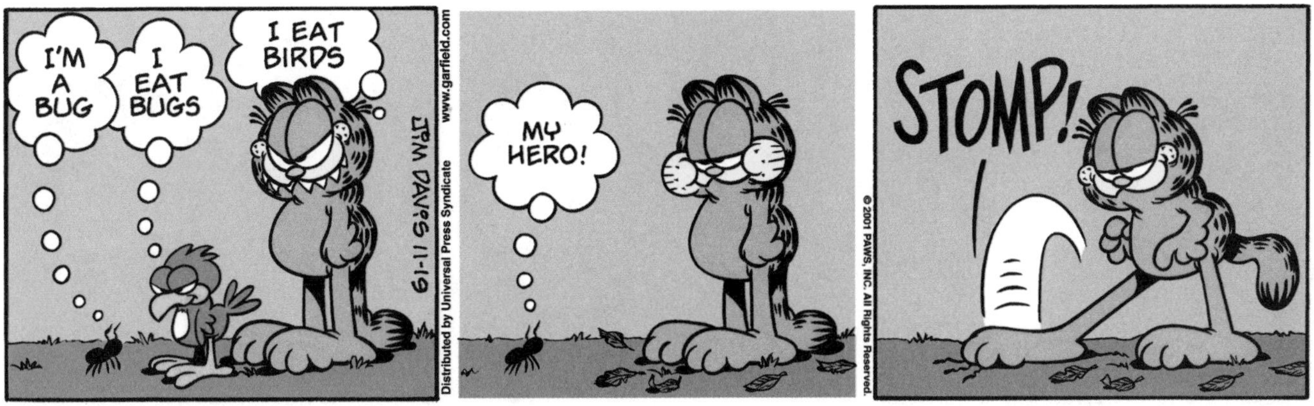
I'M A BUG
I EAT BUGS
I EAT BIRDS
JIM DAVIS 11-19
www.garfield.com
Distributed by Universal Press Syndicate
MY HERO!
© 2001 PAWS, INC. All Rights Reserved.
STOMP!

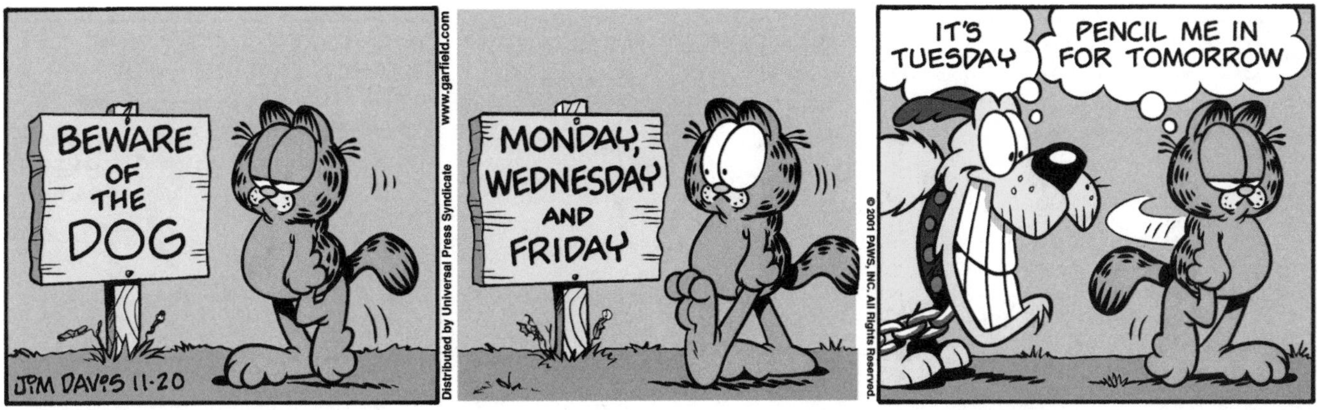
BEWARE OF THE DOG
JIM DAVIS 11-20
www.garfield.com
Distributed by Universal Press Syndicate
MONDAY, WEDNESDAY AND FRIDAY
© 2001 PAWS, INC. All Rights Reserved.
IT'S TUESDAY
PENCIL ME IN FOR TOMORROW

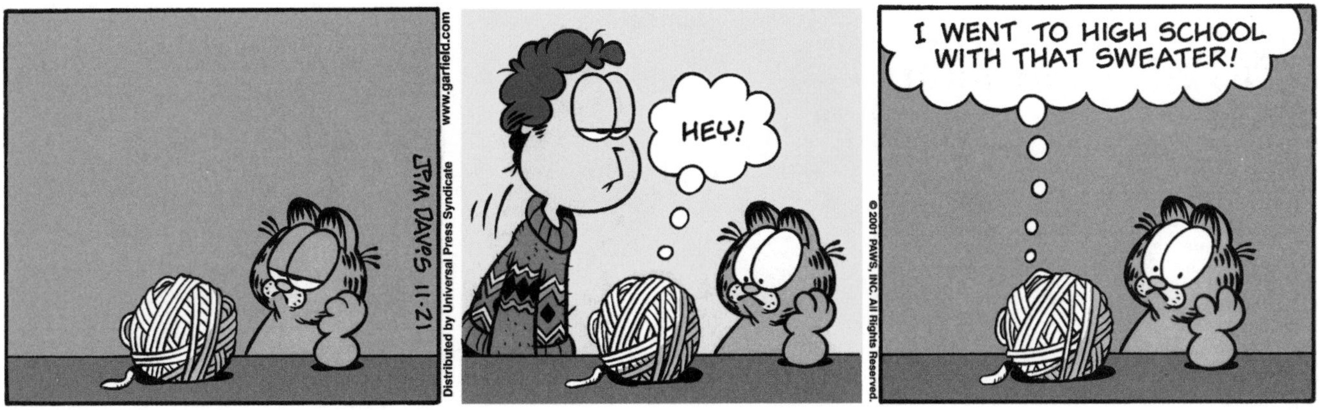
JIM DAVIS 11-21
www.garfield.com
Distributed by Universal Press Syndicate
HEY!
© 2001 PAWS, INC. All Rights Reserved.
I WENT TO HIGH SCHOOL WITH THAT SWEATER!

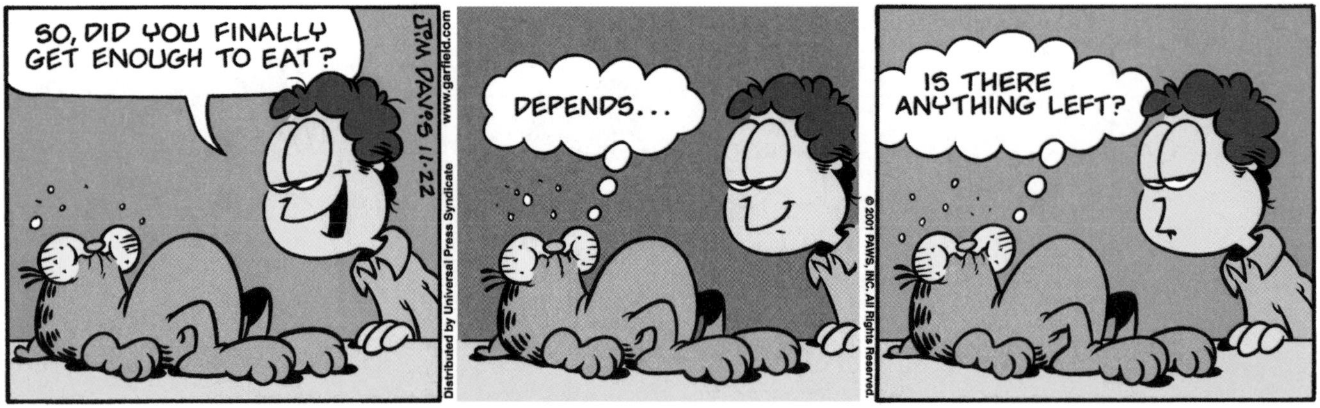
SO, DID YOU FINALLY GET ENOUGH TO EAT?
JIM DAVIS 11-22
www.garfield.com
Distributed by Universal Press Syndicate
DEPENDS...
© 2001 PAWS, INC. All Rights Reserved.
IS THERE ANYTHING LEFT?

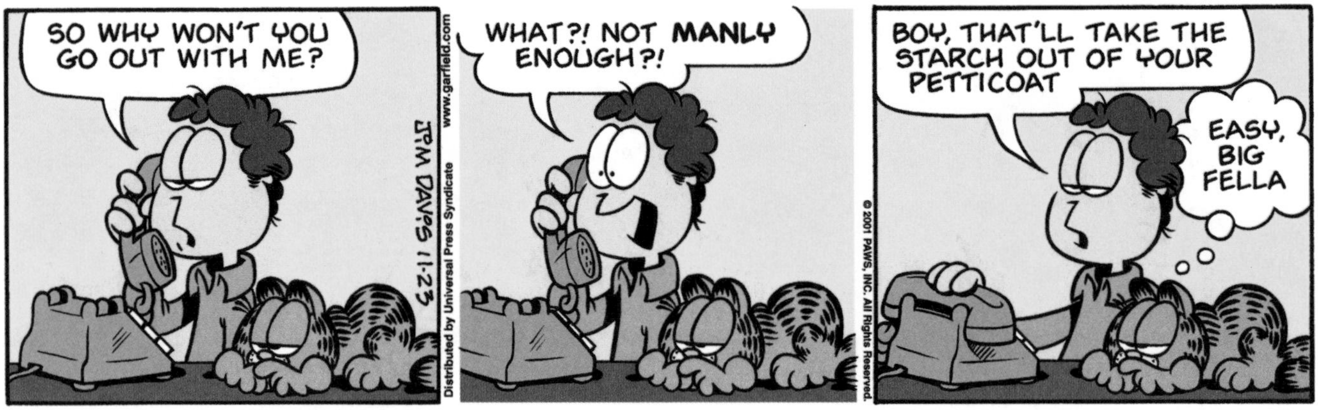
SO WHY WON'T YOU GO OUT WITH ME?
JIM DAVIS 11-23
www.garfield.com
Distributed by Universal Press Syndicate
WHAT?! NOT MANLY ENOUGH?!
© 2001 PAWS, INC. All Rights Reserved.
BOY, THAT'LL TAKE THE STARCH OUT OF YOUR PETTICOAT
EASY, BIG FELLA

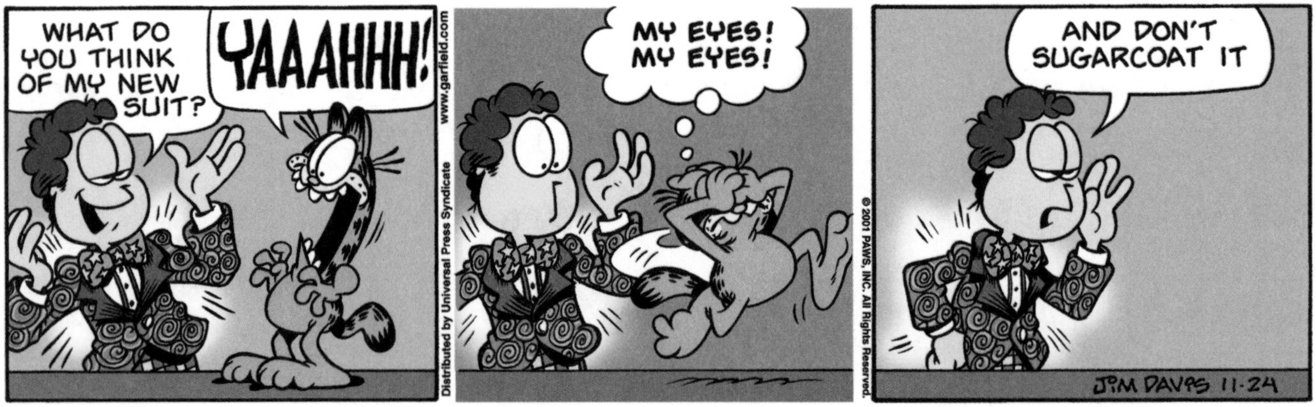
WHAT DO YOU THINK OF MY NEW SUIT?
YAAAHHH!
www.garfield.com
Distributed by Universal Press Syndicate
MY EYES! MY EYES!
© 2001 PAWS, INC. All Rights Reserved.
AND DON'T SUGARCOAT IT
JIM DAVIS 11-24

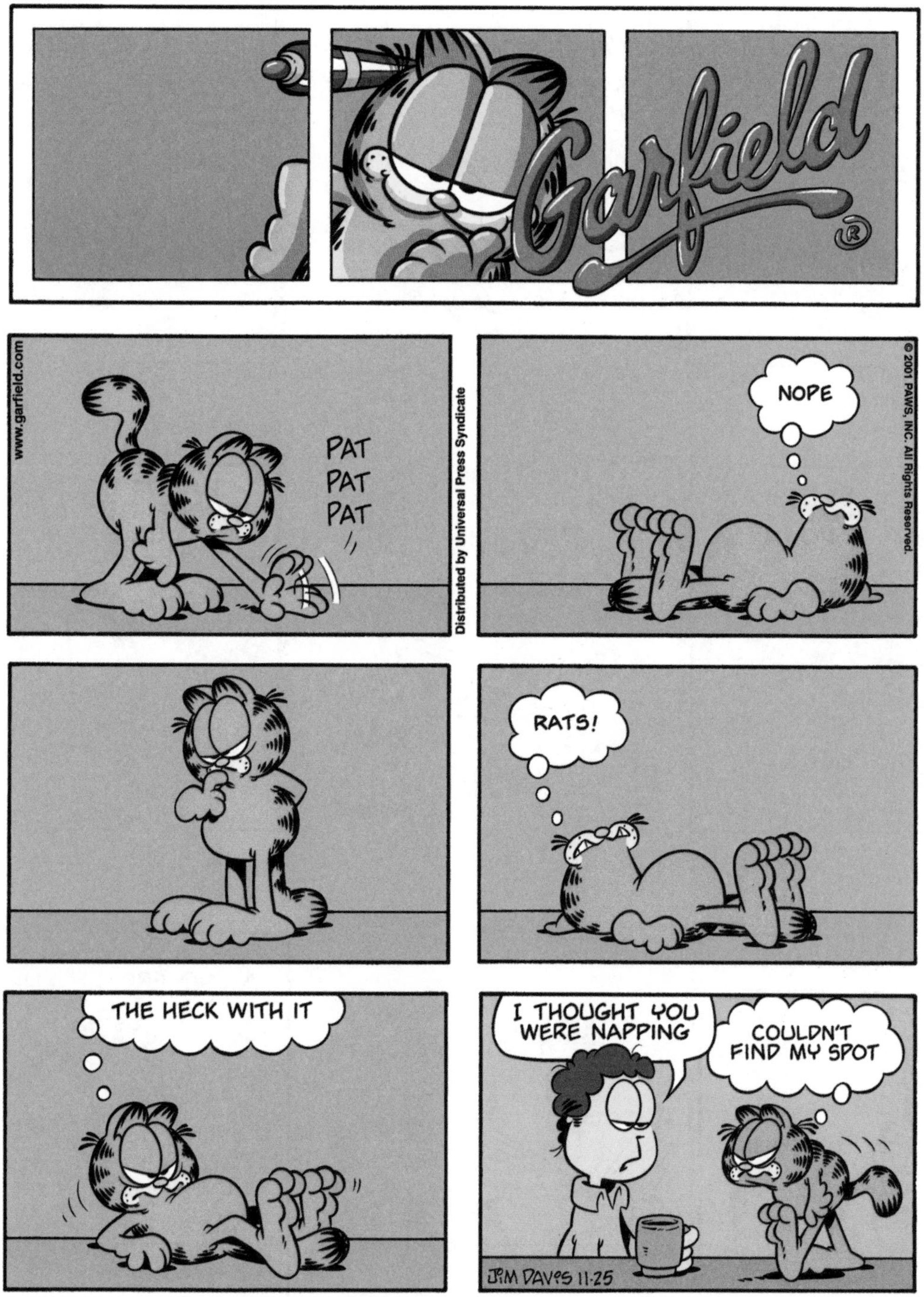
Garfield®
www.garfield.com
PAT
PAT
PAT
Distributed by Universal Press Syndicate
NOPE
© 2001 PAWS, INC. All Rights Reserved.
RATS!
THE HECK WITH IT
I THOUGHT YOU WERE NAPPING
COULDN'T FIND MY SPOT
JIM DAVIS 11-25

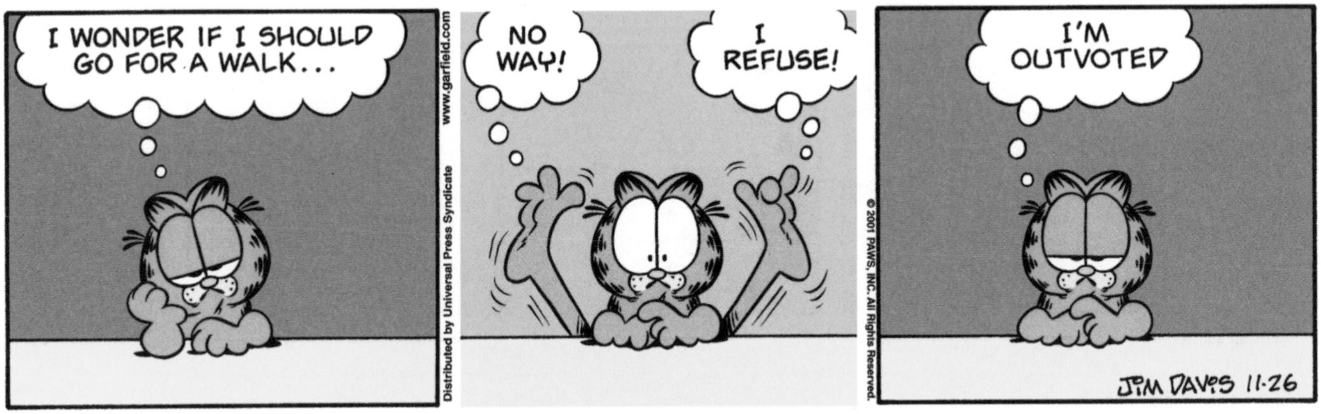
I WONDER IF I SHOULD GO FOR A WALK...
www.garfield.com
Distributed by Universal Press Syndicate
NO WAY!
I REFUSE!
© 2001 PAWS, INC. All Rights Reserved.
I'M OUTVOTED
JIM DAVIS 11-26

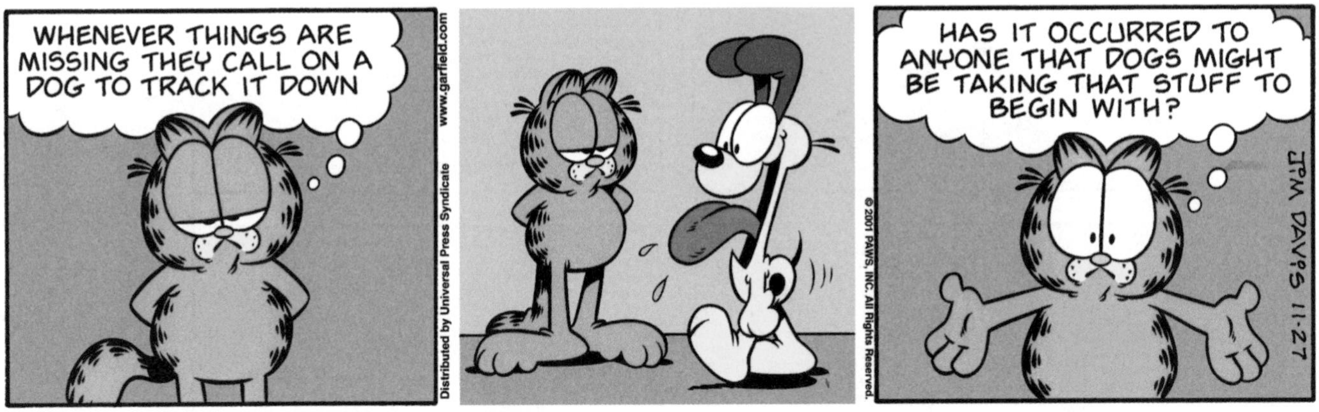
WHENEVER THINGS ARE MISSING THEY CALL ON A DOG TO TRACK IT DOWN
www.garfield.com
Distributed by Universal Press Syndicate
© 2001 PAWS, INC. All Rights Reserved.
HAS IT OCCURRED TO ANYONE THAT DOGS MIGHT BE TAKING THAT STUFF TO BEGIN WITH?
JIM DAVIS 11-27

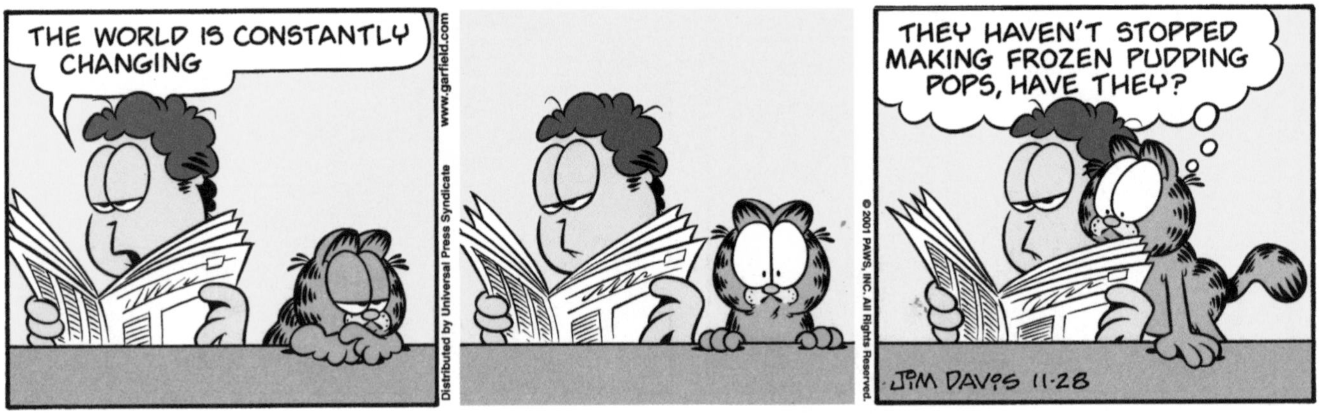
THE WORLD IS CONSTANTLY CHANGING
www.garfield.com
Distributed by Universal Press Syndicate
© 2001 PAWS, INC. All Rights Reserved.
THEY HAVEN'T STOPPED MAKING FROZEN PUDDING POPS, HAVE THEY?
JIM DAVIS 11-28

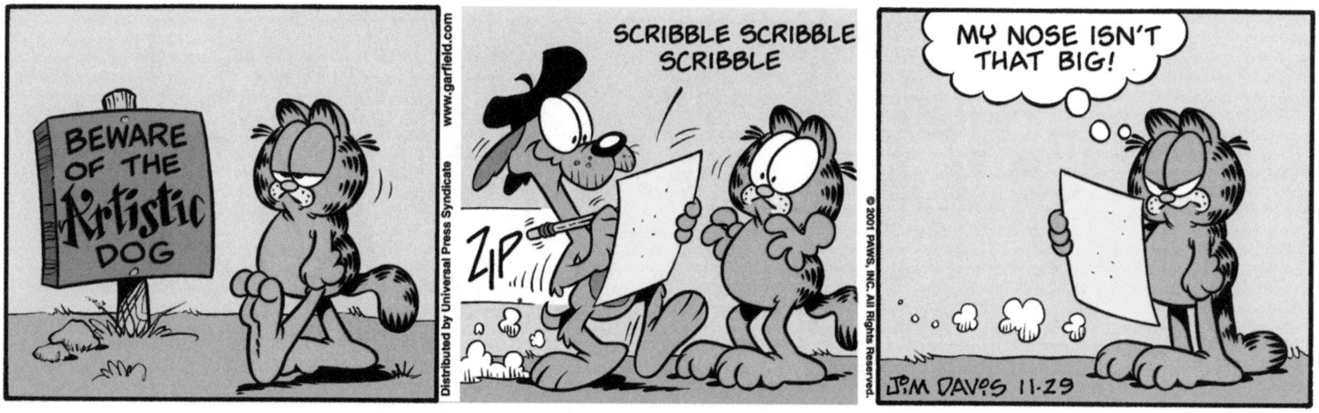
BEWARE OF THE Artistic DOG
www.garfield.com
Distributed by Universal Press Syndicate
SCRIBBLE SCRIBBLE SCRIBBLE
ZIP
© 2001 PAWS, INC. All Rights Reserved.
MY NOSE ISN'T THAT BIG!
JIM DAVIS 11-29

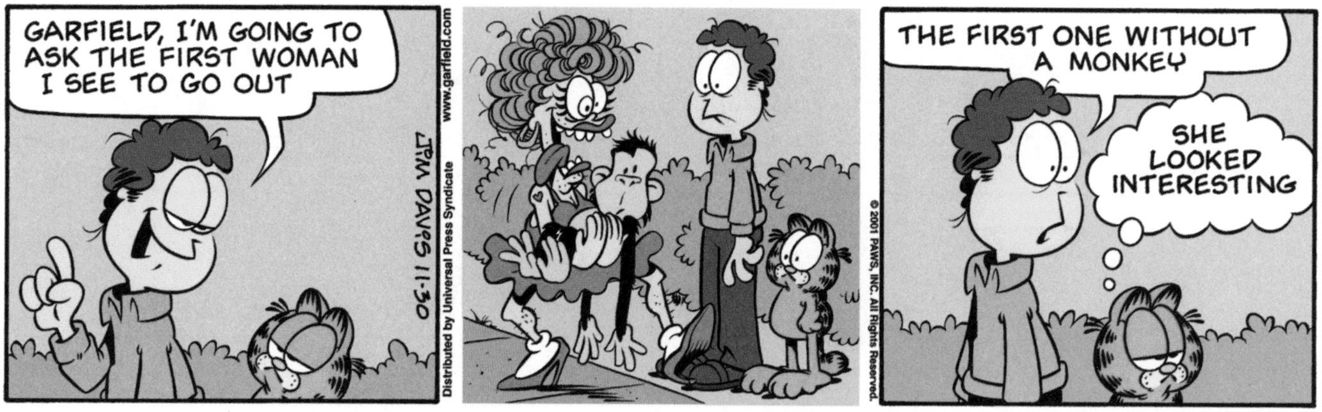
GARFIELD, I'M GOING TO ASK THE FIRST WOMAN I SEE TO GO OUT
JIM DAVIS 11-30
www.garfield.com
Distributed by Universal Press Syndicate
© 2001 PAWS, INC. All Rights Reserved.
THE FIRST ONE WITHOUT A MONKEY
SHE LOOKED INTERESTING

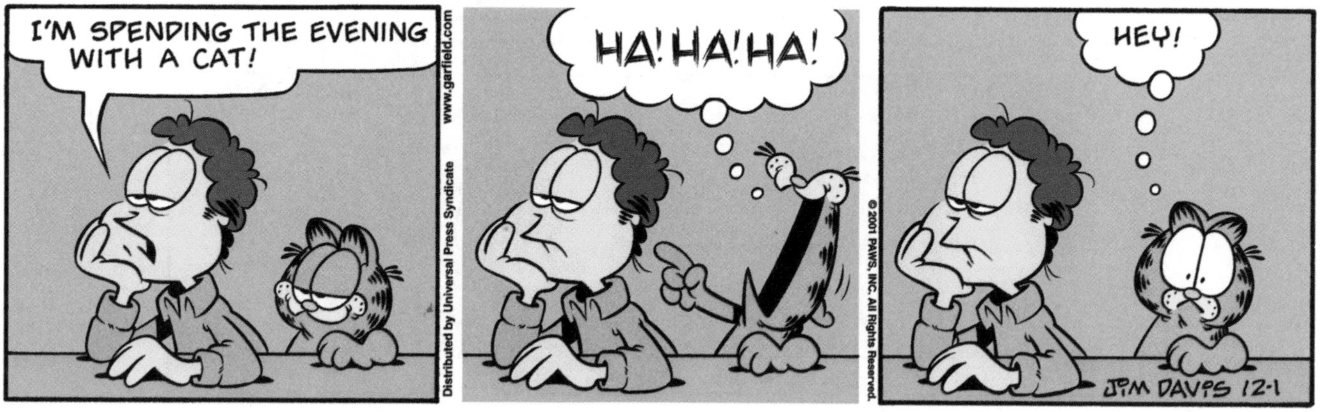
I'M SPENDING THE EVENING WITH A CAT!
www.garfield.com
Distributed by Universal Press Syndicate
HA! HA! HA!
© 2001 PAWS, INC. All Rights Reserved.
HEY!
JIM DAVIS 12-1

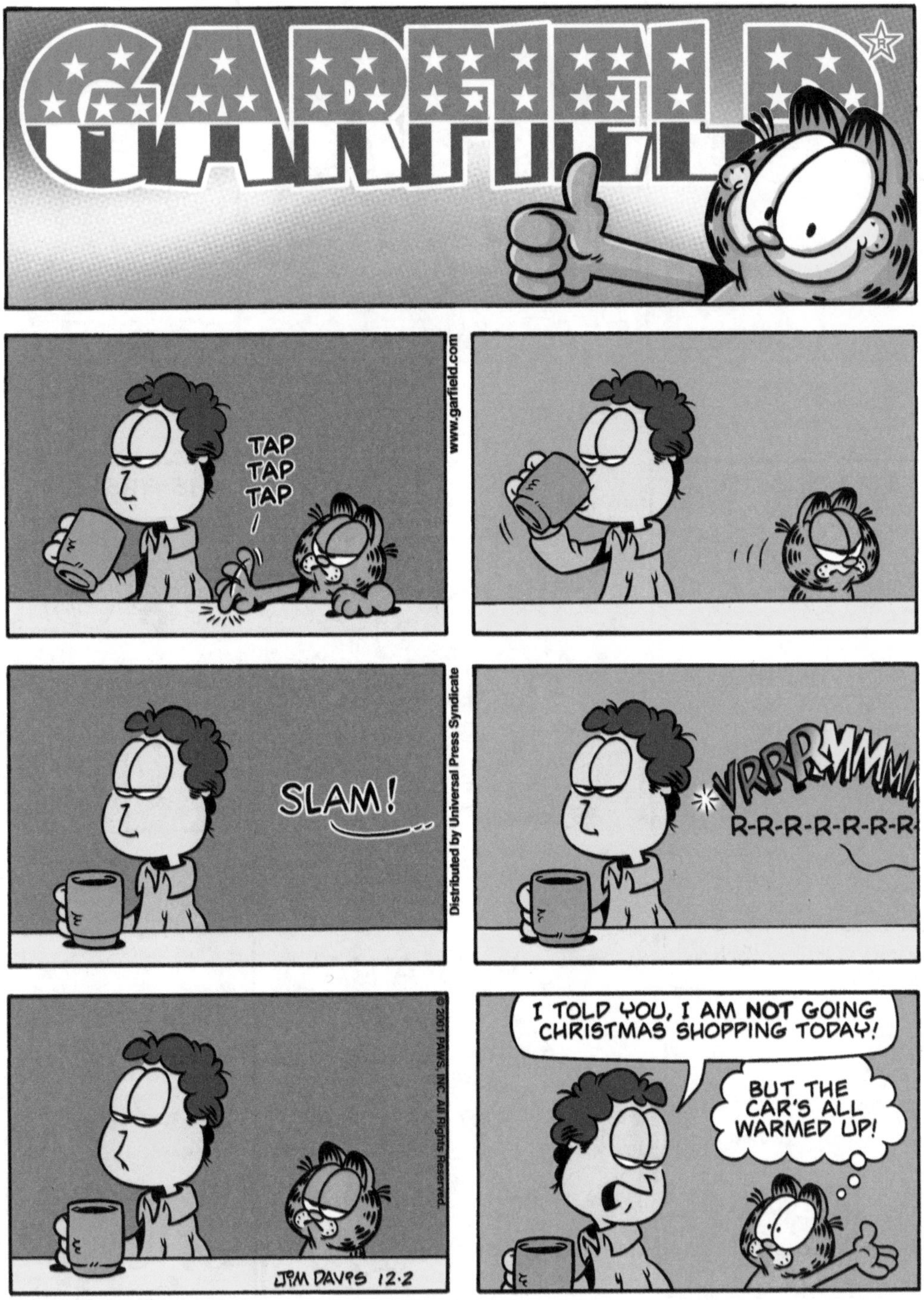

GARFIELD
www.garfield.com
TAP
TAP
TAP
Distributed by Universal Press Syndicate
SLAM!
VRRRMMMM
R-R-R-R-R-R-R-
© 2001 PAWS, INC. All Rights Reserved.
JIM DAVIS 12-2
I TOLD YOU, I AM **NOT** GOING CHRISTMAS SHOPPING TODAY!
BUT THE CAR'S ALL WARMED UP!

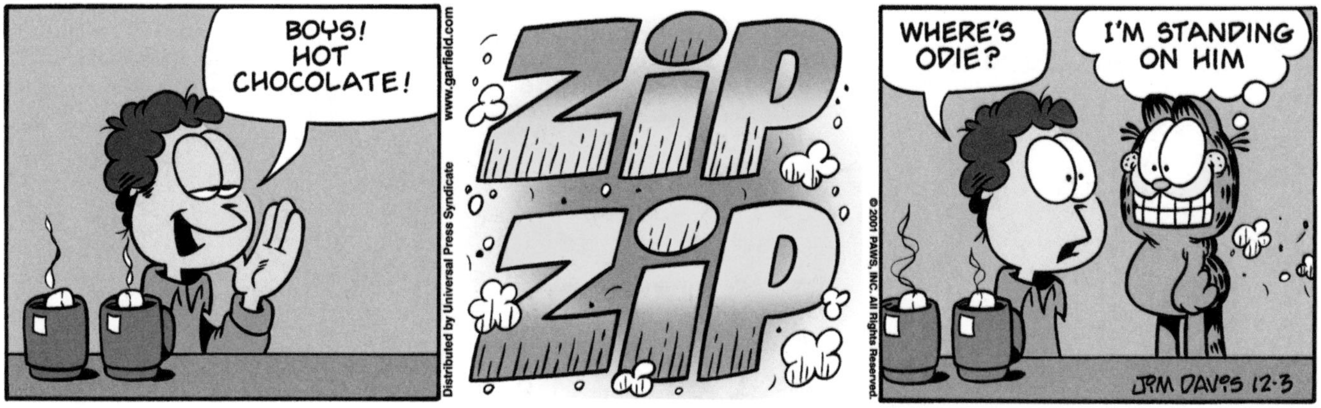
BOYS! HOT CHOCOLATE!
Distributed by Universal Press Syndicate www.garfield.com
ZIP ZIP
WHERE'S ODIE?
I'M STANDING ON HIM
© 2001 PAWS, INC. All Rights Reserved.
JIM DAVIS 12-3

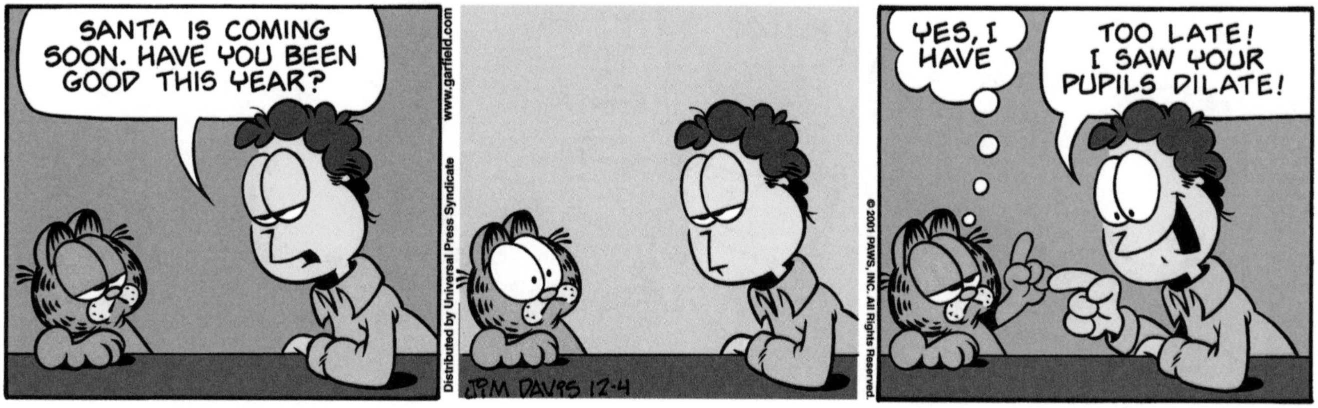
SANTA IS COMING SOON. HAVE YOU BEEN GOOD THIS YEAR?
Distributed by Universal Press Syndicate www.garfield.com
JIM DAVIS 12-4
YES, I HAVE
TOO LATE! I SAW YOUR PUPILS DILATE!
© 2001 PAWS, INC. All Rights Reserved.

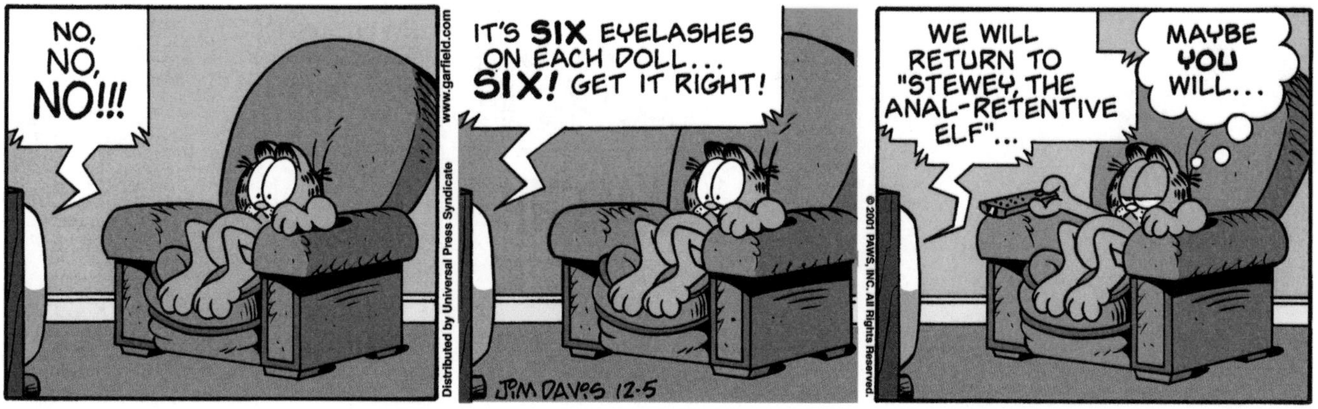
NO, NO, NO!!!
Distributed by Universal Press Syndicate www.garfield.com
IT'S SIX EYELASHES ON EACH DOLL... SIX! GET IT RIGHT!
JIM DAVIS 12-5
WE WILL RETURN TO "STEWEY, THE ANAL-RETENTIVE ELF"...
MAYBE YOU WILL...
© 2001 PAWS, INC. All Rights Reserved.

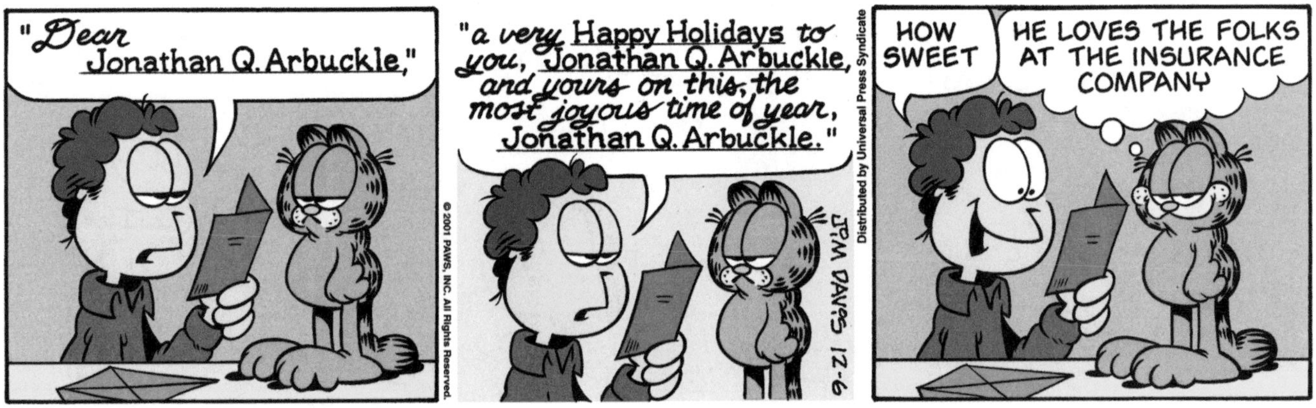
"Dear Jonathan Q. Arbuckle,"
© 2001 PAWS, INC. All Rights Reserved.
"a very Happy Holidays to you, Jonathan Q. Arbuckle, and yours on this, the most joyous time of year, Jonathan Q. Arbuckle."
JIM DAVIS 12-6
Distributed by Universal Press Syndicate
HOW SWEET
HE LOVES THE FOLKS AT THE INSURANCE COMPANY

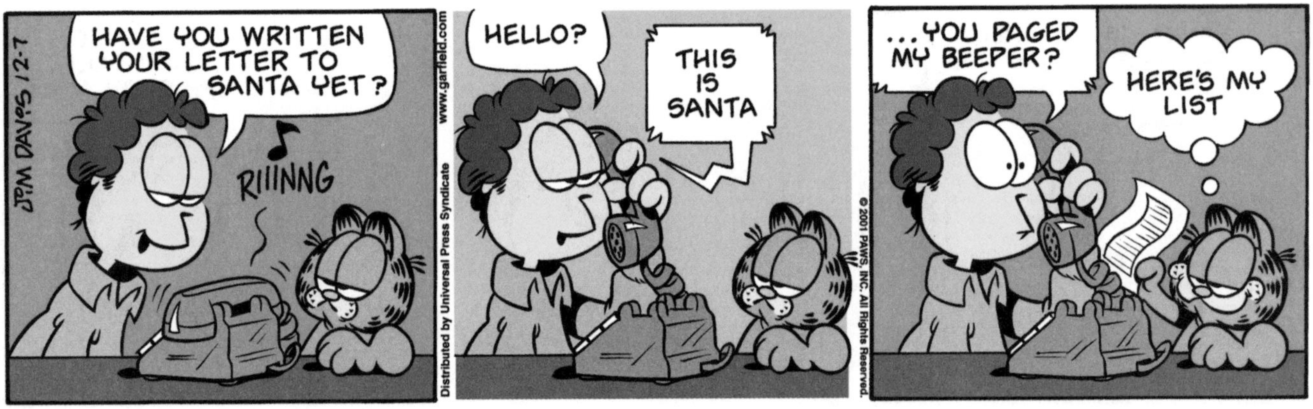
JIM DAVIS 12-7
HAVE YOU WRITTEN YOUR LETTER TO SANTA YET?
RIIINNG
Distributed by Universal Press Syndicate www.garfield.com
HELLO?
THIS IS SANTA
© 2001 PAWS, INC. All Rights Reserved.
...YOU PAGED MY BEEPER?
HERE'S MY LIST

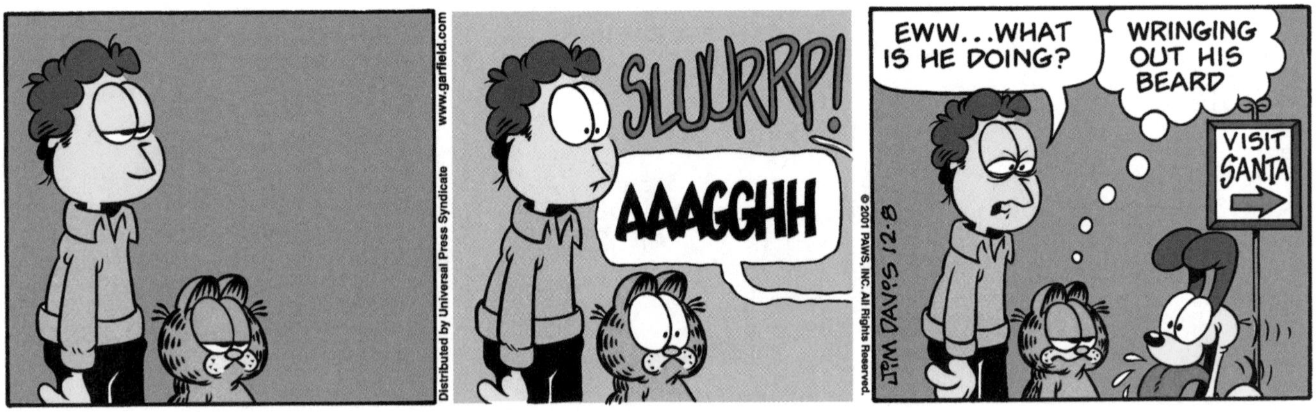
Distributed by Universal Press Syndicate www.garfield.com
SLUURRP!
AAAGGHH
© 2001 PAWS, INC. All Rights Reserved. JIM DAVIS 12-8
EWW...WHAT IS HE DOING?
WRINGING OUT HIS BEARD
VISIT SANTA

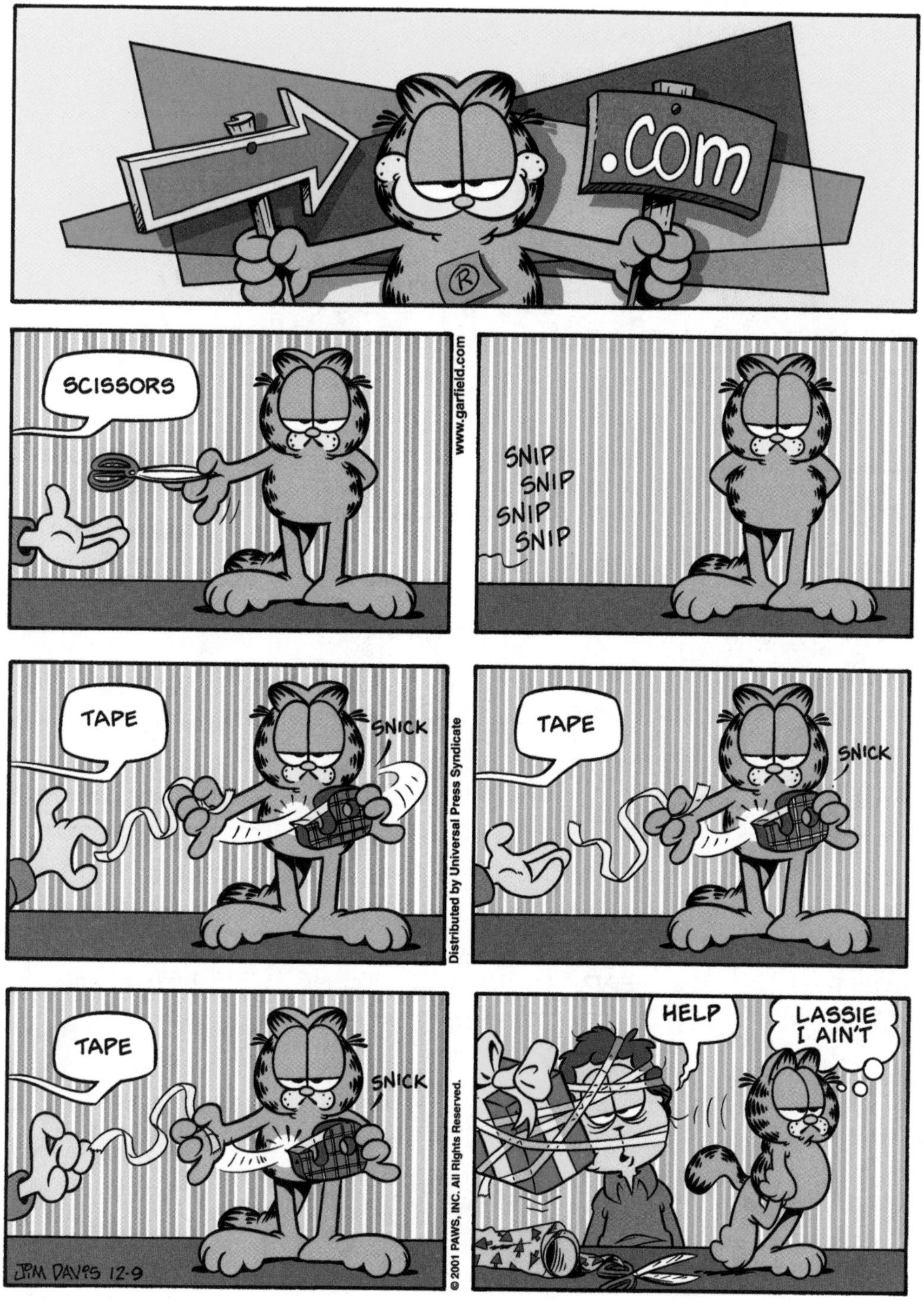
.com
SCISSORS
SNIP SNIP SNIP SNIP
TAPE
SNICK
TAPE
SNICK
TAPE
SNICK
HELP
LASSIE I AIN'T
JIM DAVIS 12-9
www.garfield.com
Distributed by Universal Press Syndicate
© 2001 PAWS, INC. All Rights Reserved.

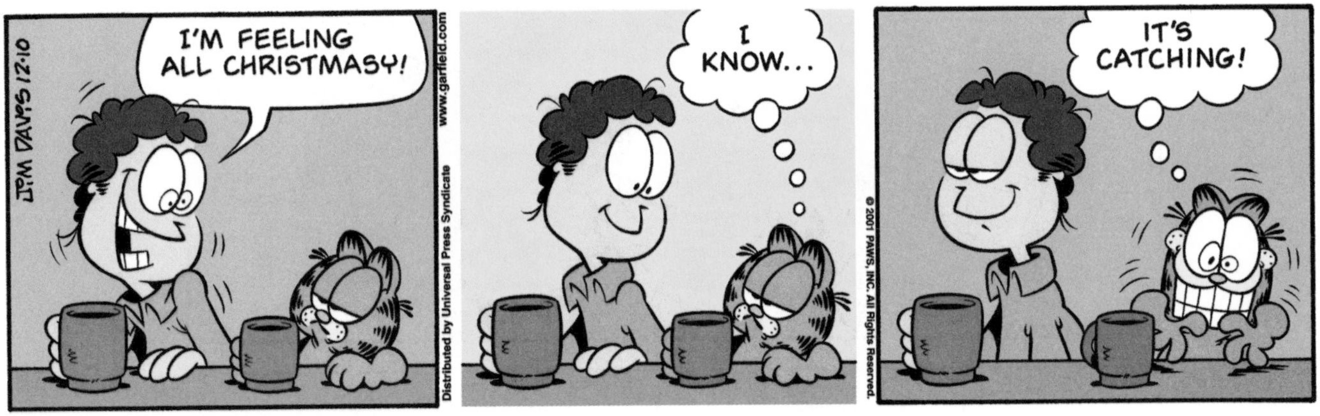
JIM DAVIS 12-10
I'M FEELING ALL CHRISTMASY!
www.garfield.com
Distributed by Universal Press Syndicate
I KNOW...
© 2001 PAWS, INC. All Rights Reserved.
IT'S CATCHING!

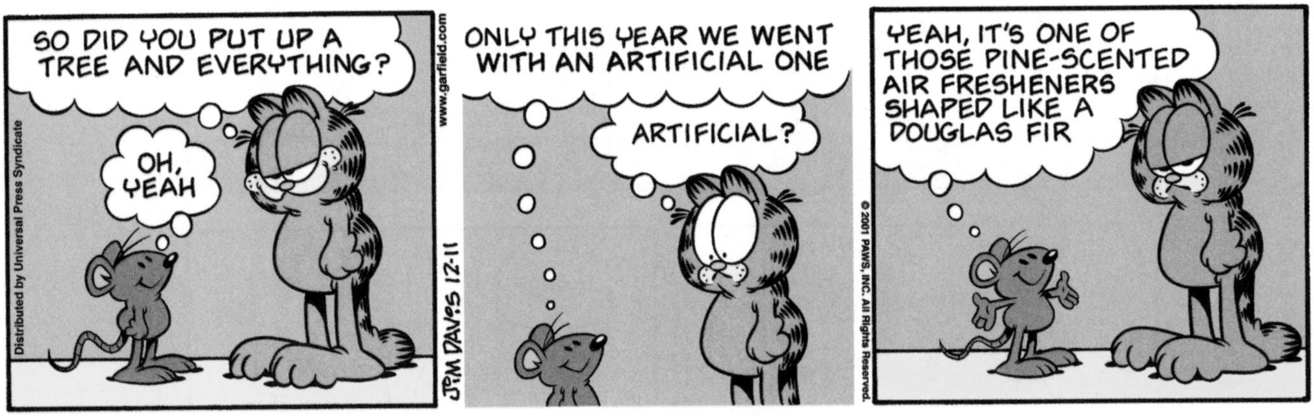
SO DID YOU PUT UP A TREE AND EVERYTHING?
OH, YEAH
Distributed by Universal Press Syndicate
www.garfield.com
JIM DAVIS 12-11
ONLY THIS YEAR WE WENT WITH AN ARTIFICIAL ONE
ARTIFICIAL?
© 2001 PAWS, INC. All Rights Reserved.
YEAH, IT'S ONE OF THOSE PINE-SCENTED AIR FRESHENERS SHAPED LIKE A DOUGLAS FIR

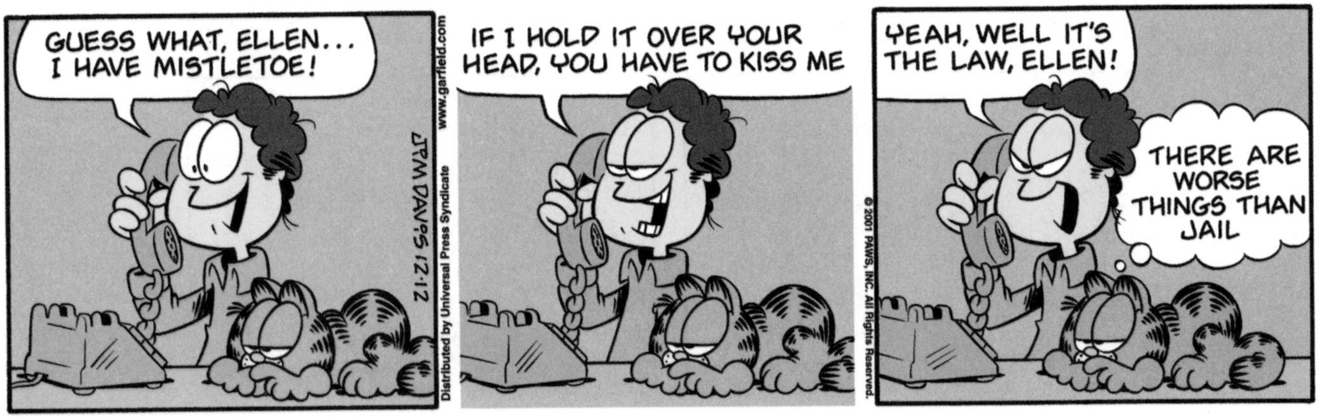
GUESS WHAT, ELLEN... I HAVE MISTLETOE!
JIM DAVIS 12-12
www.garfield.com
Distributed by Universal Press Syndicate
IF I HOLD IT OVER YOUR HEAD, YOU HAVE TO KISS ME
© 2001 PAWS, INC. All Rights Reserved.
YEAH, WELL IT'S THE LAW, ELLEN!
THERE ARE WORSE THINGS THAN JAIL

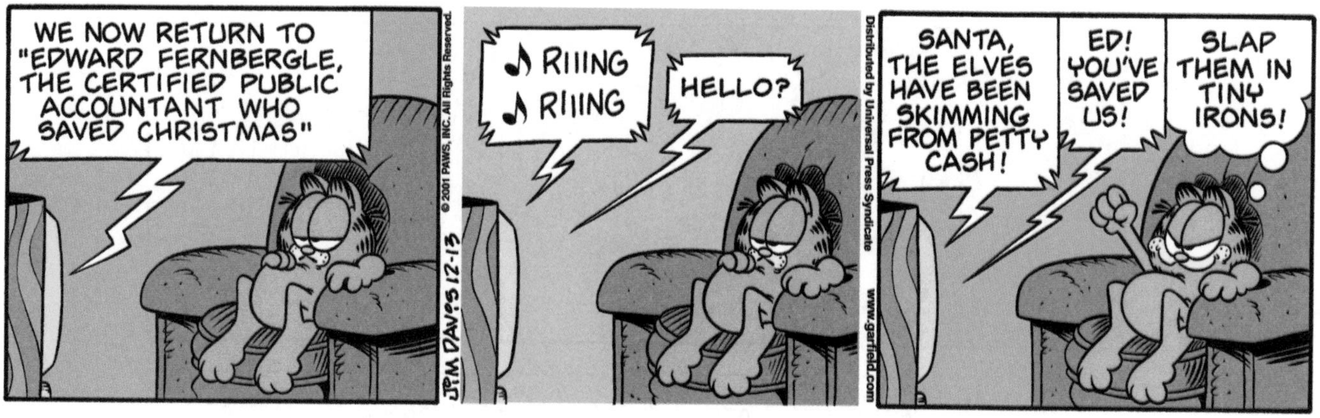
WE NOW RETURN TO "EDWARD FERNBERGLE, THE CERTIFIED PUBLIC ACCOUNTANT WHO SAVED CHRISTMAS"
JPM DAVPS 12-13
© 2001 PAWS, INC. All Rights Reserved.
♪ RIIING ♪ RIIING
HELLO?
Distributed by Universal Press Syndicate www.garfield.com
SANTA, THE ELVES HAVE BEEN SKIMMING FROM PETTY CASH!
ED! YOU'VE SAVED US!
SLAP THEM IN TINY IRONS!

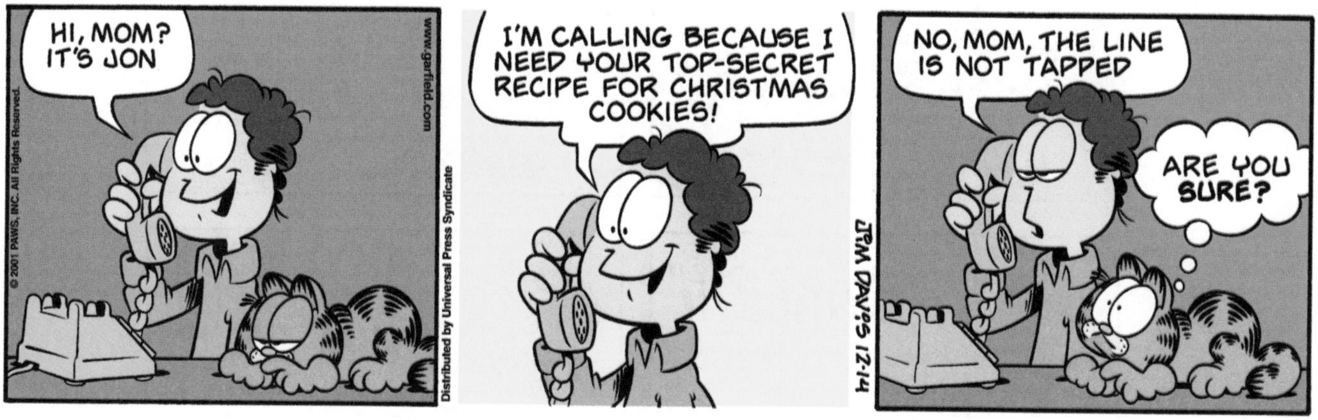
HI, MOM? IT'S JON
© 2001 PAWS, INC. All Rights Reserved.
www.garfield.com
Distributed by Universal Press Syndicate
I'M CALLING BECAUSE I NEED YOUR TOP-SECRET RECIPE FOR CHRISTMAS COOKIES!
JPM DAVPS 12-14
NO, MOM, THE LINE IS NOT TAPPED
ARE YOU SURE?

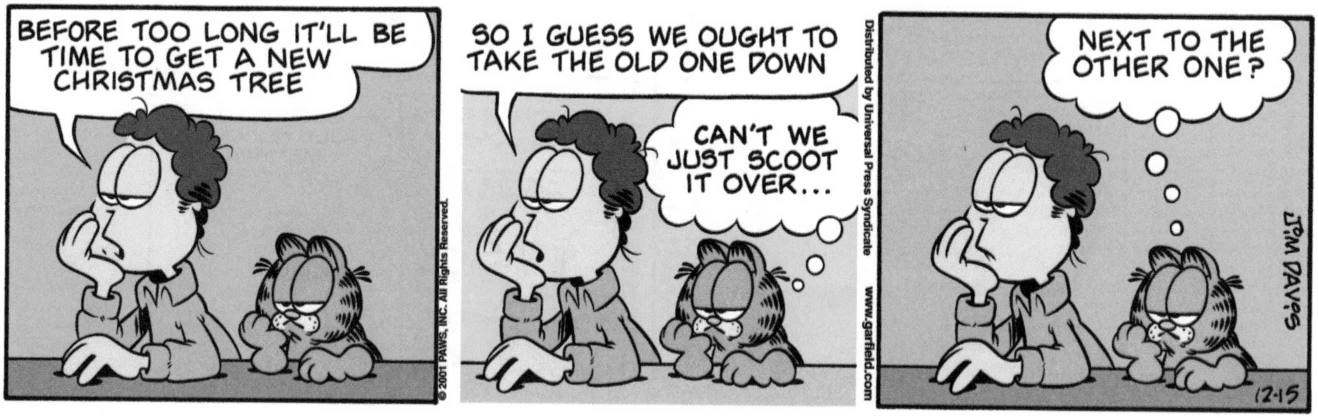
BEFORE TOO LONG IT'LL BE TIME TO GET A NEW CHRISTMAS TREE
© 2001 PAWS, INC. All Rights Reserved.
SO I GUESS WE OUGHT TO TAKE THE OLD ONE DOWN
CAN'T WE JUST SCOOT IT OVER...
Distributed by Universal Press Syndicate www.garfield.com
NEXT TO THE OTHER ONE?
JPM DAVPS
12-15

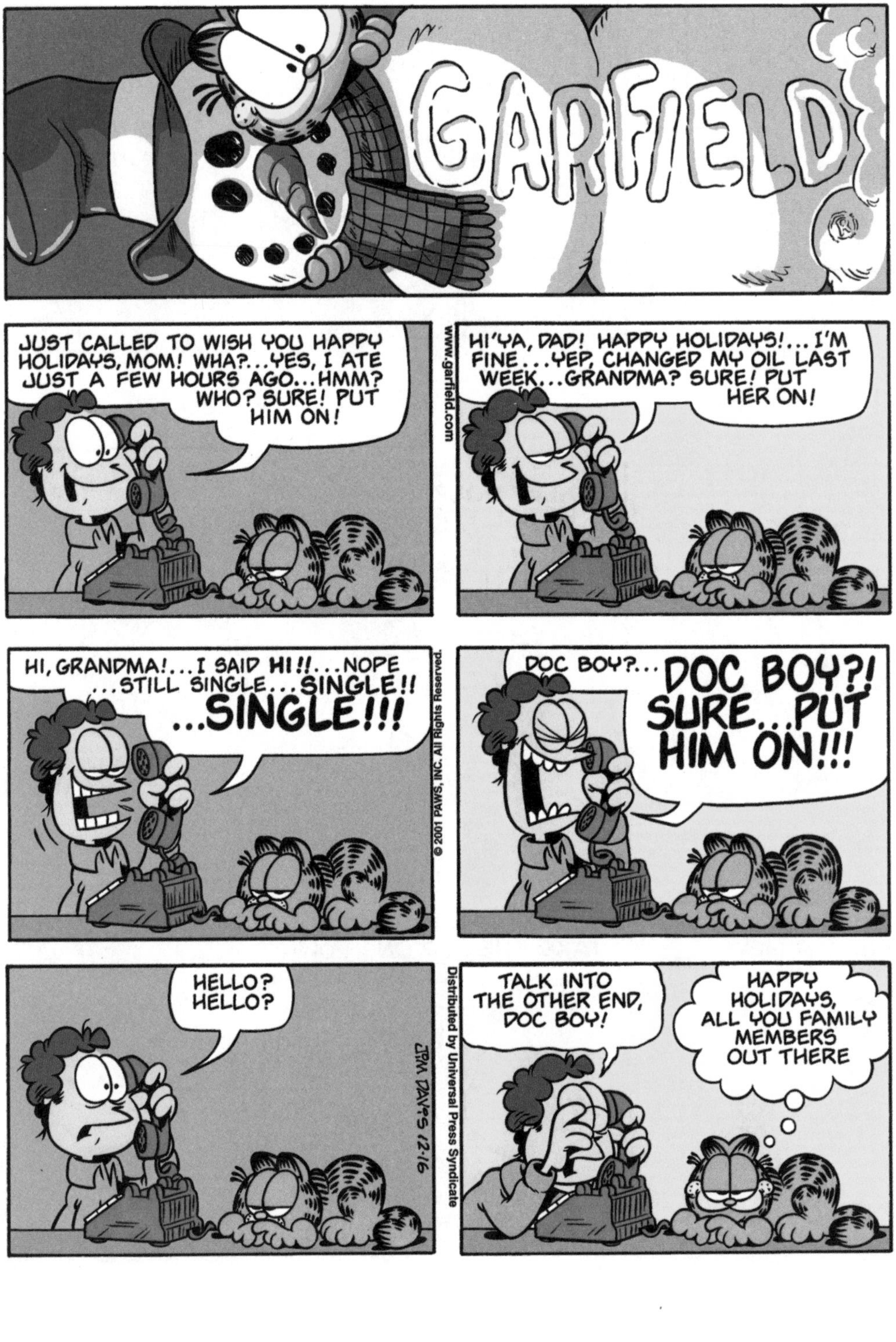
GARFIELD®
JUST CALLED TO WISH YOU HAPPY HOLIDAYS, MOM! WHA?...YES, I ATE JUST A FEW HOURS AGO...HMM? WHO? SURE! PUT HIM ON!
www.garfield.com
HI'YA, DAD! HAPPY HOLIDAYS!...I'M FINE...YEP, CHANGED MY OIL LAST WEEK...GRANDMA? SURE! PUT HER ON!
HI, GRANDMA!...I SAID HI!!...NOPE ...STILL SINGLE...SINGLE!! ...SINGLE!!!
© 2001 PAWS, INC. All Rights Reserved.
DOC BOY?... DOC BOY?! SURE...PUT HIM ON!!!
HELLO? HELLO?
JIM DAVIS 12-16
Distributed by Universal Press Syndicate
TALK INTO THE OTHER END, DOC BOY!
HAPPY HOLIDAYS, ALL YOU FAMILY MEMBERS OUT THERE

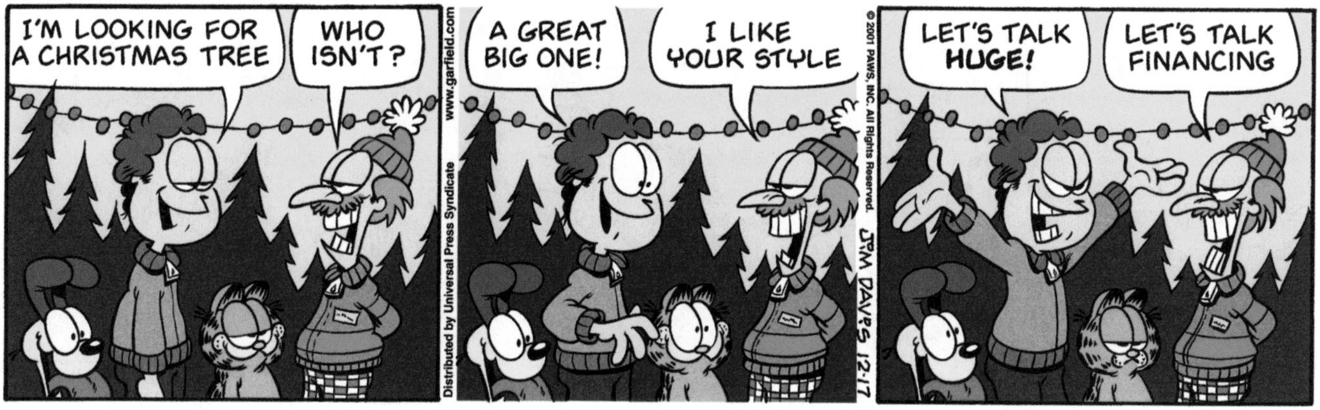
I'M LOOKING FOR A CHRISTMAS TREE
WHO ISN'T?
www.garfield.com
Distributed by Universal Press Syndicate
A GREAT BIG ONE!
I LIKE YOUR STYLE
© 2001 PAWS, INC. All Rights Reserved.
JIM DAVIS 12-17
LET'S TALK **HUGE!**
LET'S TALK FINANCING

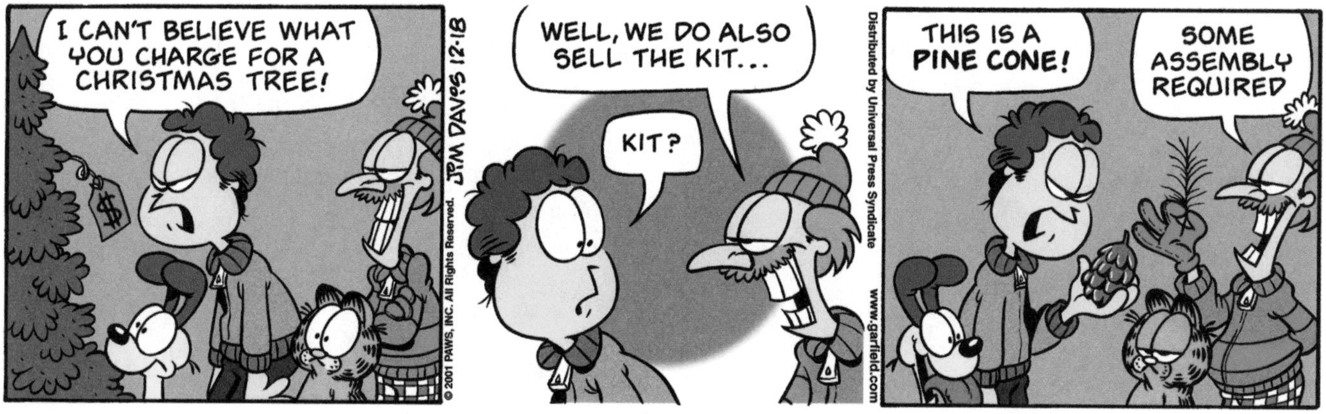
I CAN'T BELIEVE WHAT YOU CHARGE FOR A CHRISTMAS TREE!
$
JIM DAVIS 12-18
© 2001 PAWS, INC. All Rights Reserved.
WELL, WE DO ALSO SELL THE KIT...
KIT?
Distributed by Universal Press Syndicate
www.garfield.com
THIS IS A **PINE CONE!**
SOME ASSEMBLY REQUIRED

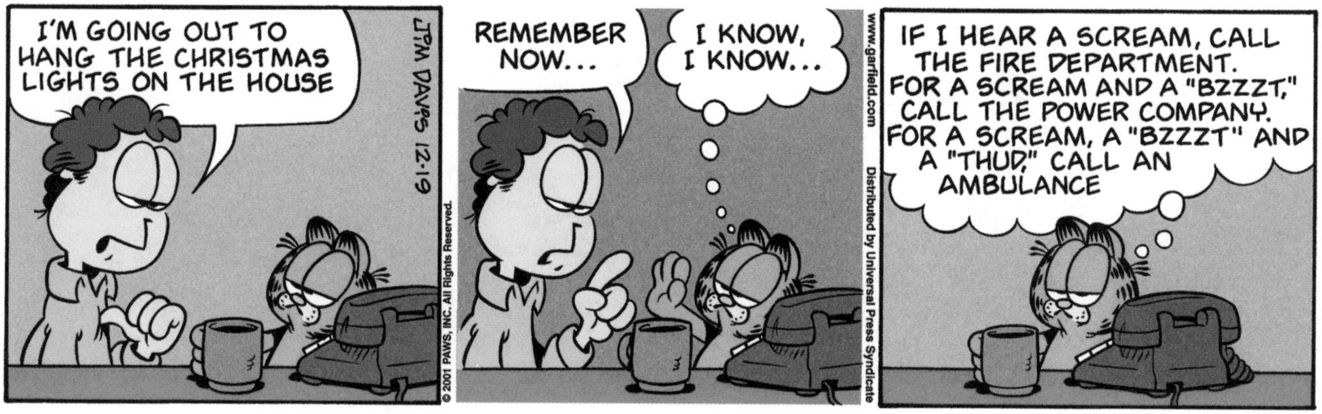
I'M GOING OUT TO HANG THE CHRISTMAS LIGHTS ON THE HOUSE
JIM DAVIS 12-19
© 2001 PAWS, INC. All Rights Reserved.
REMEMBER NOW...
I KNOW, I KNOW...
www.garfield.com
Distributed by Universal Press Syndicate
IF I HEAR A SCREAM, CALL THE FIRE DEPARTMENT. FOR A SCREAM AND A "BZZZT," CALL THE POWER COMPANY. FOR A SCREAM, A "BZZZT" AND A "THUD," CALL AN AMBULANCE

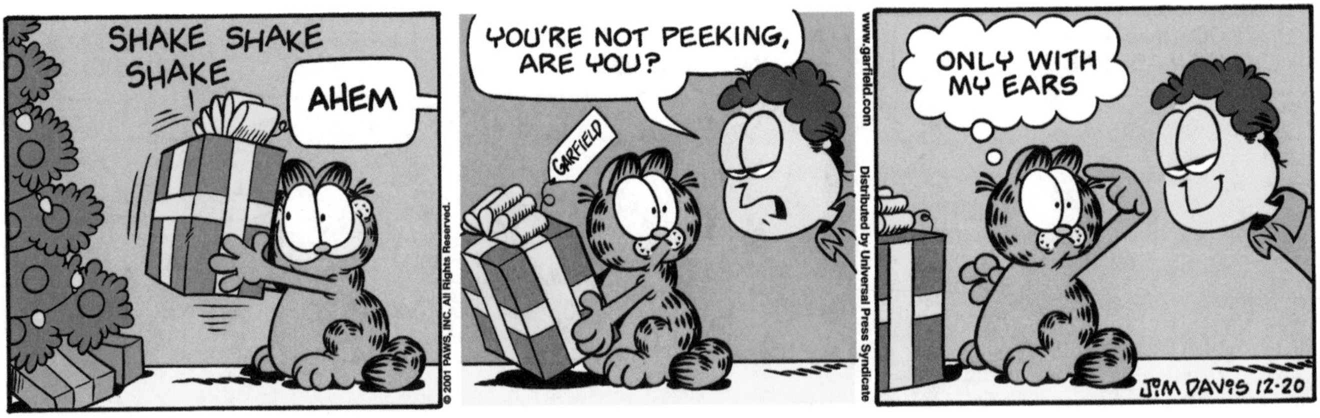
SHAKE SHAKE
SHAKE
AHEM
© 2001 PAWS, INC. All Rights Reserved.
YOU'RE NOT PEEKING, ARE YOU?
GARFIELD
www.garfield.com Distributed by Universal Press Syndicate
ONLY WITH MY EARS
JIM DAVIS 12-20

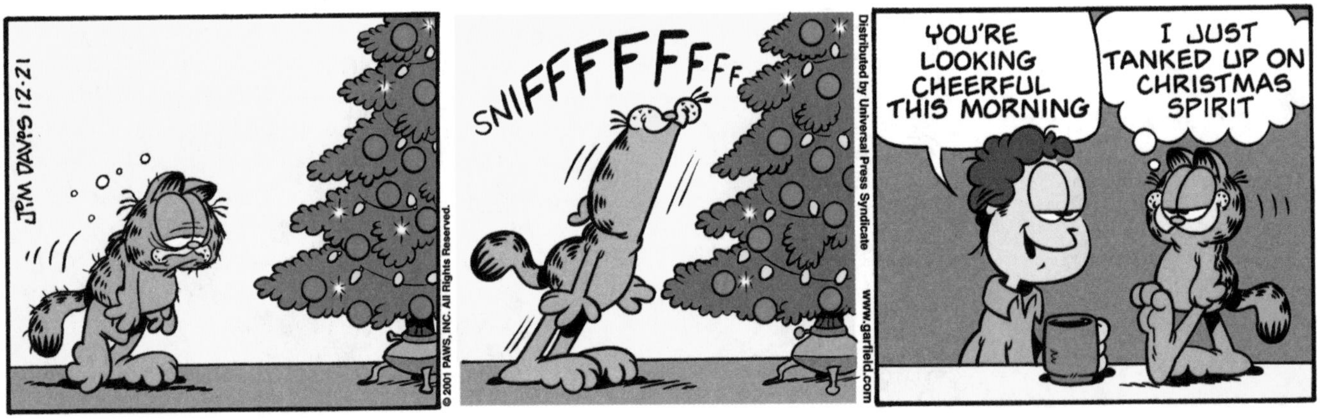
JIM DAVIS 12-21
© 2001 PAWS, INC. All Rights Reserved.
SNIFFFFFFFF
Distributed by Universal Press Syndicate www.garfield.com
YOU'RE LOOKING CHEERFUL THIS MORNING
I JUST TANKED UP ON CHRISTMAS SPIRIT

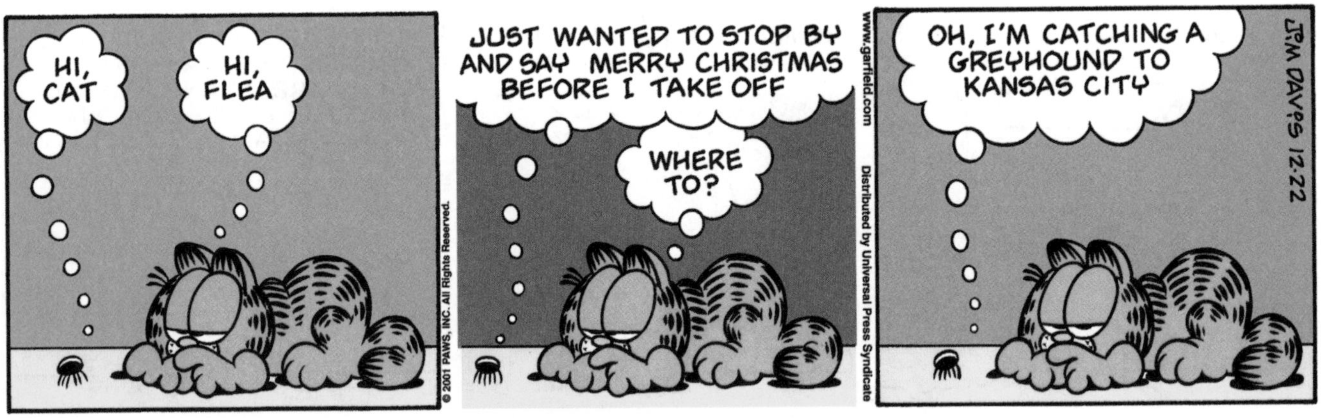
HI, CAT
HI, FLEA
© 2001 PAWS, INC. All Rights Reserved.
JUST WANTED TO STOP BY AND SAY MERRY CHRISTMAS BEFORE I TAKE OFF
WHERE TO?
www.garfield.com Distributed by Universal Press Syndicate
OH, I'M CATCHING A GREYHOUND TO KANSAS CITY
JIM DAVIS 12-22

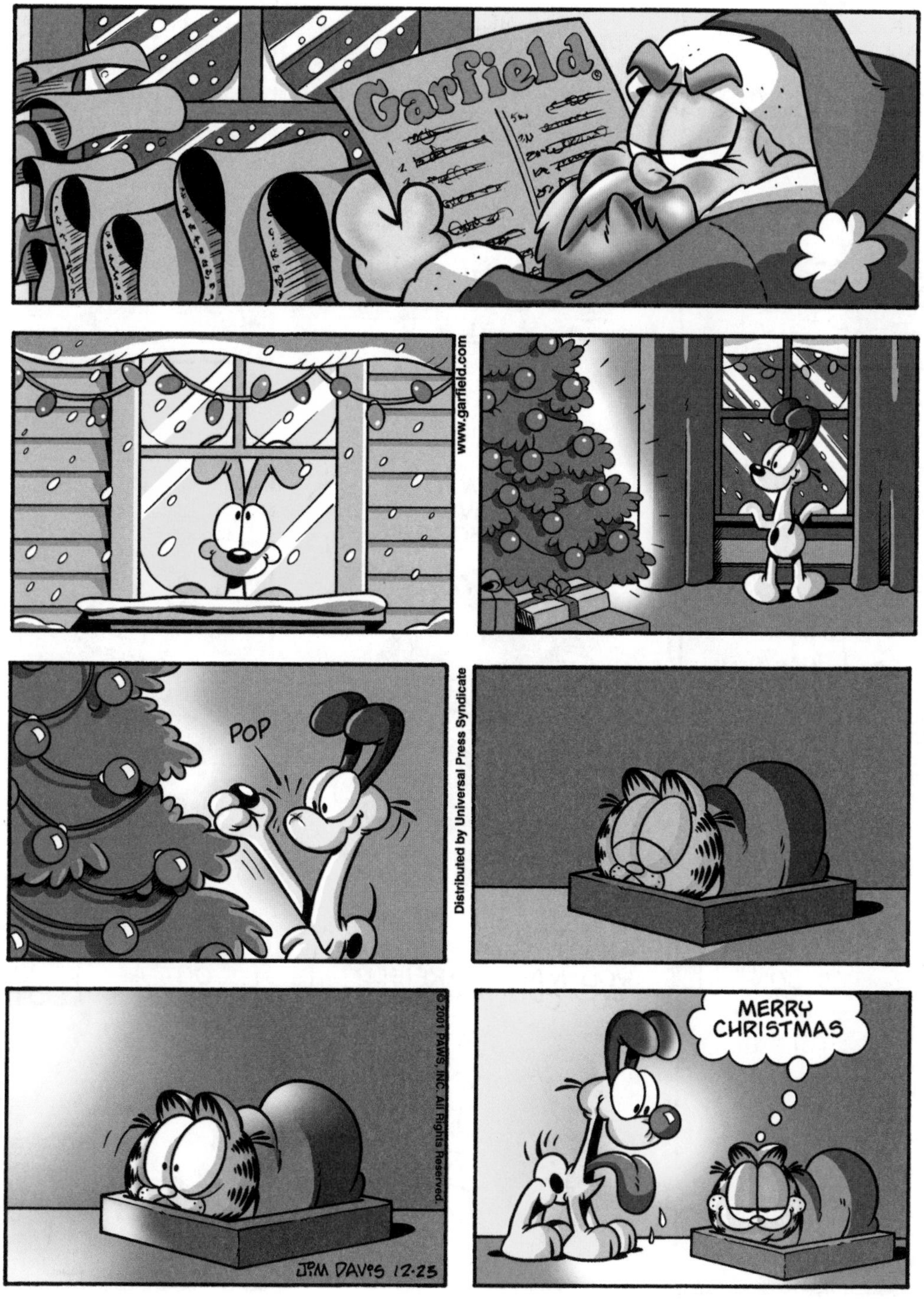
Garfield®
www.garfield.com
Distributed by Universal Press Syndicate
POP
© 2001 PAWS, INC. All Rights Reserved.
JIM DAVIS 12-23
MERRY CHRISTMAS

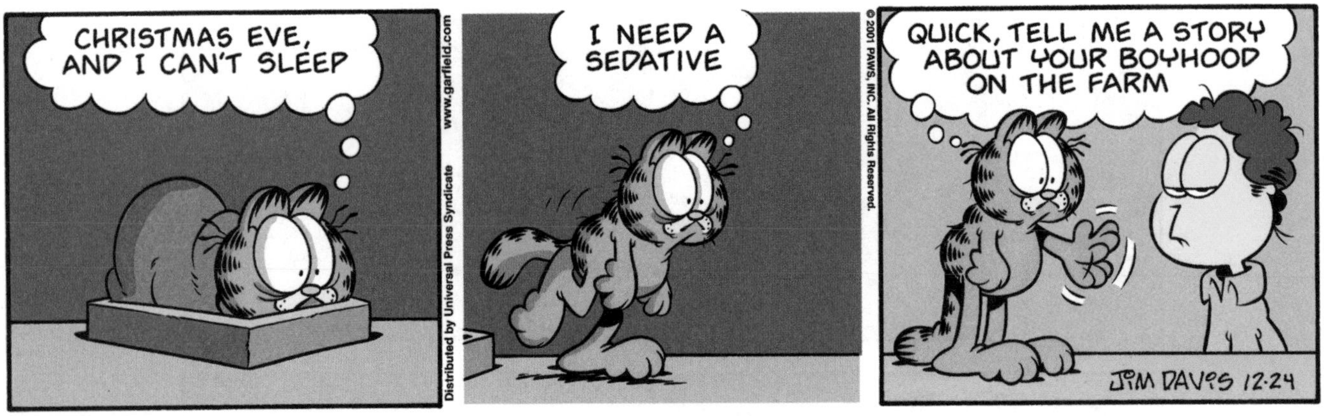
CHRISTMAS EVE, AND I CAN'T SLEEP
I NEED A SEDATIVE
QUICK, TELL ME A STORY ABOUT YOUR BOYHOOD ON THE FARM
JIM DAVIS 12-24
Distributed by Universal Press Syndicate www.garfield.com
© 2001 PAWS, INC. All Rights Reserved.

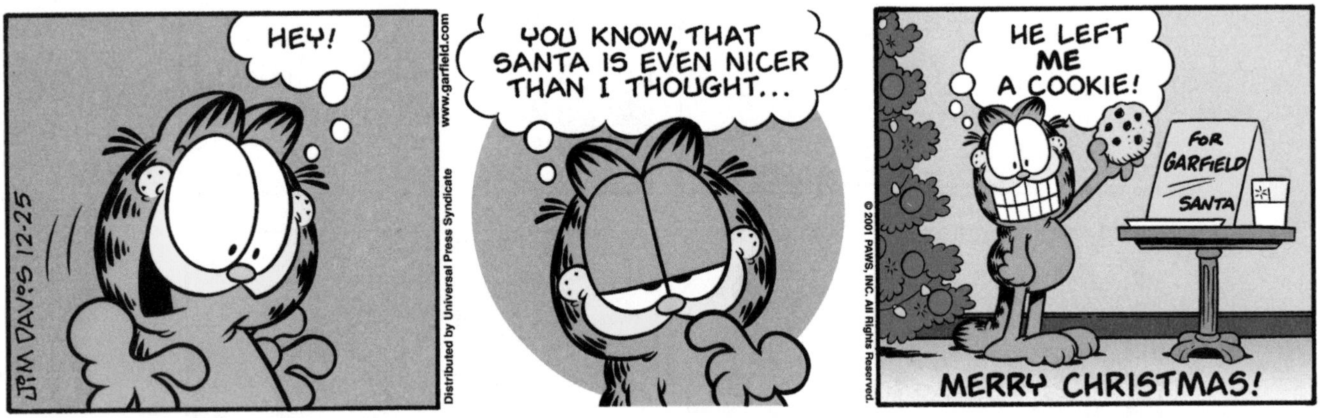
HEY!
JIM DAVIS 12-25
YOU KNOW, THAT SANTA IS EVEN NICER THAN I THOUGHT...
HE LEFT **ME** A COOKIE!
FOR GARFIELD
SANTA
MERRY CHRISTMAS!
Distributed by Universal Press Syndicate www.garfield.com
© 2001 PAWS, INC. All Rights Reserved.

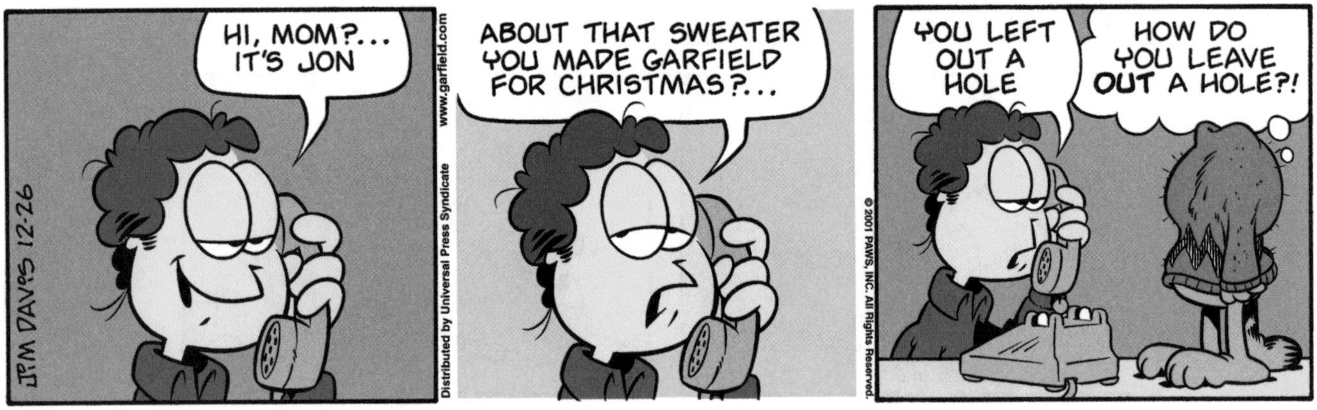
HI, MOM?... IT'S JON
JIM DAVIS 12-26
ABOUT THAT SWEATER YOU MADE GARFIELD FOR CHRISTMAS?...
YOU LEFT OUT A HOLE
HOW DO YOU LEAVE **OUT** A HOLE?!
Distributed by Universal Press Syndicate www.garfield.com
© 2001 PAWS, INC. All Rights Reserved.

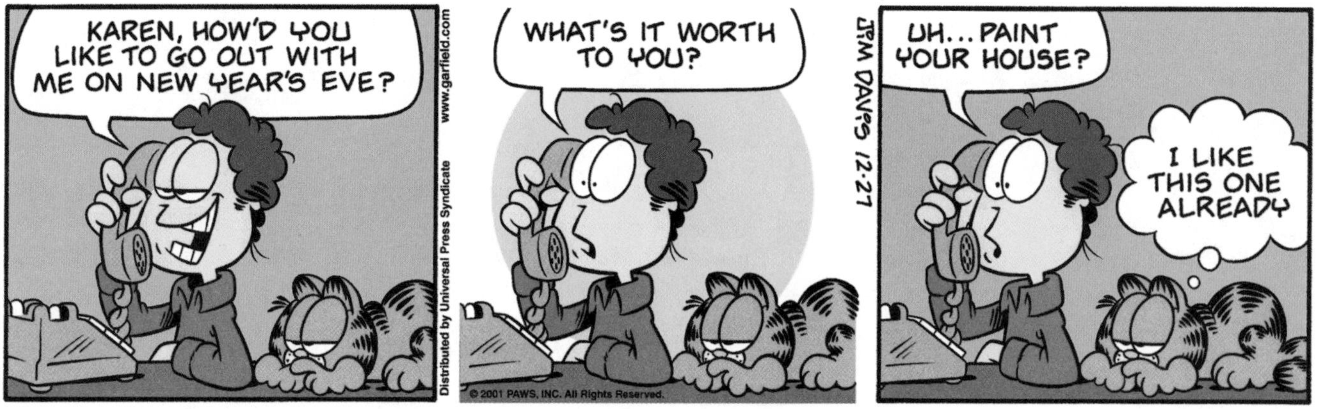
KAREN, HOW'D YOU LIKE TO GO OUT WITH ME ON NEW YEAR'S EVE?
www.garfield.com
Distributed by Universal Press Syndicate
WHAT'S IT WORTH TO YOU?
© 2001 PAWS, INC. All Rights Reserved.
JIM DAVIS 12·27
UH... PAINT YOUR HOUSE?
I LIKE THIS ONE ALREADY

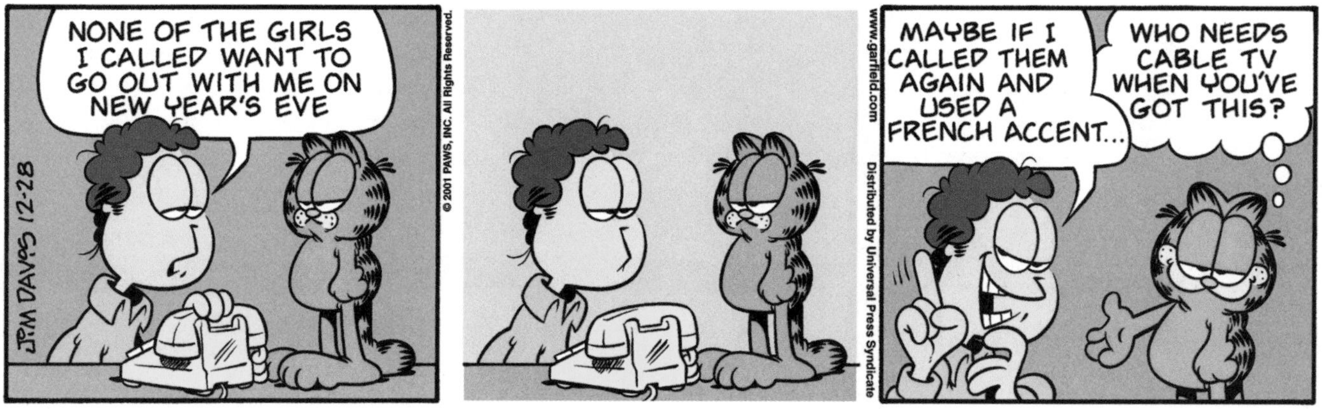
NONE OF THE GIRLS I CALLED WANT TO GO OUT WITH ME ON NEW YEAR'S EVE
JIM DAVIS 12·28
© 2001 PAWS, INC. All Rights Reserved.
www.garfield.com
Distributed by Universal Press Syndicate
MAYBE IF I CALLED THEM AGAIN AND USED A FRENCH ACCENT...
WHO NEEDS CABLE TV WHEN YOU'VE GOT THIS?

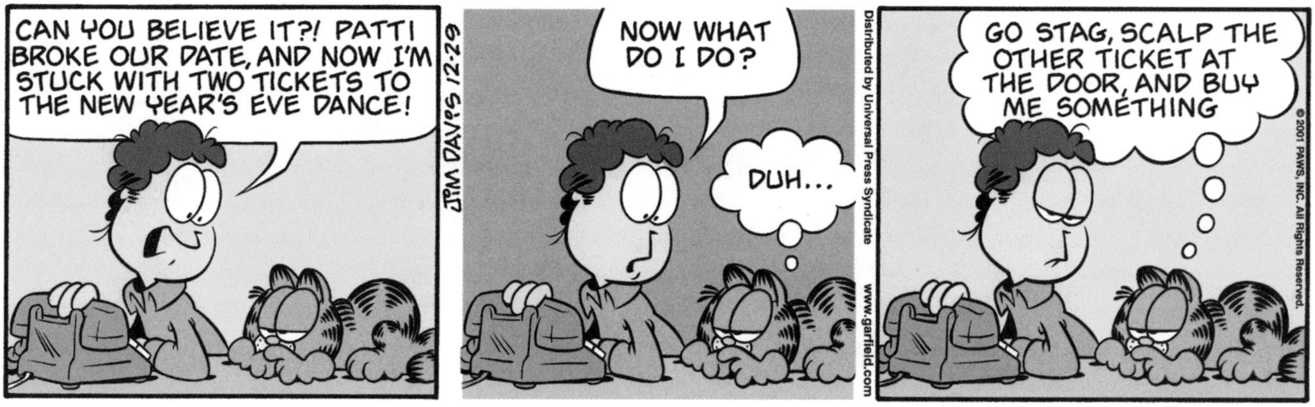
CAN YOU BELIEVE IT?! PATTI BROKE OUR DATE, AND NOW I'M STUCK WITH TWO TICKETS TO THE NEW YEAR'S EVE DANCE!
JIM DAVIS 12·29
NOW WHAT DO I DO?
DUH...
Distributed by Universal Press Syndicate
www.garfield.com
GO STAG, SCALP THE OTHER TICKET AT THE DOOR, AND BUY ME SOMETHING
© 2001 PAWS, INC. All Rights Reserved.

Outrageous Outtakes Part Deux

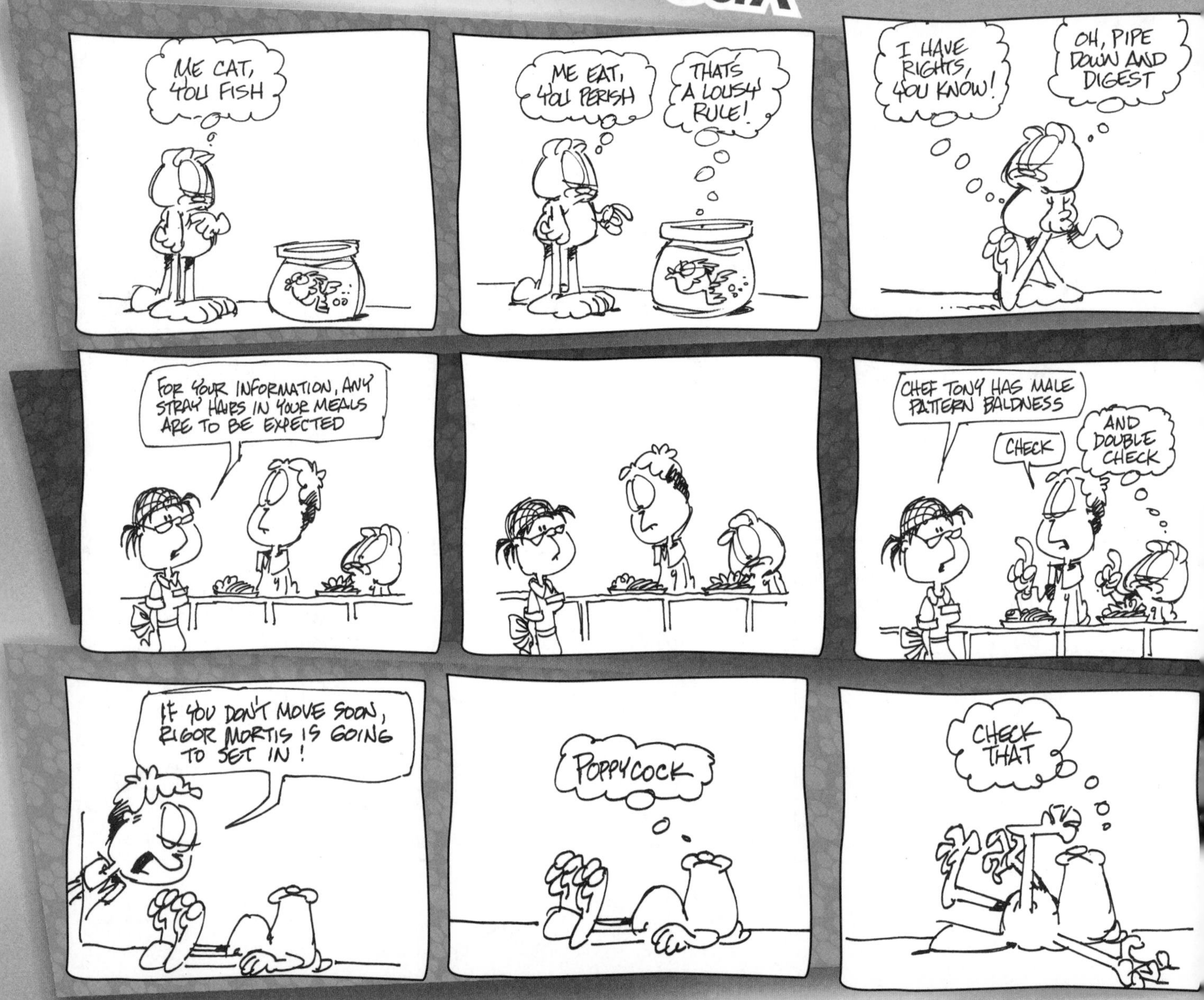

ME CAT, YOU FISH
ME EAT, YOU PERISH
THAT'S A LOUSY RULE!
I HAVE RIGHTS, YOU KNOW!
OH, PIPE DOWN AND DIGEST
FOR YOUR INFORMATION, ANY STRAY HAIRS IN YOUR MEALS ARE TO BE EXPECTED
CHEF TONY HAS MALE PATTERN BALDNESS
CHECK
AND DOUBLE CHECK
IF YOU DON'T MOVE SOON, RIGOR MORTIS IS GOING TO SET IN!
POPPYCOCK
CHECK THAT

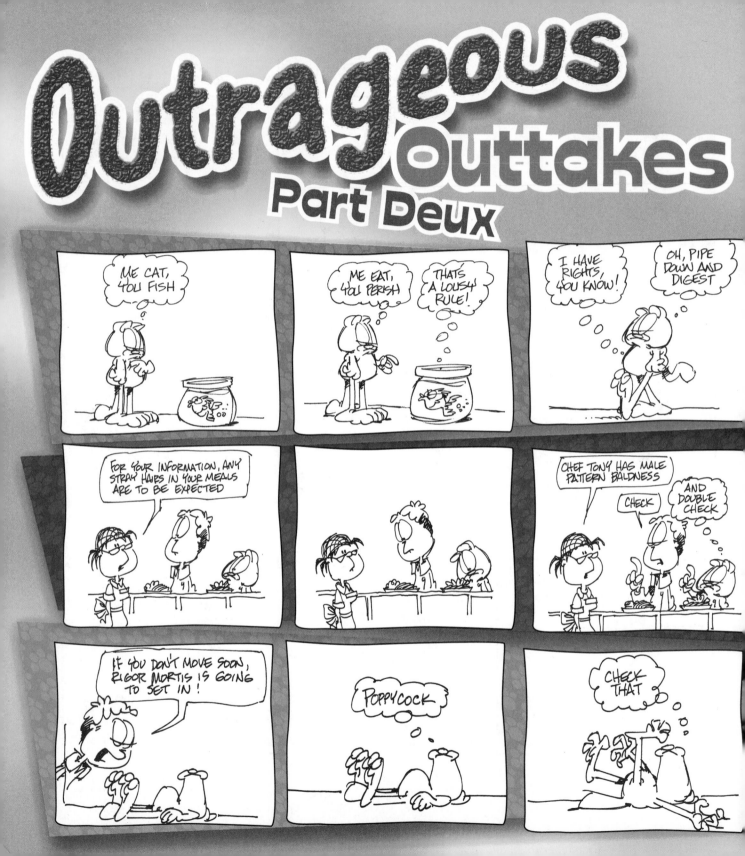

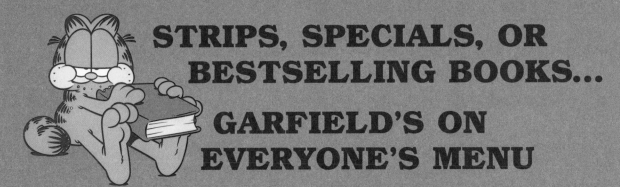

STRIPS, SPECIALS, OR BESTSELLING BOOKS...

GARFIELD'S ON EVERYONE'S MENU

Don't miss even one episode in the Tubby Tabby's hilarious series!